Power and Global Sport

Sport has changed. Traditions and territorial distinctions are dissolving as a result of new global political, economic and cultural conditions. In *Power and Global Sport*, Joseph Maguire and his co-authors examine these changes, investigating the power relations that govern global sport and assessing the consequences for the future of sport. In doing so, they provide a paradigm case of globalisation at work.

The book is founded on a series of case studies, linked by a common process-sociological approach. It is divided into four parts, each dealing with an important aspect of sport and globalisation:

- The local–global nexus – how global sports processes are played out at the level of local communities.
- Lived experiences – the reality of global sport for players and supporters.
- Identity politics – the impact of global sport on national consciousness.
- Sporting futures – the emergent political, economic and cultural forces that are shaping global sport, and their implications for its development.

Case-study structure and clear style of writing make *Power and Global Sport* a highly accessible text, which will be enjoyed by undergraduates and researchers alike. The text introduces new approaches to the study of sport and globalisation, updating and extending Joseph Maguire's previous work, and is therefore an essential resource for all those working in this fast-changing area.

Power and Global Sport contains contributions from Mike Burrows, Mark Falcous (University of Otago, New Zealand), Catherine Possamai, David Stead (Loughborough University, UK) and Jason Tuck (University College Winchester, UK).

Joseph Maguire is Professor of Sociology of Sport and Co-Director of the Centre for Olympic Studies & Research at Loughborough University, UK, as well as Past President of the International Sociology of Sport Association (1995–2003). Joseph Maguire has written extensively in the area of globalisation, sport, culture and society.

Power and Global Sport

Zones of prestige, emulation and resistance

Joseph Maguire

LONDON AND NEW YORK

First published 2005
by Routledge
2 Park Square, Milton Park,
Abingdon, Oxon OX14 4RN

Simultaneously published in the USA and Canada
by Routledge
270 Madison Ave, New York, NY 10016

Routledge is an imprint of the Taylor & Francis Group

© 2005 Joseph Maguire

Typeset in Goudy by
GreenGate Publishing Services, Tonbridge, Kent
Printed and bound in Great Britain by
TJ International Ltd, Padstow, Cornwall

British Library Cataloguing in Publication Data
A catalogue record for this book is available from the British Library

Library of Congress Cataloging in Publication Data
Power and global sport : zones of prestige, emulation, and resistance /
edited by Joseph Maguire.
      p. cm.
   Includes bibliographical references and index.
   ISBN 0-415-25279-2 (hardback) – ISBN 0-415-25280-6 (pbk.)
1. Sports–Political aspects–Cross-cultural studies. 2. Nationalism and
sports–cross-cultural studies. 3. Globalization–Cross-cultural studies.
I. Maguire, Joseph A., 1956–
   GV706.35.P69 2005
   796–dc22

                                                      2004021895

ISBN 0-415-25279-2 (hbk)
ISBN 0-415-25280-6 (pbk)

Contents

Preface

Joseph Maguire deserves to be called the pioneering figure in the study of sport globalisation. He's been at it for more than fifteen years, and has developed a corpus of work that has to be admired by all of us who have struggled to keep up with him. It doesn't matter where – on the theoretical spectrum – you fall, Maguire's work has become a benchmark for where the rest of us take off. *Power and Global Sport* is the latest instalment, and continues the path that Maguire has been blazing for decades.

The questions being asked of globalisation and sport have remained constant. Does sport unite or divide us (people, nations, regions)? Maguire prefers 'civilising' and 'decivilising' to refer to the same thing, but however it is put, the question remains the same. Others have addressed it, as well they should; since it is the most fundamental socio-emotional question to be asked. What distinguishes Joseph Maguire from all of the others is his addressing the question from so many differing angles, with so many different sports. If you look at any one of his studies, you won't get the answer, nor the whole picture (his early work on the impact of American football upon England is my personal favourite, however). It is only when you see Maguire coming at the issue of globalisation from virtually every corner of the globe that you begin to understand the importance of his work. By looking at so many venues, we are privy to a sophisticated examination of the global/local dichotomy at the macro level. No one has managed to speak to this with the authority that Joe Maguire has.

One of his favourite themes in discussing sport, globalisation and power is one he has worked to perfection: diminishing contrasts and increasing varieties. The ability of sport to act as an agent in homogenising disparate sporting traditions exists in a very real way; but as Maguire shows, so does the ability of independent sporting traditions to remain autonomous and even to forge new identities. This collection, undertaken in collaboration with former students, covers these issues in updated fashion. Whether one is looking at the attempted encroachment of such American sport colossi as the National Football League or National Basketball Association, or the use of national identity in sport, or the influence and meaning of colonial cricketers, these readings develop a sense of authority that is as compelling in its expansiveness as it is stellar in its specific examinations.

Rather than reduce these discussions to a mono-causal set of explanations, the authors all sense that globalisation is a set of constructions and configurations that require the ability to be comfortable with economic, political, cultural and sociological perspectives of global sport. In fact, even though Maguire's preferential paradigm is 'figurational sociology' he (and the other authors) regularly move beyond it to incorporate the diversity of thinking required to deal with so weighty a matter. Hence, marketing and consumer behaviour can be woven into discussions of identity politics, transnational labour migration, and cultural hegemony. The richness of national/cultural comparisons that this collection offers is one of its most compelling features. Another is that it seeks to be inclusive rather than exclusive; that is, Maguire and company seek to extend our thinking on globalisation by showing the close proximity between differing perspectives on sport globalisation, rather than confront other theories as hostile forces. They enable the rest of us to find the linkages and enrich our view of this very real and interesting dimension of globalisation.

One of the most important contributions we can make to our disciplines is to foster the development of a collection of case studies that encourage sound theoretical formulation and conclusions. But, of what use is a convincing analysis if it doesn't contain a moral imperative replete with policy? *Power and Global Sport* doesn't shy away from this either as it pushes this agenda forward. It is a very welcome addition to the growing body of literature on sport and globalisation.

Professor Alan Klein
Northeastern University, Boston

Acknowledgements

I was not sure that I would write another book on globlisation. I guess I have my former and current students to thank for keeping me 'up to speed' and making me think again on some issues. I should also thank my former students, and now colleagues, with whom I have co-written several of the chapters. Without them the richness of the case studies contained in this work would be missing. I hope they like how what we have done contributes to the book overall.

During the course of the writing for this book I became Past President of the International Sociology of Sport Association (ISSA). That, in itself, freed up time to finish this work, but without the experience of being President of ISSA, and thus coming into contact with colleagues from different cultures, and also visiting various parts of the globe, my sensitivity to a global perspective would be that much less developed. I thank my colleagues and friends in ISSA for sharing their time, insights, and cultures.

Work of this kind is never done in isolation: without the support, advice and sharp editorial eye of my wife, Jennifer, this book would be the lesser for it. I also thank her for my membership of The Wine Society – that has helped too! Finally, let me thank colleagues at Routledge, particularly Samantha Grant, for her patience when deadlines were not *quite* met!

Introduction

Power and global sport

Joseph Maguire

Writing in the post-apartheid period, Nelson Mandela, a boxer in his youth, commented on the role that sport plays across the globe:

> Sport is probably the most effective means of communication in the modern world, bypassing both verbal and written communication and reaching directly out to billions of people world-wide. There is no doubt that sport is a viable and legitimate way of building friendship between nations.

We do not need to question the global reach that Mandela attributes to sport – it is supported by a range of evidence (Bairner, 2001; Guttmann, 1994; Maguire, 1999; Maguire *et al.*, 2002; Miller *et al.*, 2001; Van Bottenburg, 2001, 2003). What is necessary to assess, however, is the actual impact that global sport has on people, nations and civilisations across the globe. Is Mandela right to be so optimistic, or are there other aspects of global sport encounters that need highlighting?

Clearly, the development and diffusion of modern sport is bound up in global processes (Maguire, 1999; Maguire *et al.*, 2002). The growth and development of worldwide sport organisations, the global acceptance of the rules of sport, and the establishment of international and global competitions are bound up in a series of flows that structure the interplay of sport worlds (see also Chapters 1 and 8). On first impression, sport seems to reinforce the international diminishing of contrasts, with numerous global events producing a coming together of the world – however fleeting. Nevertheless, the close affiliation between sport and national cultures also means that international sport (which even in global events is fundamentally national in nature) undermines, and will continue in the foreseeable future to undermine, more regional political integration such as that championed by the European Union (EU) and its European Commission, and indeed the sentiments expressed by Mandela (see also Chapters 5 and 6).

Yet, Mandela is not alone in associating global sport with the attributes and potential he identifies. In a development symptomatic of its contemporary global status and visibility, sport was the subject of a United Nations inter-agency task force report. Entitled *Sport for Development and Peace: Towards Achieving the Millennium Development Goals* (2003), the report made a series of claims for the role and potentiality of sport that would affect the lives of people, nations and civilisations across the globe. The report concluded:

> The world of sport presents a natural partnership for the United Nations system. By its very nature sport is about participation. It is about inclusion and citizenship. Sport brings individuals and communities together, highlighting commonalities and bridging cultural or ethnic divides ... Sport can cut across barriers that divide societies, making it a powerful tool to support conflict prevention and peace-building efforts, both symbolically on the global level and very practically within communities. When applied effectively, sport programmes promote social integration and foster tolerance, helping to reduce tension and generate dialogue. The convening power of sport makes it additionally compelling as a tool of advocacy and communications.
>
> (2005, p. v)

These are major claims to make about global sport, and indeed the report makes a series of others regarding the role sport can play in connection with health, disease control, economic development and environmental concerns. Several of these themes have been taken up by DEMOS, a left-leaning UK-based think tank, who sought to use the role of the Olympic truce at the Athens Games to promote the cause of peace (Briggs, McCarthy and Zorbas, 2004). Whatever our views about the (worthy) aims that the UN and DEMOS have set for themselves, and for sport, in achieving UN millennium goals and assisting in conflict resolution, our task as social scientists is to provide a realistic picture of sport. We have to critically assess, for example, the extent to which sport can and does achieve the role that Kofi Annan, UN Secretary General, claims it plays:

> Sport can play a role in improving the lives of individuals, not only individuals, I might add, but whole communities. I am convinced that the time is right to build on that understanding, to encourage governments, development agencies and communities to think how sport can be included more systematically in the plans to help children, particularly those living in the midst of poverty, disease and conflict.
>
> (UNDP and Sport and Development for Peace, 2003, p. 1, online)

The fact that the UN Secretary General places such importance on sport highlights its growing global significance (though at the time of writing no UN funds had been allocated). Our task is to examine this significance, noting the potentiality as well as the problems of global sport. In so doing, we will be better able to contribute to and assess policy formulation and implementation regarding sport at local, national and global levels. This book seeks to assess some of the claims made in support or critique of global sport. The four parts and eight chapters address some, but by no means all, key issues and concerns regarding global sport. This Introduction is designed to map out some of the conceptual tools that are needed in assessing the role and potentiality of global sport. Here, sport is also being used as a critical case study to assess the character and impact of global processes more generally.

That is, does sport assist in building friendship between people and nations? In doing so, as part of broader global civilising processes, does it extend some degree of emotional identification between members of different societies and civilisations? With the flow of athletic talent across the globe and with the holding of worldwide contests played out in front of people from different nations, and watched by billions via the media–sport complex, has an array of more cosmopolitan emotions developed within and between the peoples of different nations? Or, conversely, have globalisation processes been accompanied by a more powerful decivilising counter thrust, in which groups, within and between societies and civilisations, have reacted aggressively to the encroachment of alien values, artifacts and cultural products, of which modern sport is an example par excellence. If that be so, then the nationalism and violence that characterise aspects of global sport are more easily understood. Indeed, the feeling of wilful nostalgia, and the desire to have 'one of our own' representing the nation may be symptomatic of the sense of insecurity people feel in an increasingly globalised world and their rejection of more cosmopolitan values.

These are important questions about global sport, but also raise what Andrew Linklater argues is the most important question to ask about globalisation more generally. That is, whether the primary effect of globalisation is to extend, or contract, emotional identification between members of different societies (Linklater, 2004). The general question regarding globalisation will be returned to later. Let us, at this stage, briefly consider sport. During the twentieth century, modern sport was indeed to become a global idiom – Mandela and the UN report are correct in that sense. Yet, sport can play a seemingly contradictory role in global processes and identity formation. From a process-sociological perspective, it is not surprising that sport both extends emotional identification between members of different societies and civilisations and, at the same time, fuels decivilising counter thrusts. These are part of the same process that can be understood in terms of the interconnected concepts of established-outsider relations and diminishing contrasts–increasing varieties. While Alan Bairner does not use these words or theoretical approach per se, much common ground can be detected in his assessment of these issues:

> If the world is becoming homogenized, then nationalism or national identities in all their manifestations are rapidly losing their social significance, if, however, one adopts [a] more sophisticated approach . . . then it becomes obvious that nationalism coexists alongside globalization and is at times strengthened by it.
>
> (2001, p. 163)

From the evidence to hand it is clear that the diffusion of sport out of its British/European heartland was closely connected to an intensified global spurt (1870–1920). Its standardisation, organisational development and global diffusion reflected and reinforced the global processes that were being powered by the West and, as the twentieth century unfolded, by representatives of the US – in both the public and private sectors. The power geometry of globalisation and global sport always involve a complex, unequal balance within and between groups, nations and civilisations. Here, in this Introduction, two broad areas are addressed: globalisation, power and established-outsider relations; and civilisational encounters and global processes. Attention is then given, briefly, to the structure of this book.

Globalisation, power, and established-outsider relations

> Previously the doings of the world had been, so to say, dispersed, as they were held together by no unity of initiative, results, or locality; but ever since this date history has been an organic whole, and the affairs of Italy and Africa have been linked with those of Greece and Asia, all leading up to one end.

Observations of this kind seem quite appropriate as a commentary on contemporary aspects of globalisation. Yet, these words were, in fact, written about the Roman conquest of the Mediterranean world in the second century BC (Polybius, Histories 1.3, cited in Milleker, 2000, p. 3). Such comments alert us to the idea that discussion about inter-civilisational relations is nothing new – long-term processes are at work. Throughout the 1990s and into this century, attention has been paid to globalisation and, increasingly, to the inter-civilisational relations to which Polybius drew attention (Albrow, 1996; Beck, 2000; Beynon and Dunkerley, 2000; Giddens, 2000; Held, 2000; Held and McGrew, 2000; Hoogvelt, 2001; Sassen, 1996; Therborn, 2000). This interest has been matched in the connections researchers have made between globalisation and sport. Just as with its study more generally, the study of sport and globalisation is characterised by a diversity of perspectives, a number of competing concepts and ideas, and, in popular discussion, not a little ideological baggage.

However, some degree of consensus has been reached with regard to the fact that globalisation has undoubtedly changed the relationship between time and space, and that the globe is a more compressed space. In addition, there appears greater agreement that terms and concepts like interdependency, networks, multicausality, multidirectionality and glocality enhance the ability of researchers to grasp the dynamics of globalisation. Indeed, Held *et al.* (1999, p. 11) go so far as to conclude: 'contemporary globalisation is not reducible to a single, causal process, but involves a complex configuration of causal logics'. Such a view finds support in some work on sport (Bairner, 2001; Maguire *et al.*, 2002), while other work focuses more exclusively on the role of capital (Miller *et al.*, 2001).

Less consensus is evident in assessments regarding the consequences and trajectories of global sport processes. Opinion is as divided in this connection as it is with regard to cultural globalisation more generally. On the one hand, and reinforcing the views of the sports–industrial complex (see Chapter 8), global sport is viewed as a thoroughly progressive and liberating phenomenon that opens up the potential for greater human contact, dialogue and friendship. Global sport events, such as those planned for the 2008 Beijing Olympics, are said to promote the spread of human rights and democracy, improve inter-cultural understanding, and thus – in the marketing speak of the International Olympic Committee (IOC) – 'Celebrate Humanity' (see Chapter 7). Note that the IOC have conducted extensive marketing research, in conjunction with their TOP (The Olympic Partnership) sponsors and potential media outlets. Such research focused on what consumers know, and highlighted several themes associated with Olympism – hope, dreams and aspirations, friendship and fair play, and joy in effort. Some or all of these themes have been co-opted by corporate concerns and underpinned the global/local advertising campaigns of TOP sponsors in the build-up to the Athens games.

Sentiments of this kind underpin the words of Mandela cited earlier, and also find expression in observations made by Kofi Annan regarding the Games of the XXVII Olympiad, held in Sydney in 2000:

> The Olympic games display the very best of our common humanity. Coming together across virtually every line of race, ethnicity, language, religion, gender and national identity, the athletes – on their own or as members of a team – will scale new heights, set new records and give the world a lesson in international understanding. The games are a true celebration of humanity.
> (UN Press Release SG/SM/7523, 31 August 2000, p. 1)

In contrast to such sentiments, the present structure of global sport can also be seen as symptomatic of a new and consumer dominated phase of Western capitalism. As such, global consumer sport imposes its cultural products on vulnerable communities across the globe (for further discussion of the issues of space, place and community see Chapters 2 and 4). One consequence of this imposition is the eradication of cultural difference – whether this is a result of Americanisation and/or global capitalism is not of immediate relevance. The West dominates the economic, technological, political and knowledge resources and controls the levers of power of global sport (see Chapter 8). Global sport is thus tied to the opening up of new markets and the commodification of cultures – its consumption is a hallmark of late capitalism in a postmodern age.

These competing interpretations of global sport raise several questions regarding the origins, dynamics and characteristics of globalisation. They do not, of course, exhaust the possible analyses that can be made with regard to global sport. While further attention needs to be given to these questions, it is perhaps worthwhile recording that these interpretations are not as contradictory as they seem, and that the tendencies they describe may well, in a seemingly paradoxical manner, be part of the same overall process. Cultural globalisation, of which global sport is a part, can thus be viewed as unifying, universalising, progressive and liberating, or as divisive, fragmenting, constraining and destructive, of local cultures. There appears to be evidence for both. On the one hand, a world market for capital, commodities, labour and communications has developed, which is dominated by, and differentially favours, developed countries in general and the civilisation of the West in particular. Materially, people, at an everyday level, and nations, at a geopolitical level, are bound up in the matrix of global financial transactions (FIFA's World Cup and UEFA's Champions League being good examples); culturally, global brands structure the availability of and meanings associated with products consumed at a local level (consider the association football products provided by Adidas and Nike); personally, the media supplies us with images of far-off places and superstars who act as cultural icons, thereby sensitising the individual to the need to be globally aware and to think globally (the hosting of the Korea–Japan association football World Cup of 2002 and the celebrity status of footballer David Beckham highlight these trends; see also Chapter 3).

On the other hand, people, nations and civilizations appear adept at reacting differently to similar experiences of the global and of global sport. Globalisation has sparked anti-globalisation movements whose members not only wish to resist the processes described, but also seek to promote, reinvigorate and/or establish local organisations with roots in the community and based on notions of autonomy and democracy (see Chapters 2 and 4). Further, these movements, and others linked to environmentalism, are composed of people who share what Robertson, among others, has described as a 'globe-oriented perspective' (1990). Such a perspective recognises what humans share in common, while respecting difference. In addition, while globalisation may involve the development of transnational groupings, such as the EU, such centripetal forces have also, simultaneously, been matched by the acceleration of centrifugal forces, as witnessed by a surge in demands for self-government and autonomy for regions and nations. The position of the EU and the UK, and the demands of the Celtic fringe, provide a very good example of these processes at work, and such tensions also surface in a sporting context (see Chapter 5). Finally, while still highly asymmetrical, the current phase of globalisation is less dominated by Europe – a changing balance of power is evident in this new global order.

If we set aside dichotomous thinking, and emphasise a formulation that captures the twin processes of diminishing contrasts and increasing varieties, these tendencies are not as mutually exclusive as some of their more ardent exponents claim. This conclusion holds true for studies of sport (Maguire, 1999), and assessments regarding cultural globalisation more generally. Waters (1995), for example, concludes that in contemporary globalisation we are witnessing a 'complex interweave of homogenising with differentiating trends' and that:

> The globalization of popular culture has apparently paradoxical, but actually consistent, effects in simultaneously homogenizing and differentiating. Certainly it can homogenize across the globe in that what is available at any locality can become available in all localities, but at any particular locality it can increase the range of cultural opportunity.
>
> (p. 40)

These observations raise questions regarding theoretical stance, the timing and development of globalisation, and the power relations that govern such processes. Three broad approaches have been identified by Held *et al.* (1999). These are hyperglobalisers, sceptics, and transformationalists. The debates focus around three key issues: the extent to which globalisation has led to the elimination of local culture and the concomitant growth of a global Americanised culture (see Andrews, 1997); the notion that globalisation is a myth, or has had a superficial impact on the global, and that nation is where the action is (see Rowe, 2003); and that globalisation is leading to unique cultural networks and hybridity (see Rail, 1998).

Whatever the merits of these positions, an equally contentious debate surfaces regarding the timing and development of globalisation. Here, the work of Giddens, Held and Robertson are to the fore. While I am sympathetic with the approach of Robertson (see Maguire, 1999), there is much to gain from drawing on the work of Held (2000) and the insights provided by Goran Therborn (2000). Held's work highlights the need to consider questions of global governance – see also McGrew (2000) and Chapter 8 for how issues of governance connect to a critical analysis of the sports–industrial complex. Therborn identifies a series of historical waves, beginning with the spread of world religions, predating Robertson's timing of globalisation and enhancing our understanding of the complexity of long-term global processes. It is worth restating that the emergence of modern sport in the context of English society in the early 1700s was also part of a longer-term inter-civilisational sequence (Maguire, 2004).

In all of these discussions regarding globalisation, questions of power repeatedly surface. How best, then, to make sense of power, sport and global relations? Richard Gruneau, in a new postscript to his 1988 work, *Class, Sports and Social Development*, offered a fair account of aspects of a figurational approach to the sociology of sport, yet still concluded:

> I never felt that Dunning's work – or Elias's either, for that matter – offered an adequate theory of power or an engaged standpoint for social criticism. Power is discussed in various ways in Elias and Dunning's work, but it is rarely connected directly to a broader theory and critique of domination in social life, especially in respect to the changing social organization of capitalism. Even today, after a decade and a half of theoretical development and refinement, more recent figurational approaches to the sociology of sport, such as Maguire's, only pay passing attention to the specific dynamics of global capitalism.
>
> (Gruneau, 1999, p. 121)

These comments deserve to be taken seriously. Gruneau is right to point to the fact that the question of power, and its link to a broader theory and critique of domination in social life, have not been sufficiently spelt out in accounts on sport – though in *Global Sport* (Maguire, 1999) these issues were addressed. Nevertheless, there is a genuine debate to be had about the nature of power. In the section that follows, the question of power and the link to questions of established-outsider relations is more fully articulated. In addition, this linkage is more fully examined with reference to the dynamics at work in inter-civilisational relations and global processes. This may not be sufficient for Gruneau, for he would wish a greater emphasis placed on the changing social organisation of capitalism. I agree, and the original work on American football (Maguire, 1990), and the updated account that compares this with the activities of the NBA in the UK (see Chapter 1), do address the linkage of sport and capitalism. Where we differ, I suspect, is the relative emphasis given to the economic in conjunction with the political and the cultural.

His own position, like that of fellow neo-Marxists and/or cultural studies writers, connects the question of power to the centrality of economics in human societies. Whereas in some accounts of sport, such as the work of Brohm (1978), economics plays a causal role, more recent work, by Silk and Andrews (2001), tends to soften this line and places greater emphasis on the role of local culture, along with economics, in global sport. Despite this more nuanced approach, Andrews (1997, pp. 79–80) felt able to claim that global popular culture 'has largely, but by no means exclusively, been influenced by the interconnected technological, capital and media flows emanating from the United States'. More recently, Miller *et al.* (2001, p. 10) concluded: 'What began as a cultural exchange based on empire has turned into one based on capital'. There is much of worth in these positions, but the analysis of power and global sport offered here takes a different tack.

Process-sociology sees power as an essential feature of the networks of interdependency that people form with each other. The types and forms of interdependency are contoured by power relations – these are the capillaries of power to which Foucault also refers. Elias (1978) used what he called game models as didactic devices to capture the pervasive effects of interdependence and power. Studies informed by such an approach can examine the exercise of power at the level of social interaction, but also in far more complex, multifaceted organisational structures such as the IOC, or in relations within and between nation-states regarding sport and domestic or foreign policy objectives. These game models seek to capture the ways in which the numbers of players and the extent of structural complexity increase, and power differentials within contests decrease. The more power relations become relatively equal among large numbers of groups, the more likely is it that the outcome will be somewhat different to what any single person or group has planned or anticipated. These figurations that people form with each other are always governed by a dynamic operation of power (note the linkage with Foucault in this regard). As Elias (1978) noted:

> At the core of changing figurations – indeed the very hub of the figuration process – is a fluctuating, tensile equilibrium, a balance of power moving to and fro, inclining first one side and then the other. This kind of fluctuating balance of power is a structural characteristic of the flow of every figuration.
>
> (p. 131)

Power, then, is a structural process and an inherent characteristic of figurations in flux.

Two related ideas also assist in making sense of these power relations, and thereby global processes: functional democratisation and the monopoly mechanism. The former relates to the process whereby, as noted, the more relatively equal become the power ratios among people and groups, the more likely is it that the outcome is something that no single person or group planned or intended. In terms of cycles of violence, for example, double-bind processes trap people in a position of mutual fear and distrust or cumulative weakening or reciprocal destruction; only rarely do they resolve themselves in a condition of compromise without absolute victors or absolute vanquished (Elias & Dunning, 1986, p. 58). The term monopoly mechanism seeks to capture the structured processes at work over time and place as social differentiation and integration among increasingly larger groups become dominant, and greater concentrations of power occur. As chains of interdependency grow longer – at a national and at a global level – the monopoly mechanism can take effect. The emergence and global consolidation of the IOC is a case in point.

Crucially, this monopoly mechanism is not confined to the sphere of economics. Rather, in a multicausal and multidirectional way, this occurs in the area of military struggle, political domination, cultural relations and economic activity. These processes were a major feature of state formation, but such questions of power also govern small-scale social interaction and community relations. In order to make sense of social relations within and between communities, Elias (in conjunction with John Scotson) developed a model that focused on the power balances between established and outsider groups. Its significance for the study of global sport has not been fully recognised (Maguire, 1999), but Martin Albrow (1997, p. 42) views Elias's work on established-outsider relations as 'a prescient forerunner of globalisation research'.

This model can thus be applied to a broad range of stratification phenomena, including ethnic/race issues, class struggles, gender relations and indeed relations at a global level. Established-outsider studies of this kind avoid giving primacy to economic and class relations, yet acknowledge the fundamental importance of power differentials in society. Such differentiation is multidimensional in character and finds expression in people's self-esteem and images of others. Status, prestige, power and control underpin established-outsider relations. As Elias & Scotson (1965, p. 155) observed: 'Without their power the claim to a higher status and a specific charisma would soon decay and sound hollow whatever the distinctiveness of their behaviour'.

Power differentials of this kind generate contrasts between group charisma and group stigma – established groups enjoy the former, while outsiders suffer the latter. Established groups are better able to organise, within specific zones of prestige, their high-status public image while at the same time constructing a negative image of outsider groups. This uneven balance of power – at local, national and global levels – is the decisive condition for any effective stigmatisation of an outsider group. The stigma of collective disgrace can thus be made to stick. It is therefore difficult, though not impossible, for outsider groups to resist internalising the negative characteristics attributed to them by the established group. One strategy in these zones of prestige is to emulate the established group; another is to resist and react with hostility. These issues of prestige, emulation and resistance will be returned to when considering civilisational relations more generally. If such images are internalised, outsiders may well come to experience this power inferiority as a sign of human inferiority. Thus, the sense of stigma is developed at the level of culture and group dynamics, and individuals internalise this sense of disgrace into their personality structure. While such processes remain a feature of day-to-day relations, they are, nevertheless, deeply embedded within the shared histories and collective memories of individuals and the communities/nations they compose. Such processes are always contested and involve the exercise of a range of power resources. Here, we may note the linkage to issues of habitus, on which Elias focused in his study of *The Germans* (1996). Ideas of this kind also surface in the work of Bourdieu (1984), though he did not probe questions of cultural power in global civilisational terms.

When the balance of power shifts in the direction of the outsiders, however, the power to stigmatise diminishes and the former outsider groups tend to retaliate. Such retaliation may well be directed to the former masters or other groups, who, though themselves outsiders, were formerly closer to the established group. The history of Indian cricket, and the relations between representatives of the former colonial power and the different communities that compose the nation-state, vividly highlight these processes at work (Guha, 2002). Crucially, however, whichever way the balance of power tips, at the level of the nation-state, and civilisational relations more broadly, established groups almost invariably experience and present themselves as more civilised, while constructing outsiders as more barbaric. This is vividly evident in the geo-identity politics following the events of what have become known as 9/11. Thus, the ongoing development of established-outsider relations and the zones of prestige, emulation and resistance that accompany them are built into the characteristics of group relations – at community, national and global levels. It should also not be a surprise to discover that the established-outsider relations that contour such zones play a crucial role in the identity politics of cultural globalisation, and in the dynamics underpinning the longer-term and contemporary aspects of global sport.

In the diffusion of sport throughout the empire, the British, whatever their own ethnic origin, acted as the established group dealing with a range of outsider groups. The degree to which they viewed the local culture as barbarian may well have varied, but they were convinced of their own civilised status. Their sports confirmed their gentlemanly civilised status – for it was men who composed the established group within the imperial elite. The clubs and playing fields acted as zones of prestige, which helped stratify relations not only among the British themselves, but also in their dealings with the 'natives'. These zones of prestige thus conferred distinction, and allowed gentlemen to embody the qualities of honour, chivalry and fair play. Access to such prestigious clubs and playing fields could be regulated – only chosen outsiders would be allowed to emulate their imperial masters and become, through the adoption of their sports, more British than the British. Such individuals, acting as players, teachers and administrators, could thus spread British sports, and thus British influence, more widely and deeply within a colony (Cashman, 1988; Mangan, 1986, 1988; Stoddart, 1988).

Such established-outsider relations were always contested, even though the manner and form of resistance would vary from 'white' to 'non-white' colonies. And the British themselves were to experience the same double-bind that can be traced to the processes associated with functional democratisation – try as they might to maintain their own civilised status, gradually the cultural markers of power and prestige seeped out from beneath their exclusive control, and in the case of sport, the imperial masters began to be beaten at their own games. Questions of power, culture and control are thus at the heart of global sport processes (see Maguire, 1999, pp. 47–56; and Chapter 8). In writing about these civilisational zones of prestige, emulation and resistance, questions concerning civilisational analysis more broadly are raised. It is to these that attention now turns.

Civilisational encounters and global processes

Until relatively recently, use of the term civilisation had fallen out of favour in cultural anthropology, history and sociology. In globalisation research, little attention had been given to the idea of global civilising processes (Linklater, 2004). It became fashionable to view such terms as flowing from Christendom, and as a product of the Enlightenment, and thus containing a built-in value judgement that emphasised the superiority of the West. In contrast, in post-colonial thinking, what matters is the decentring of the West and the proclaiming of voices on the margins. This approach has much merit. Indeed, given that globalisation processes are marked by double-bind processes such as functional democratisation, little wonder then that the waning of the West may already be underway. In addition, demographic changes are decentring the West from within. Further, national and regional economies and political structures are being reconfigured in the context of a quickening globalisation spurt. Debunking Eurocentric or Western-based world-views has thus proved a powerful corrective in making sense of the longer-term and contemporary aspects of globalisation.

Yet, such an approach also brings with it certain conceptual blind spots. The sociological roots of the term civilisation are far more complex than the debunking motif would suggest (Sanderson, 1995). While it is not possible to outline its history here, three waves of sociological usage of the term can be identified. The first wave involved Max Weber, Emile Durkheim and Marcel Mauss; the second wave included Norbert Elias, Pitirim Sorokin and Benjamin Nelson; the third wave finds expression in the work of Shmuel Eisenstadt and Samuel Huntington (see Tiryakian, 2001). Use of the terms civilisation, civilising processes, and global civilising processes can cast important light on both the development of globalisation and contemporary globalisation processes. In this connection, examination of sportisation processes can provide a powerful paradigmatic study of broader global phenomena.

If the terms civilisation and global civilising processes are shorn of the assumptions associated with claims of Western superiority, the task remains to develop further the vocabulary, concepts and evidence concerning inter-civilisational encounters on a global level. Analyses by Francis Fukuyama and Huntington, summed up in book titles such as *The End of History and the Last Man* (Fukuyama, 1992), or *The Clash of Civilizations and the Remaking of World Order* (Huntington, 1996), only go so far in capturing the complexity of what is involved. So what is the alternative? First, it is necessary to outline certain key assumptions. Second, consideration is given to the internal structures of civilisations. Third, examination of the forms, dimensions and contexts of inter-civilisational encounters will be undertaken. Using the resulting perspective, aspects of the sociology of sport could be reoriented so as to more effectively grasp relatively neglected features of global sport.

The term civilisation can be understood in a singular and a plural sense. It is possible to equate the term solely with modernity, and to link it with the emergence of a globalised technoscientific civilisation. In this sense, one civilisation is emerging, or has emerged, but many cultures remain (Schäfer, 2001). Thus, technoscientific civilisation can be embraced, while the products and ideas of specific cultures, e.g. Americanisation, can be resisted or rejected. Considered in this light, global civilisation has no fixed territoriality. Its structure is made up of a worldwide matrix of technoscientific networks – the media–sport complex can be understood in such terms (see Chapter 1). For Wolf Schäfer (2001, p. 312), this 'essential constituent defines the civilisation of our time as a deterritorialised ensemble of networked technoscientific practices with global reach'. Such an approach fruitfully alerts us to the globalised nature of technoscience (for discussion of how this finds expression in sport worlds see Chapter 8). In addition, its very spread enables us to grasp the dynamics at work.

Schäfer (2001) arguably provides us with an even more significant insight when he concludes:

> Not too many people care about global civilization at this moment, in fact, most people are prepared by their local culture to dismiss a singular civilization or consider it a dangerous thing. Yet, world music, global email, human rights, green politics and other global pursuits and holistic interests are sowing the seeds for more intense global identifications. Collective symbolising has begun to shore up support for the global environment of the human species. People could embrace the civilization of this planet with such loyalty as they now embrace their local culture.
>
> (p. 312)

World music (along with dance) may have this potentiality but the diversity of musical forms, as with ludic culture, is also under threat. Such sentiments regarding world music can also, like the comments of Mandela, Annan and the UN report noted at the outset, be connected to global sport and its potentiality. Schäfer's more general point returns us to Linklater's (2004) observation with regard to globalisation. That is, whether the primary effect of globalisation is to extend, or contract, emotional identification between members of different societies. Considered in this light, the task for studies of global sport should include an assessment of whether sport assists in building friendship between people and nations, and in so doing, and as part of broader global civilising processes, extends some degree of emotional identification between members of different societies and civilisations. (For an alternative view of global sport based on a human development model that links with the issues raised by Schäfer see Chapter 8.) Global sport may well also fuel decivilising counter thrusts. One of the tasks for sociologists examining global sport is to gauge its effects in a detailed cross-cultural fashion – exploring established and outsider groups and nations in the global civilisational hierarchy. That task remains to be done. Then again, perhaps world music and dance have a greater potentiality to sow the seeds for more intense global identifications?

The work of Tiryakian (2001) and others sensitises global analyses to the existence of dynamic and interactive cultural units that are larger than nation-states, but smaller than a single socio-economic totality. Stress needs to be placed on the plurality of civilisations, noting the nature and extent of their interdependence, while also establishing their distinctive and formative features. Understood in this way, civilisations are total phenomena: they entail economics, politics and culture, which in various combinational syntheses move civilisations and their contacts with others in different directions. Considered in this light, the study of these civilising processes at local, national and global levels facilitates the generation and testing of hypotheses regarding comparative and historical aspects of human development. The study of play, games and sports provides an important context in which work of this kind could be undertaken (Galtung, 1982; Huizinga, 1949/1970). Though now somewhat neglected, Gunther Luschen's (1967) study of the interdependence of sport and culture provides some clues in this regard.

Before considering the dynamics, nodal points and power relations of these inter-civilisational exchanges, it remains necessary to map out further the internal structures of civilisations. In ideal-type terms, Arnason (2001) identifies several civilisational blocs: Chinese, east Asian, Indian, Islamic, Byzantine and Western Christian; however, this does not exhaust the possible range. The cultural codes of these civilisations have both overlapping features as well as distinctive elements. Arnason is less concerned with the specifics, and focuses more on providing a provisional model of the common properties of civilisations. Arnason's work, in conjunction with insights drawn from Randall Collins and Norbert Elias, provides the basis of the schemata presented here.

Civilisations, then, have distinctive cultural orientations and interpretations of the world. Galtung (1982, 1991), studying sport as a carrier of deep culture and structure, was on the right lines when he concluded that Western sports serve as fully fledged carriers of the socio-cultural codes 'typical for expansionist occidental cosmology' (1991, p. 150). The potential of this insight was not fulfilled as it remained disconnected from broader civilisational analysis. In addition to these cultural codes, the institutional constellations of civilisations – the frameworks of political and economic life – need examination. Civilisations also express representative ideologies, in texts, and in the embodied strategies and self-images of elites. Again, the study of play, games and sports can highlight these embodied strategies – the high status habitus of British gentlemen was clearly evident in their games and pastimes played on the fields of empire. Studies of the diffusion and differential adoption of polo and rugby union in places like Argentina and Japan provide important clues to the processes at work.

These civilisational complexes can encompass whole families of societies (Arnason, 2001). Such complexes clearly have long-term temporal dimensions, stretching across successive generations and societal formations. It would be wrong, however, to think that the application of this approach is confined to long-term processes. Contemporary globalisation and inter-civilisational relations can be understood in the same terms. It is also important to note that within these overall complexes, regional figurations arise and relatively distinctive patterns emerge. Although the British had an empire on which the sun was said never to set, its various outposts were forging quite distinct cultural codes, institutional arrangements, and ideologies.

While these features help in understanding the internal structures of civilisations, it is also necessary to highlight the characteristics of what has been termed the civilisation of modernity and the modernity of civilisations (Tiryakian, 2001). Eisenstadt (2001), for example, detects several characteristics, including: the use of advanced technologies that compress distance and alleviate traditional diseases of humankind; the expression of a wide variety of lifestyles and patterns of individuation; decentred zones of prestige; and extensive contacts and interactions, virtual and physical, that occur between and within regions. While it is not clear what values underpin this global civilisation of modernity, it is no longer the exclusive domain of the West, or even of Westerners experiencing the civilisation of the other. Despite this, the West may still be said to have triumphed because so much — but not all — of its civilisation moved beyond its British/European/Western homelands and established itself as an integral part of the civilisation of modernity (see Chapter 7 for a consideration of the 2008 Beijing Olympic games in these terms).

Examination of the internal structures of civilisations is a necessary but not sufficient analysis of global civilisational processes. This must be interwoven with the study of inter-civilisational encounters. Unidirectional, monocausal explanations, focusing on the role of capital or Americanisation, do not do full justice to the heterogeneity of these inter-civilisational encounters. In making sense of encounters of this kind, as with global consumer culture more generally, the analysis has to deal with questions of production and consumption. The dynamics of inter-civilisational encounters are characterised by both a diminishing of contrasts and an increase of varieties.

The relative hegemony of the West has ensured that the production of its civilisational wares has globalised over the past two centuries and more. As a result of the colonisation strategies of the established (designed to impose their culture or co-op that of the other), and the emulation and imitation actions by outsiders (seeking to close the status gap), there has been a tendency towards civilisations overlapping. That is, the contrasts between them become more muted. Such processes are at work between Western and non-Western civilisations: they are also present in relations *between* outsider civilisations. Inter-civilisational encounters are multidimensional; a global mosaic of power struggles, within and between established-outsider groups, at local, regional and global levels is at work. These crossovers and fusions involve the co-adoption of similar skills and techniques, the development of ever denser communication networks, and structures of consciousness, at practical and discursive levels (Arnason, 2001). The diffusion of Western ludic body culture and the sporting habitus can be understood in such terms.

This diminishing of contrasts is only one side of the coin. There has also occurred an increase in the varieties of identities, styles, products and practices. Such a process is again underpinned by a complex power geometry involving established-outsider relations. That is, the representatives of more powerful civilisations wish not only to colonise other cultures, but also ensure that their own styles and practices are distinctive enough to reaffirm their group charisma and sense of civilised high status and taste. Power struggles *within* established groups also prompt the incorporation of aspects of other cultures and civilisations into the established civilisational form. In contrast, the representatives of less powerful civilisations seek to resist colonisation and the civilisational assumptions, styles and practices of others. In doing so, they too restyle their own behaviour, customs and ideas, and reaffirm outsider civilisational traditions in a more intense way.

There are, however, other dynamics at work in the production and consumption of new varieties. A process of crossover, fusion and creolisation of cultures and civilisations takes place. Writing about this in more general terms, Elias (1939/1994) noted:

> In accordance with the power-relationship, the product of interpenetration is dominated first by models derived from the situation of the upper class, then by [the] pattern(s) of conduct of the lower, rising classes, until finally an amalgam emerges, a new style of unique character.
>
> (p. 464)

Although Western civilisation, at this stage in human development, can be regarded as the established group in global terms, its history suggests that it too is part of a specific multi-civilisational sequence. In making this case, the analysis returns to a point previously made. Civilisations are not fixed, closed or isolated entities – they have a long-term history as well as contemporary features.

Established groups are able to develop a collective we-image, based on a sense of civilisational superiority and group charisma, as well as a they-image, in which outsiders (and their play and games) are viewed with disdain and mistrust. Outsiders and their civilisation are stigmatised as inferior, and their practices as childlike and unsophisticated. With the shift towards greater interdependency, and the decrease of contrasts, however, a functional democratisation process is at work. High-status civilised behaviour seeps out from the zones of prestige. Established groups, despite refining their own behaviour in response, find it more difficult to control outsiders – either those who have successfully emulated their former masters, or those who chose to resist. The case has already been made that the making of modern sport, and the role that the British and their empire played in the global diffusion of sports, can be understood in these terms (Maguire, 1999, pp. 50–55). Here, then, the analysis is extended to a discussion of the role that zones of prestige, emulation and resistance play more generally in such inter-civilisational encounters.

Though Collins (2001) does not use concepts such as established-outsider relations and diminishing contrasts–increasing varieties, his analysis of zones of prestige dovetails with this broader schematic. These zones can be more adequately understood if linked to global civilising processes, which involve phases of colonisation and repulsion (Elias, 1939/1994). Such zones can also prompt decivilising counter thrusts in which groups react aggressively to the promotion and encroachment of alien values (Linklater, 2004).

Zones of prestige refer to multiple or singular centres where culturally impressive activities are produced, displayed and consumed. These zones perform three main tasks, which may be connected to sportisation processes. First, they renew and confirm the identities of members of civilisations. London, for example, played this role, but in the context of nineteenth-century sport and games, so too did high-status public schools. In terms of sport and the empire, there were also regional and local zones of prestige – think of the role that cricket clubs in Kuala Lumpur and Singapore played in the exercise of imperial power.

Second, zones of prestige attract sojourners, students and visitors. Drawn to the civilisational magnetism and cultural charisma of nineteenth-century imperial Britain, fellow Europeans and representatives of other civilisations sought to understand the success of the British. For Baron Pierre de Coubertin, his visits confirmed his belief that this success was connected to the play and games of British public schools. He was not alone in such beliefs – a range of students and visitors returned home, established inter-civilisational networks, and brought with them the values and practices of the British, including their sports. Third, these zones of prestige acted, and act, as networks, where ideas, religious beliefs and social formations could be examined, discussed and, crucially, exchanged. In examining the early making of modern sport Elias and Dunning (1986) pointed to the significant role of private clubs and their relative autonomy which was more pronounced in Britain then elsewhere in Europe. In terms of sports and games, British zones of prestige acted as magnets, but this involved not only the outflow and diffusion of games and sports. The established imperial centre also experienced the inflow of ideas and practices. These included attempts to develop Swedish and Danish gymnastics, and German Turnen (McIntosh, 1968). In addition, sports such as polo and badminton flowed back from outposts of empire and contained within them the imprint of other civilisational traditions.

Zones of prestige can rise and fall in terms of the civilisational magnetism and cultural charisma they project and contain. The role they play in inter-civilisational encounters is also contoured by the relative distances and modes of communication available in different parts of the globe. In addition, the degree of identification with and loyalty to a specific civilisational tradition also influences whether its impact is short term and ephemeral, or long term and more enduring with the ideas, customs and practices entering the other civilisation's cultural interpretation of the world, its institutional constellations, representative ideologies, or we-group habitus codes.

Zones of prestige can, however, also prompt rejection and hostility on the part of people from outsider civilisations. In phases of colonisation, indifference to or outright rejection of the civilisational practices of the more powerful established group also occurs (Elias, 1939/1994, p. 464). Rejection can also be a feature of long-term antagonism between civilisations – the response by sections of the Islamic world to the ludic body traditions of the West is a case in point (Mazrui, 1987). In this regard, it is worth noting that neither geopolitical nor economic hegemony automatically creates a centre of civilisational prestige (Collins, 2001). Yet, the intention of such zones is clear. As Elias (1939/1994) remarked in this regard:

> It is not a little characteristic of the structure of Western societies that the watchword of its colonizing movement is 'civilization' . . . But it is not only the land that is needed but the people; these must be integrated, whether as workers or consumers, into the web of the hegemonial, the upper-class country, with its highly developed differentiation of functions.
>
> (p. 509)

The cultural shift from emulation and imitation to hostility does not, however, always follow from a change in the balance of power between established and outsider groups. As Collins (2001, p. 427) notes: 'a struggle for military liberation or economic upward mobility may occur without a concomitant rejection of imports from a zone of civilizational prestige'. The longevity of cricket in the Caribbean and in the Indian subcontinent, long after the imperial masters left their former colonies, are examples of these processes at work (Beckles & Stoddart, 1995; Guha, 2002).

This insight leads to a more general observation about sport, civilisational encounters and globalisation. While established-outsider relations are contoured and shaped by an amalgam of political, economic and social processes, a movement for cultural or civilisational autonomy is not a mere reflex of geopolitical or economic relations. Inter-civilisational encounters are also based on dynamics that involve social networks of intellectuals, cultural workers and organisations that provide a base for cultural production and consumption (see Chapter 3 for discussion of sport migrants). Attracted to the zone of prestige, sojourners become pupils and followers. On returning home they may become keen advocates of what they have learned and, in so doing, build successful careers – in the case of sport, as players, coaches, teachers or administrators. Alternatively, such visitors may return home convinced of the superiority of their own civilisational tradition, and thus work with equal vigour to reject cultural products and practices from the established civilisation.

The differential diffusion of Olympism via the Olympic movement may well prove to be a classic example of these dynamics at work, but much more work needs to be done on how this diffusion unfolded in different civilisations. Its importance was clearly highlighted by Kofi Annan's message to the Games of the XXVII Olympiad, held in Sydney in 2000. A clear link was made with Olympism and the ideals of the UN:

> Olympic ideals are also United Nations ideals: tolerance, equality, fair play and, most of all, peace. Together, the Olympics and the United Nations can be a winning team. But the contest will not be won easily. War, intolerance and deprivation continue to stalk the earth. We must fight back. Just as athletes strive for world records, so must we strive for world peace ... Interest in the power of sport as a means of promoting a culture of peace is on the rise.
> (UN Press Release SG/SM/7523, 31 August 2000, p. 1)

Reinforcing the diffusion of Olympism in general and sport in particular, the centres of prestige have long sent out missionaries and pioneers. Think, for example, of the role that the YMCA played in the diffusion of global sport and that the Catholic church played in the development of Kenyan athletics. These missionaries also make their careers as carriers of a civilisational culture eager to proselytise on the periphery (Mangan, 1988). Over time, sports and games became part of the formal policy of the nation-states of different civilisations, directed at citizens in the form of physical education and at elite athletes, who become part of the global sports–industrial complex (see Chapter 8). As such, these strategies, in an unintended manner, reinforce and reflect the geopolitical, economic and cultural established-outsider figuration.

To acknowledge this is not to overlook the role of cultural producers, to which Collins directs our attention. Rather than seeing such careers as autonomous from issues of geopolitical and economic hegemony, a more adequate portrayal would be in terms of the relative autonomy within specific figurations of production and consumption. Nevertheless, it is important to note that it is factions in the culture-producing networks that have the strongest interests in inter-civilisational imports and exports, in terms of promoting or inhibiting such flows. The dynamics underpinning the global diffusion of sport can also be linked to these processes (Maguire, 1999; Van Bottenburg, 2001, 2003).

One final observation regarding civilisational encounters and global processes needs to be made. It has already been noted that even when the balance of power changes between established and outsider civilisations, the representatives of the latter do not necessarily reject the previous imports from the zone of prestige. A related question arises concerning how the former established civilisation retains its prestige and its network centrality after it is eclipsed by the superior military and/or economic power of another world region. Here, a pertinent example is the case of the British. While having lost economic and military supremacy, London, and some of the cultural wares of the British, retain their prestige. How? Part of the answer lies in what Collins (2001) argues in the following passage:

> A region becomes a civilizational center, a zone of prestige attracting outsiders, because it has the social structures which promote intellectual creativity: organisational bases for a small number of opposing schools of thought, lineages which are built up over several generations and which intersect with one another in creative rivalry at a few centers of intellectual action.
>
> (p. 431)

In this connection, the BBC, the British Council and its high-status universities would be examples of British organisations and institutions that encourage innovation and expression, and thus allow for the retention of prestige. Long-standing sporting events, such as Wimbledon, Royal Ascot and the Henley Regatta, perform similar functions. Yet, this is only part of the explanation. Zones of prestige are also linked to how its advocates view themselves. In this regard, the we-image and we-ideal of the British needs to be considered (see also Chapters 5 and 6). Modelled on an idealised image of themselves in the days of their imperial greatness (in political, economic, military and sporting terms), their group charisma and we-ideal lingers on for many generations as a model they feel they ought to live up to, but are often unable to do so.

As Elias (1939/1994) observes with regard to declining nations and civilisations more generally:

> Yet, the dream of their special charisma is kept alive in a variety of ways – through the teaching of history, the old buildings, master-pieces of the nation in the time of its glory, or through new achievements which seemingly confirm the greatness of the past.
>
> (p. xliv)

The media framing of, and popular reaction to, the men's England rugby union team victory in the 2003 World Cup in Australia highlights such processes at work. The fantasy shield of their imagined charisma and the retention of specific zones of civilisational prestige gives the British the resources to carry on. But, defeats on and off the playing field undermine that civilisational prestige. What will the reaction be if Great Britain fail to secure the award of the 2012 Olympic Games? Whatever other zones of prestige the British maintain, sport may no longer be as central, even if, as the historian Ensor noted in 1936, 'the development of organised games ... may rank among England's leading contributions to world culture' (1936, p. 164). The study of power, established-outsider relations and inter-civilisational encounters allows us to make a more sober assessment of this export, and of the globalised nature of sport more generally.

Final remarks

This book is divided into four parts. Part I focuses on what has been termed the local–global nexus. Here, attention is given to two case studies that involve different aspects of space, place, locality and global processes. In Chapter 1, with Mark Falcous, attention is given to a comparison of the activities of the NFL and the NBA in the UK. Chapter 2, with Catherine Possamai, provides an analysis of how a local London community reacted to changes in association football in the 1990s. Part II looks at the lived experiences involved in aspects of global sport. Case studies on cricket, with David Stead, and of rugby league, with Catherine Possamai, are presented. Attention is paid to the experience of both players and supporters. In this way, the focus is on the here and now and everyday experience of global sport.

Part III focuses on questions of national identity and the impact that global sport has in this regard. While specific attention is given to rugby union (with Jason Tuck), and association football (with Michael Burrows), both chapters are tied together by a common interpretation derived from process-sociology. Part IV looks to the future and examines areas that may illuminate deeper trends at work in global sport. In Chapter 7, attention is given to what the success of the Beijing bid for the 2008 Olympic Games reveals about civilisational relations and cultural struggles more broadly. The final chapter offers both a critique of the sports–industrial complex and an alternative vision of the path that global sport could take. It will be for the reader to make an assessment of the merit of this critique and the value of the alternative proposed. My hope, however, is that these final observations offer some resources of hope to those who wish to build more democratically based sport worlds and civilisational encounters.

Part I
Local–global nexus

1 'Making touchdowns and hoop dreams'

The NFL and the NBA in England

Joseph Maguire and Mark Falcous

This chapter explores processes of market expansion, cultural diffusion and dissemination as they coalesce around the operations of 'sporting transnationals'. Debates surrounding the interplay of local and global processes have attracted increasing attention from sociologists of sport (Andrews, 1997; Guttmann, 1994; Maguire, 1999; Maguire *et al.*, 2002; Miller *et al.*, 2001, 2003; Van Bottenburg, 2001, 2003). The prominent role of sport in constructions of cultural identities has meant that it is highly visible in the transformations and entrenchments of local cultures in the context of globalisation. Consequently, the analysis of sport provides fertile ground to consider local–global interdependence. The intensity of this interplay has been heightened within the emergent political economy of sport, contingent to which, in what Maguire (1999) has referred to as the most recent sportisation phase, is an accelerated phase of corporate–media–sport alignment and global expansion of various sporting 'brands'.

Such issues are captured in the comments made by television commentator Mark Webster, who speculated on the likely impact of the National Basketball Association (NBA) compared to the National Football League (NFL) in England:

> It [the NBA] ain't going to suddenly be the new soccer, but it's got a better chance than any other American sport. It's a great game to play: you don't need anything but a ball and a basket. The NFL peaked in England around the turn of the decade. It was never really a great game. What it was, was the first American piece of culture we could buy, like McDonald's.
> (Webster, cited in Campbell, 1997)

In arguing that American basketball was likely to have greater success during the 1990s than American football had achieved during the 1980s, Webster highlights several significant factors in the cultural diffusion and reception of North American sports within the UK, including: the rival appeal of established local sports; the resilience of the local commercial sports market; and the playing appeal and accessibility of basketball. He also proposed that the cultural resonance of American sports equates to that of American cultural products per se (McDonald's specifically).

In this chapter, we take the opportunity for comparative analysis afforded by the presence and operations of the National Football League (NFL) and National Basketball Association (NBA) in the UK (the commencement of which were separated by a 13-year spell). The chapter focuses on the presence of the NBA within the UK during the 1990s, and makes comparisons with the operations and impacts of the NFL during the 1980s as detailed by Maguire (1990, 1991b, 1993b). In considering their strategies, impacts and relative success, systematic parallels are instructive. These comparisons provide the opportunity to reflect on wider questions of the local–global nexus. Specifically, they reveal the dynamic nature of local–global interdependence and highlight issues of reception, resistance and transience within the context of the cultural politics of the 'Global Age' (Albrow, 1996). They also afford scope to briefly reflect on theoretical debates which have informed conceptualisations of the cultural impacts of the operations of global sports transnationals. Too often, the local–global debate has been characterised by an obtuse polemic between advocates of homogeneity or heterogeneity. A way out of this false dichotomy is to view the debate in terms of the twin concepts of diminishing contrasts and increasing varieties (Maguire, 1999). Likewise, Uri Ram, examining the impact of McDonald's on Israeli society, is equally uncomfortable with adopting an either/or position. He argues that 'while both homogenization and heterogenization are dimensions of globalization, they take place at different societal levels: homogenization occurs at the structural–institutional level; heterogenization, at the expressive–symbolic level' (2004, p. 11). This chapter is then guided by such observations and seeks to avoid falling into the trap of seeing such processes as unidirectional or monocausal.

Transnational corporations, global sport and cultural identities

The geographical diffusion of playing forms, institutions, governance and associated ideologies is an integral feature of the emergence of modern sport as a global idiom. The more recent expansions of sporting 'brands' to foreign markets, however, is symptomatic of recent developments in the political-economy of sport (see Andrews, 1997; Maguire, 1999; Maguire et al., 2002; Miller et al., 2001, 2003). These developments include an accelerated phase of corporate–media–sport alignment, resulting in sport being reconfigured according to more instrumentally rational approaches to capital accumulation on a global scale. Consequently, mass consumption, media collusion, integration with transnational corporations, marketing and branding, and diversified accumulation through the sale of ancillary branded products characterise the structural–institutional patterning of global sport. With market expansion, the extension of 'core operations' (for example, extending the geographical spread of franchises/teams), media broadcasting and merchandising operations have become integral to the operations of numerous commercial sports. Subsequently, the global presence of some transnational sports brands has extended rapidly.

The role of transnational corporations (TNCs) within the economic restructuring that is a component of globalisation is considerable, though the enduring role of the nation-state should not be overlooked. One consequence of the application of economic logics of globalisation underpinning desires for market expansion has been the emergence of global products (Robins, 1997): consumer goods that are consistent across world locations. These products, Robins notes, are entwined with an ideology of global awareness – one element of which is the emergence of the global consumer. Such global awareness has also spawned anti-global and green movements that use aspects of globalisation to make their own case. Nevertheless, global products and brands are myriad, the most prominent of which include Coca-Cola, McDonald's, Sony, Mastercard, Calvin Klein, Motorola, Fuji and Nike. These developments also have manifestations within the global sports economy. Indeed, the development of transnational industries has emerged as a 'significant feature of the global sport system' (Maguire, 1999, p. 128).

Global consumer marketplaces feature increasing numbers of sporting 'brands' that compete for visibility, market share and capital return. Commencing in the 1980s, the major professional sport leagues in North America — the NFL, the NBA, National Hockey League (NHL), and Major League Baseball (MLB) – made concerted efforts to expand their markets globally (Bellamy, 1999). Transcontinental formations, such as the Southern Hemisphere 'Super-12' rugby union, spanning Australia, New Zealand and South Africa, also emerged during the 1990s. Pan-European competitions – most notably the association football 'Champions League' and the 'Suproleague' and 'Euroleague' for basketball — are further symptomatic of these shifts. More transient world circuits in tennis, golf, athletics, cycling, skiing and Formula One motor racing also compete globally (Maguire, 1999). Furthermore, nationally based competitions, such as association football's English Premiership, the Italian Serie A, and Australia's National Rugby League (NRL), are prominent in competing with North American leagues for global appeal through broadcasting and merchandising operations. The presence of these brands within global markets has resulted in a degree of homogenisation at the level of consumer choice. Thus, a significant feature of the global sports economy is that the same global brands and images vie for consumer share on a worldwide scale. Yet, expansion of this kind is also marked by cultural encounters; local diversity and new varieties of cultural forms must also be considered.

Primarily conveyed through the communication industries, sporting brands are entwined with particular values and consumption patterns that encounter a multiplicity of languages and discourses through which local people envision their social worlds (Held and McGrew, 2002). Accordingly, the globalisation of sporting brands is not associated with a simplistic homogenisation and/or erosion of local cultures, but involves encounters and modulations of complex and multi-layered discourses of cosmopolitanism and parochialism, in differing ways across varied locales and zones of prestige, emulation and resistance (see Introduction). This is precisely the complexity of local–global interplay characteristic of the actions of sporting TNCs. They have the capability to embody simultaneously particularising and universalising trends. The homogenising effect of sporting TNCs at the level of consumer choice across local cultures is mediated by the interpretations grounded in specific local cultural meanings and identities. Thus, sporting transnational expansion is bound up in wider processes of local reconfiguration arising from intensified global interconnectivity.

The local impacts of and responses to expansion point to varied local scenarios. These range from 'defensive localism', involving the reassertions of local identities and/or resistance to cultural 'otherness', to the active local incorporation of cultural differences (Maguire, 1994a). Invariably, co-existing yet disparate responses are present in local contexts. In the case of the NBA, active receptivity, most notable among youth markets, *and* resistance have been evident in the cases of France (Emerson, 1994), and Poland and New Zealand (Andrews *et al.* 1996).With reference to the NBA 'Europe Tour' to Paris in 1994, a spokesman for the French amateur basketball federation, Jean Pierre Dusseaulx, derided the 'schtick' of the exhibition game in Paris as a 'basket show', and complained of the 'rude and overbearing' American formats (Emerson, 1994). In contrast, French teenagers viewed local players as lacking 'the little things on the side that give the NBA style: buzz cuts, baggy shorts, high tops without socks, the street cool' (Emerson, 1994, p. 77). Such examples of variations in response to the NBA presence highlight the capacity for disparate reactions in local contexts. Indeed, the response of Paris teenagers is commensurate with 'expansive localism' (Andrews, 1999), whereby the incorporation and identification with cultural otherness is implicated in challenging established local cultural mainstreams.

In this way sport is like other successful post-war American cultural exports, such as rock and roll, rap, blue jeans, fast food, Hollywood movies and glam-teen television serials. Yet, the position of American sports in this regard is ambiguous. Specifically, a lack of successful diffusion of American sports in that same post-war period demonstrates the cultural resilience of sport within local cultures. This lack of diffusion, Van Bottenburg (2001, p. 143) notes, is 'in sharp contrast to the success of other elements of American popular culture, from Levi's and Coke to *Ally McBeal*'. Such observations highlight the significance of sport as a marker of place and space related cultural formations, particularly its role within local and, significantly, national identities. Reactions toward the global presence of sporting transnationals, emerging from historically informed formulations of locality, provide fertile terrain to explore the identity politics of local–global interdependence. Prior to exploring some of the substantive issues of the operations of sporting transnationals, some discussion of how global sport has been theorised is appropriate.

Theorising the local–global sports nexus

Local and national identities, although sometimes represented as united, currently appear to be in a state of flux, yet, despite this, have tended to win out over other sources of cultural identity. This dislocation is arguably connected to globalisation processes. Here, the issue concerns the extent to which local and national identities are being *weakened*, *strengthened* or *pluralised* by globalisation processes. A series of double-bind processes are at work. At various points, in different places, local cultures or identities (such as the Britishness/Englishness also considered in Chapters 5 and 6) are strengthened, show resistance or increase in variety. At other points, the contrasts between cultures diminish. Viewing the issue in this way depends on the adoption of a long-term or developmental perspective. It also requires tracing the lengthening chains of interdependencies that characterise global culture. Here, a sensitivity to the compression of time–space issues is vital. Further, in order to think relationally, the researcher must bear several elements in mind, including: the interconnections between concepts of diminishing contrasts and increasing varieties; the idea of the commingling of Western and non-Western cultures; the subsequent emergence of a new amalgam; and the ongoing attempts by established groups to integrate outsider peoples' as workers and/or consumers (see Introduction). All of these concepts shed important light on the debate regarding local/national cultures and globalisation.

If the double-bind tendencies of diminishing contrasts and increasing varieties are uncoupled, however, then support for arguments emphasising either cultural homogenisation or a global cultural pastiche is possible. Homogenisation theories that claim that national cultural identities are weakened by the processes of globalisation are correct to point out that aspects of globalisation are powered by Western notions of civilisation. Cultural industries do provide a staple diet of Western products and the cult of consumerism has spread around the globe. In some respects, the media–sport production complex, highlighted here with reference to North American/US sporting products, also ensures the marketing of the same sport forms, products and images. The local does not freely choose which cultural products are available for consumption. There is a political economy at work regulating global flows. An unresolved question is whether this political economy is shaped by the concerns of global capitalism *per se*, or the concerns of the elites of Western societies more generally.

An over-emphasis on the marketing of sameness, however, leads the analysis to overlook that global marketing strategies also celebrate difference. That is, the cultural industries constantly seek out new varieties of ethnic wares. These ethnic wares are targeted at specific niches within a local culture. This targeting can lead to a strengthening of local ethnic identities. It is also important to note that 'indigenous' cultures and peoples are responsive and active in the interpretation of the global flow of people, ideas, images and technologies. Those national cultures and identities most affected by these processes appear to be those at the centre, not the periphery, of the global figuration of interdependencies. Globalisation processes are also unevenly distributed within central regions. Given this, there is reason to doubt the full-blown homogenisation thesis.

Within globalisation of sport research, process sociologists and those applying cultural studies approaches have been foremost in advancing theoretical explanations. The wider nature of debates between these camps concerning the study of sport have been well rehearsed (see Dunning and Rojek, 1992; Hargreaves and

Macdonald, 2000; Murphy, Sheard and Waddington, 2000; Rojek, 1992). A starting point in benefiting from these ongoing dialogues may be found in the continuities and discontinuities of these approaches, which provide both a common ground and a basis to enhance explanatory frameworks of global sport.

In terms of continuities, both figurational approaches and cultural studies 'have a common respect for history, analysis of power relations at the core of their general frameworks, and a common emphasis on the cultural diversity and richness of social reality' (Jarvie and Maguire, 1994, p. 59). This common ground has, sometimes, been reflected in globalisation of sport debates. As Horne (1998) has observed:

> Both process [figurational] sociology, in which globalization involves flows and resistances, marked by the diminished contrasts and increased varieties of the civilizing process ... and post-Marxist cultural studies ... share with cultural hegemony theory the notion of hegemony as a contingent phenomenon, with the possibility of reversals.
>
> (p. 173)

In this sense, it is clear that figurational sociology and variants of cultural studies share similarities in conceptualising the nature of globalisation processes in and through sport.

Key distinctions surround the relative emphasis on the intentional actions of powerful groups/elites in shaping the limits and possibilities of global sport. Whilst highlighting the intended actions of the powerful, Maguire's (1999) process-sociological approach posits that globalisation is characterised by both intended and unintended processes. Cultural studies proponents have, in turn, focussed more centrally upon the intentions of hegemonic groups – along with the associated practices and outcomes — which connect to globalisation processes. In conceptual terms, the issue is one of relative emphasis rather than fundamental disagreement. For example, Rowe has argued for the need for the mechanisms of capital accumulation to be given 'sufficient weight' (1995, p. 104), and at the same time, Maguire's (1999) work acknowledges the role of the dynamics of capitalism within the shifting and contested power dynamics of global sport development. The practices of transnational corporations, organisations and capitalist classes, Maguire argues, 'figure strongly' (1994a, p. 401).

Clearly, others have pressed the need for greater emphasis on these specific dynamics (see Gruneau, 1999; Greer and Lawrence, 2001). In turn, Maguire has argued for the need to incorporate the potential for globalisation processes to have 'blind, unplanned dimensions and a relative autonomy from the intentions of specific groups of people' (1999, p. 40). The significance of these, he argues, is that 'unintended consequences provide the seedbed in which future power struggles are played out' (Maguire, 1999, p. 215). These critiques and counter-critiques, under scrutiny, primarily surround questions of emphasis in conceptualising the key foci of the analyses of global sport.

In exploring the continuities and discontinuities between existing research, the particular analytical strengths of varying approaches are made clear whilst recourse to alternative approaches may signal directions for progression and more sophisticated theorisations. Such an approach to theory has found expression in recent calls for 'theories ... to be read not just as isolated perspectives, but as elements in an ongoing conversation' (Maguire and Young, 2002, p. 4). In this manner, theorisations of global sport dynamics can potentially become more sophisticated in accounting for the interdependence of cultural politics, economic dynamics, the intentions of powerful/established groupings and the unintended outcomes which might arise from global cultural interchange. Such an approach may overcome the damaging 'gladiatorial' debates which have tended to emphasise distinction between 'rival camps' alone, and have ultimately hindered theorisations of sport (Rojek, 1992).

Such an approach might also help overcome conceptual tensions which tend to characterise existing accounts. For example, Whitson (1998) has speculated that sports are increasingly detached from place attachments and loyalties in favour of discourses premised upon personal and consumer choice. At the other end of the spectrum, Rowe has recently argued that 'sport's compulsive attachment to the production of national difference may, instead, constitutively repudiate the embrace of the global' (2003, p. 292). That is, conceptualisations oscillate between cosmopolitan consumer identifications with little national and local significance, and nationalistic identification with and through sport, to the exclusion of 'globality'. In this regard, there is a need for conceptual clarifications and dialogue in coming to terms with the place of sport at the local–global nexus. Ultimately, differing theoretical frameworks remain at the level of conjecture in the absence of real-life applications to test theoretical positions and/or conceptualisations. Thus, there is a need for substantively grounded empirical work to locate sport within the global field. Again, this is common ground shared by process sociology and Marxist historical sociology, and to which this chapter and book are directed. The chapter now explores the operations of the NFL and NBA in the UK, which provide a useful case study of the dynamic nature of the local–global sports nexus. Through the case of the UK, we explore issues of expansion, reception and the consequences of the operations of North American sports brands, within the context of contemporary cultural politics.

From touchdowns to hoop dreams: US sports in the UK market

The NFL achieved considerable, albeit fleeting, success in penetrating the UK sports market during the 1980s. The making of American football in England during the 1980s was underpinned by strategic alliances between the NFL, media groups and corporate partners (Maguire, 1990). This rise was evident in several areas: considerable merchandising sales – rising from £125,000 in 1983–1984 to over £25 million in 1987; television viewing figures that superseded prominent indigenous sports, such as rugby union and motor racing; considerable brand recognition within British households; and extensive sales of Super Bowl XXI programmes – over 150,000 in three days in 1987 (Maguire, 1990). Central to the expansion of the NFL were the interdependent marketing strategies of American beer manufacturer Anheuser Busch and the television company Channel 4. The creation of markets by the meshing of interests of these key players extended beyond the game of American football and included merchandising, sponsorship and endorsement operations (Maguire, 1990). Such associations made with the game, and the NFL specifically, were central to heightening the visibility of the league within English markets.

Maguire (1990) also noted some of the wider cultural impacts of NFL expansion in England, including the creation of a spectator/consumer niche, which began to impact upon the dominant sporting culture in England by potentially marginalising indigenous sports, in terms of popular appeal and viewing figures. For example, American football had no television exposure in 1981. By 1988, American football ranked seventh in terms of the number of scheduled hours on television amongst all sports (Barnett, 1990), outranking the television presence of long-standing established sports such as athletics and motor racing. Indicating the emergence of a specific niche market, survey data suggested that, by 1988, watching the NFL had overtaken soccer in television popularity amongst 15–24 -year-olds (Barnett, 1990). This presence was entwined with the emergence of 'indigenous' American football leagues, such that by 1988 there were 198 senior teams and 16,000 registered players throughout the UK. As Van Bottenburg (2001, 2003) points out, this is meagre compared to participation levels of established local sports (for example 500,000 golfers and more than a million association footballers at that time). However, it clearly demonstrates an impact of some scope. The context of the national sporting landscape ensured that the English marketplace was more receptive. In particular, the largely embryonic commercial orientation of sport during the 1980s presented weak competition to the attractively packaged televised American football product. These conjunctural processes facilitated the 'fairly significant impact on English society' of American football (Maguire, 1990, p. 233).

The activities and impacts of the NFL within the UK were followed by market expansion attempts by the NBA, commencing in 1995 (see Falcous and Maguire, 2005). The approach adopted by the NBA to penetrate UK markets during the late 1990s bears close similarity with those of the NFL during the 1980s. These similarities are demonstrated in Figure 1.1, which shows that the interdependent pillars of NFL and NBA – their strategy, media groups, the leagues themselves, and corporate sponsors – are almost identical. Furthermore, the strategic approaches were markedly similar: media exposure, events and promotions, underpinned by mutually reinforcing corporate alliances. Notably, these included the promotion of the core product, with the direct staging of one-off NBA and NFL games in London, as well as grassroots involvement.

In the case of the NBA, grassroots programmes consisted of three strands: the 'Mad Skillz' Tour, NBA-2-Ball school initiatives and 'Jam' sessions. Alternatively, NFL grassroots involvement centred upon the establishment, support and ownership of an English-based American Football League. For both

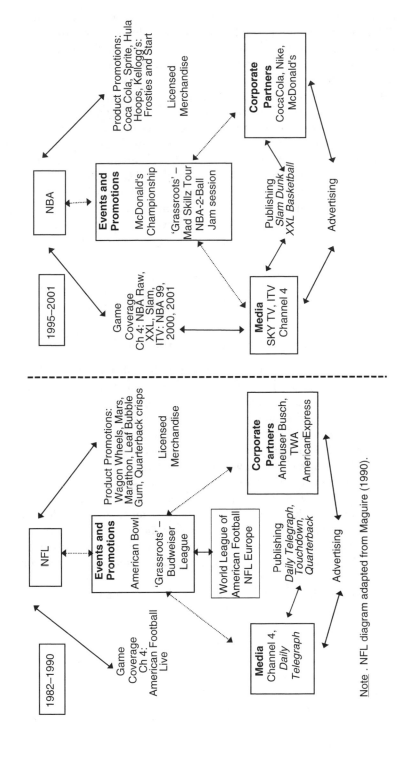

Figure 1.1 Comparison of the presence of the NFL and NBA in Britain

1995–2001

NBA

Game Coverage
Ch 4: NBA Raw,
XXL, Slam,
ITV: NBA 99,
2000, 2001

Events and Promotions
McDonald's Championship

'Grassroots' –
Mad Skillz Tour
NBA-2-Ball
Jam session

Product Promotions:
Coca Cola, Sprite, Hula
Hoops, Kellogg's:
Frosties and Start

Licensed Merchandise

Corporate Partners
CocaCola, Nike,
McDonald's

Publishing
Slam Dunk
XXL Basketball

Advertising

Media
SKY TV, ITV
Channel 4

1982–1990

NFL

Game Coverage
Ch 4:
American Football
Live

Events and Promotions
American Bowl

'Grassroots' –
Budweiser
League

World League of
American Football
NFL Europe

Product Promotions:
Wagon Wheels, Mars,
Marathon, Leaf Bubble
Gum, Quarterback crisps

Licensed Merchandise

Corporate Partners
Anheuser Busch, TWA
AmericanExpress

Publishing
Daily Telegraph,
Touchdown,
Quarterback

Advertising

Media
Channel 4,
Daily Telegraph

<u>Note</u> . NFL diagram adapted from Maguire (1990).

leagues, these initiatives were entwined with synergistic corporate alliances. The NBA 'Mad Skillz' Tour, for example, was sponsored by Nike, and the 2-Ball initiative by Kellogg's. In the case of American football, the fledgling indigenous competition was underpinned by the involvement of Anheuser Busch, and operated under the brand title – Budweiser League. These alliances were further manifest in TV coverage and advertising, player appearances, and the sale and promotion of licensed merchandise in the case of both leagues.

The key distinction between the two leagues lies in attempts by the NFL to develop their core product within the British market, with the creation of a World League of American Football (WLAF). The WLAF was an NFL-backed venture that was created as a developmental league for the NFL, intended to expand the market for American football throughout the world. When the WLAF first kicked off, there were ten teams (six in the US, one in Canada, and three in Europe), including a 'Monarchs' franchise in London. Later re-branded as the NFL Europe in 1992 with an all-European format, the competition featured franchises in London (renamed the England Monarchs for the 1998 season, then suspended the following year) and Edinburgh (established in 1995) (see Bellamy, 1993; Guttmann, 1994; Wilcox, 1994). Despite speculation surrounding pan-European initiatives, the NBA has yet to directly sponsor or establish activity in Britain.

Sports space: the NFL and NBA within the UK

Gauging the impact of the NFL and NBA within the UK is complex. Their presence is multifaceted, and the impact, in both economic and cultural terms, is manifest in both intended and unintended ways. Specifically, difficulties underpin the indices around which 'penetration' may be evaluated. The notion of *sports space* (Markovits, 1990) provides an insightful conceptualisation of the factors underpinning the relative prominence and success of sports within the UK, and the challenges faced by those who seek global markets. The concept refers to the cultural meanings of a sport and the capacity of a society to value a particular kind of sport and render it of social significance. Hence, it is possible for sports to achieve prominence within cultural space, but also for them to recede from that status – to become more residual – in a dynamic manner. The concept of sports space as contested terrain is thus of value in the context of the nexus of sporting transnationals and local cultures (see Chapter 2 with reference to the concepts topophilia and *heimat*).

Despite parallels in the strategies of the two leagues noted above, several indicators tentatively suggest that the NBA has been less successful in establishing itself within UK sports space. Cursory observations of national print media coverage and the low visibility of merchandising, for example, are suggestive of a less significant impact than the NFL. The most readily available index of NBA success is television audience figures. Comparisons with NFL audience figures suggest that the 'sporting touchdown' (Maguire, 1990) in the case of the NFL does not appear to have been matched by a 'slam dunk' in the case of the NBA (see Table 1.1).

Table 1.1 Comparison of NFL (1982–1990) and NBA (1996–2001) viewing figures

NFL		NBA	
Year	Viewing figures (average audience)	Year	Viewing figures (average audience)
1982–83	1.1 million	1996	0.507 million
1983–84	1.5 million	1997	0.264 million
1984–85	2.3 million	1998	0.521 million**
1985–86	3.1 million	1999*	0.72 million
1986–87	2.9 million	2000*	0.66 million
1987–88	3.7 million	2001*	0.766 million
1988–89	3.32 million		
1989–90	2.39 million		

*   ITV took over coverage of these seasons from Channel 4.
** Figures only available for February of 1998. [NFL figures taken from Maguire (1990).]

The figures in Table 1.1 demonstrate that the NBA has attracted smaller television audiences during the 1990s than the NFL in the 1980s. It is notable that the latter trend of NBA figures, following its switch from Channel 4 to Independent Television (ITV) in 1999, appears to be one of marginal increase. Nevertheless, viewing figures are considerably short of the peak attained by the NFL of an average audience close to 4 million viewers in the late 1980s. Indeed, NFL figures rose to 5–6 million for the Superbowl, despite a start time of shortly before midnight (Barnett, 1990). This disparity in success is perhaps made more significant given the long history of basketball within Britain, relative to American football. Taken as an indicator of the ability of the two leagues to secure sports space, this data shows the NBA to have been markedly less successful.

Explanations of this disparity in the success of the two leagues is multifaceted. First, consideration of the shifting conjunctural dynamics within Britain is necessary. Notably, the wider political and cultural context of Britain during the 1990s represents a significantly differing 'local' market and conditions of cultural reception from that encountered by the NFL during the 1980s. Second, the rapid commercialisation of British sport during the last decade and a half presented the NBA with a more competitive sports marketplace than the NFL faced. Third, the pre-existing cultural location of the sport of basketball is a potential factor in the failure of the NBA to achieve penetration on the same scale as the NFL. Specifically, this cultural positioning is entwined with a series of American and racialised associations of the game. Let us address how each of these factors impacted the ability to secure 'sports space'.

Changing conjunctural dynamics: from enterprise culture to 'cool Britannia'?

Facilitators of 'receptivity' regarding both the English cultural landscape and the wider political context of Anglo-American relations were central to the success of the NFL during the 1980s (Maguire, 1990). Notwithstanding the capability for multidirectional influences, resistance and reinterpretation, the US enjoyed 'relative dominance' within Anglo-American relations. Accordingly, the 'enterprise culture' prevalent within Thatcherite Britain 'proved a highly favourable climate for the spread of American cultural forms' (Maguire, 1990, p. 234). Paradoxically, during the 1980s, suspicion regarding the threat of Americanisation to British values and national identities was apparent from both sides of the political spectrum. In terms of sport, however, any cultural critique of Americanisation per se remained muted and lagged behind wider criticism. Also notable was the marketing of the NFL through discourses of masculinity. In this case, American football, underpinned by a 'cult of individualism', found a particular cultural resonance with sections of English society – notably a 'young, affluent, predominantly male group' (Maguire, 1990, p. 221).

Alternatively, the NBA encountered a significantly different figurational dynamic and conjunctural moment, informed by several interwoven processes. Culturally, suspicion of Americanisation in broad terms had continued and heightened by the late 1990s – and is certainly evident in the early years of this century. These shifts emerged in conjunction with re-examinations of British identities in the context of wide-ranging transitions associated with the place of Britain in a post-Cold War era. These transitions include ongoing European integration, ethnic shifts associated with multi-culturalism, and political devolution, and precipitated a range of multifaceted cultural shifts. That is, the certainty underpinning national culture and identities can be threatened by the increased intensity of encounters connected to global interdependence (Held and McGrew, 2002). The consequence of the subsequent dislocation is, frequently, resistance from those who cling to, and reassert more intense versions of, regional and/or national identities (which may be neither progressive nor egalitarian). For example, ongoing processes of political devolution precipitated a re-examination of the national cultures within England, alongside reinvigorated senses of Celtic identities, particularly in Scotland and Wales. This perceived or imagined regeneration of plural British national identities is symptomatic of one of the paradoxes of globalisation processes. Politically, manifestations of this cultural shift were mobilised by the incumbent Blairite New Labour government of the late 1990s. Most evocatively captured, somewhat ironically, by the term 'Cool Britannia', this mediated vision was one of resurgent Britons in fields including fashion, popular music (notably 'Britpop'), art, cinema and other zones of prestige.

The retrenchment of local identities also featured sporting manifestations during the 1990s. Maguire (1993b), for example, has observed the empire metaphorically 'striking back' within English press coverage of the so-called 'Keating affair' and the 1992 English cricket tour of Australia – this imagery was also used by Nike following England's victory in the 2003 rugby union World Cup. These examples are in line with the broader response to globalisation processes, reflecting strengthened or resistant movements as selective representations of cultural identities. In line with this sporting retrenchment, events such as the 1996 European football championships held in England were implicated in symbolic terms with the renewed imagined sense of vibrancy of English national sporting culture. Evidence of this, often manifest in jingoism and xenophobia within English press coverage relating to Euro 96, has been provided by Maguire and Poulton (1999) and Carrington (1998). Likewise, the opening ceremony of the 1999 rugby union World Cup in Cardiff was replete with assertive Welsh national symbolism.

In this context, it is worth noting the virtual disappearance of the NFL from Britain during the 1990s. This demise is linked to the same dynamics that have proved resilient to the activities of the NBA during the 1990s. In making these comments, a complex issue needs to be addressed: the linkage between the 'imagined' regeneration of cultural identities, and the role of the culture industries — including media, advertising and film – in shaping dominant, selective representations of 'nation' or culture. Euro 96, for example, reinvigorated expressions of local identities that also signified the entrenchment of long-standing inequalities, stereotypes and habitus codes (see Chapter 6). These broader cultural and political shifts, which are implicated in a greater resilience to the infiltration of American cultural products such as the NBA, have also coincided with marked changes within the British commercial sporting landscape.

Contested 'space' in the commercial sports market

The relative lack of NBA success is also related to the changing commercial sports market in the UK during the 1990s. Specifically, this period witnessed ongoing and accelerated commercialisation in several sports, rendering UK sports space more contested, and the sports market place a more commercially competitive backdrop to market outsiders. The quest for sports space, resulting from the heightened commercial footing of indigenous sports, was subsequently more difficult. Central to the accelerated commercialisation of British sport has been men's association football, which, entwined with Rupert Murdoch's Sky TV network, has undergone a substantive transformation (Conn, 1999; King, 1997, 1998). The game has come to dominate the commercial sporting landscape, thanks in large part to extensive media exposure, aggressive and wide-scale merchandising operations, and mutually reinforcing corporate alliances.

Meanwhile, those sports that, during the 1980s, remained embryonic in commercial terms have undergone substantial commercial shifts during the 1990s. Examples of such sports include the male versions of rugby union, rugby league, athletics and cricket. The familiar foundations of media exposure and finance, alongside corporate investment, underpin these shifts. Since the 1980s, then, the domestic British sports market has become distinctly stronger, more competitive, and resilient to a new market competitor such as the NBA. Consequently, the NBA faced greater competition for the lucrative yuppie market (aspirant young professionals). Alternatively, due to cultivated attachments and consumer brand loyalty, most notably toward association football and rugby union, consumers may be less predisposed to consume the NBA in the same manner as they had done with the NFL.

The peripheral sports space of basketball

The different locations of basketball and American football within UK sports space also help explain the NBA's lack of success. Specifically, the pre-existence of indigenous basketball playing structures in the UK represents a key distinction. No such equivalent was evident in the case of the NFL, such that American football was largely unencumbered by existing cultural anchors. The sport of basketball, meanwhile, has long occupied cultural space associated with the periphery of national sporting cultures (Bale, 1982). This marginal status is manifest in a low level of visibility, in turn connected to the relatively late commercial development of the sport during the late 1970s (see Maguire, 1988), and is also entwined with the 'racialised' composition of the game. This positioning is also linked to the American origins and associations of the sport. In turn, perceptions of the peripheral cultural location of basketball have hindered the subsequent impact of the NBA and its acceptance with the UK sporting mainstream.

A series of articles appearing within the British broadsheet press during the mid-1990s give an indication of how this cultural positioning of basketball and the NBA are linked. Notably, the reportage builds upon and reinforces basketball as a marginal sport that is culturally alien to Britain. They also question the qualities of basketball relative to indigenous alternatives. The NBA brand, meanwhile, is specifically linked to stereotypes of brash, overbearing and uncouth Americanism, drawing upon broader critiques of American influences in British culture.

Commenting on the 1995 McDonald's Championship, which launched NBA involvement in the UK, Alison Kervin in *The Times* was sardonic in her assessment. The event, she observed 'was an experience but, as a sporting occasion it lacked real depth'. Hinting at a lack of subtlety associated with the game and its presentation, she continued 'comparing basketball with British team sports is almost like comparing an Oscar Wilde play, with all its subtleties, permutations and insinuations, with a Sylvester Stallone film – high drama and quick action'. Finally, Kervin reinforces the 'alien' nature of the formats of presentation, proposing sarcastically that they would be entirely inappropriate in the context of English cricket. She noted:

> It was as if the circus had come to town – and when the cheerleaders ran on for the umpteenth time, I started to wonder how this would translate in traditionally English sports. The image of Pan's People running onto Lord's dressed in sequin covered hotpants after every innings, and leap-frogging the wickets to the sounds of rock music did not rest easy.
>
> (Kervin, 1995)

Hence, the article positions the NBA as a cultural outsider of inferior quality and lacking the apparent sophistication of indigenous sports.

In a markedly similar manner, Lynne Truss commented on the McDonald's Championship held in Paris in 1997, critiquing the setting, jargon, and 'stop-start' nature of the sport. She described the event as played within a 'hideously over-lit sports hall', by 'gigantic men whose shoe size is only one step short of luggage'. Also noting the fragmented rhythm of the sport, Truss disparagingly describes the game as:

> The longest 48 minutes you will experience in your life … every time the play gets interesting in basketball, somebody calls time-out, the clock stops and you get precisely 90 seconds of acrobatics (why?), a pop music introduction (truncated), aerobic jazz dancing or mascot clowning.
>
> (Truss, 1997)

This format she describes as 'sorely irritating'. Truss concludes: 'if only they would play continuously it would be a pretty good game. But to watch it with all its interruptions is like watching a movie when the projector keeps breaking down and is too bloody tiring'. This article is indicative of the manner in which the NBA has been subject to media positioning as an alien outsider on the basis of its Americanness. In this sense, it is associated with crass razzmatazz and a crude, commercially oriented, stop-start format. Notably, it is presented as lacking the subtlety and flow of its indigenous counterparts.

A further example of such positioning was evident in a critical piece by Andrew Longmore (1995). Commenting on the McDonald's Championship held in London, he suggests that for spectators 'the most essential accessory will … be a set of ear plugs' due to the loudness of the music. He mockingly describes the NBA games as 'a cross between a rock concert, a Baptist rally and children's theatre'. That is to say, as a sporting event they are seen as lacking authenticity. Similarly, Derrick Whyte demonstrates cynicism toward the NBA's activities in Britain (1995), describing the McDonald's Championship as 'part of the NBA's grand scheme for global expansion'. He also highlights the 'gargantuan' salaries of NBA players, drawing upon stereotypes regarding the excesses associated with American sports.

Such media reportage locates basketball as a culturally alien sport and hence marginalise it within the mainstream UK – anglocentric – sports space. This is subsequently reflected in the disparaging comments regarding the NBA, reinforcing it as lacking the authenticity and subtlety of indigenous alternatives. Additionally, the presentation and razzmatazz of games evoke stereotypes of Americans as uncouth and lacking sophistication. Ultimately such positioning of the NBA within marginal sports space may hinder both the acceptance of the league and the sport of basketball more generally within UK cultures. Whilst this series of examples do not exhaust the media's cultural positioning of the NBA in Britain, they do indicate the situating of the league on the basis of national character. This array of reactions with mediated constructions of nation is linked to racialised dimensions of reception of the NBA. As Carrington and McDonald (2001) note, race and dominant constructions of the sporting nation within the UK are intimately entwined.

'Race', basketball and local–global consumption

Associations of basketball with Americanness in Britain are also laced with racial connotations. Alongside stereotypes regarding gigantic Americans there are associations with Blackness that are significant in the cultural positioning of basketball. As Gilroy (2001) argues, British national consciousness, and sporting consciousness likewise, is underpinned by the fusion of race with nation. The result, he notes, 'is the artificially whitened ... national community' (p. xiii). That is to say, race and nation and sporting nation cannot easily be disentangled. In this sense, British sport space is inherently racialised and represents a classic example of the established-outsider relations, discussed in the Introduction and in Chapter 5. The racialised cultural associations of basketball consequently reinforce its peripheral location within British sports space.

The racialised associations of basketball have implications for the reception of the NBA in Britain. Containing 77 per cent Black players, the NBA is the North American sports league with the highest proportion of Black players (Coakley, 2001). Commenting upon the case of Michael Jordan, Kellner (1996) notes 'Jordan is a distinctively *Black spectacle* and his blackness is clearly a central feature of his image' (p. 461). This observation can, in turn, be extended as a metaphor for the NBA as a whole. Given the high proportion of Black players, the NBA brand image is inherently centred on the promotion of specific constructions of Black masculinity. Subsequently, the marketing of the NBA, Wilson (1999) notes, is heavily contoured by 'cool pose'. The term captures the manner in which a symbolically empowered masculinity of Black males has emerged, constructing 'unique, expressive, and conspicuous styles of demeanour, speech, gesture, clothing, hairstyle, walk, stance and handshake' (Majors, 1990, p. 111; see also Majors, 1986). Evident across a number of sites including sports, Wilson (1999) notes that the cool pose is particularly visible in NBA basketball. Specifically, it constitutes 'a flamboyant on-court language (now popularly known as "trash talking"), and a repertoire of spectacular "playground" moves and high-flying dunks' (Wilson, 1999, p. 232). Alongside NBA expansion, this distinct form of masculinity has come to be asserted on a televised transnational stage.

Regarding consumption of the NBA within the United States, Kevin Garnett, star player of the Minnesota franchise, speculates that there may be reactionary responses from white consumers in America to such displays, which are a form of veiled racism. He notes that 'there is resentment because we're rich young black men with our own way of doing things' (cited in Starr and Samuels, 2001, p. 43). Reflecting this, a recent downturn in live NBA audiences has been linked to speculation that 'many of the middle-aged, primarily White fans who can afford choice seats in NBA arenas, are turned off by the hip-hop style of the new generation, from its music to its baggy pants and tattoos' (Starr and Samuels, 2001, p. 43). Indeed, evidence of television viewing being patterned along stratified, most notably racialised lines, has been found by Kanazawa and Fund (2001). Likewise, Wilson (1997) has noted the racialised ideologies inherent within representation of the NBA in Canadian media.

With specific reference to the NBA in the UK, Andrews *et al.* (1996) and Andrews (1997, 1999) have identified the significance of racialised readings as crucial in interpretations within the UK. For example, Andrews *et al.* (1996) highlight that the 'transnational racial kinship' felt with NBA stars, may be relevant to young Black Britons. NBA players such as Michael Jordan, they suggest, symbolise 'an assertive and empowered Black masculinity for many Black British youth' (1996, p. 451). In turn, Black British youth 'are able to re-appropriate some of the dominant discourses that surround [the league] and adapt them to a set of practices symbolizing empowered Black physicality' (1996, p. 452). The corollary of this is the implicit difficulty of the inherently Black spectacle to leverage space within the implicitly whitened national sports space. Clearly, the racialised representation of basketball is a significant factor in contouring the reception and consumption of the NBA within the cultural terrain of UK sports markets.

Conclusion

This chapter has afforded the opportunity to examine the local–global nexus in the context of the global marketing of sporting transnationals. In exploring the comparative presence of the NFL and NBA within the UK, it reveals the complex and multifaceted nature of the cultural impact, presence and reception of sports brands. Most significantly, it reveals the dynamic nature of local–global interplay. Specifically, the NFL and NBA achieved varying degrees of success despite utilising similar strategies of corporate collusion and mobilisation of promotional media. Whilst during the 1980s the NFL was able to achieve a significant degree of success within the UK market, the NBA during the 1990s was less successful in leveraging a cultural presence.

The reasons behind variations in impact and response of the two organisations employing similar strategies are manifold. As noted, the shifted political backdrop of Anglo-American relations, the limited reinvigoration of multiple British national identities as a corollary of global processes, and the greater competitiveness of the domestic sports market provided a less porous culture and market to the activities of the NBA and also helps explain the virtual disappearance of the NFL during the 1990s. Simultaneously, the cultural associations with America and Blackness are implicated in hindering the NBA within the mainstream UK marketplace. These national – specifically American – associations were manifest in the media framing of the NBA. As noted above, mainstream national press coverage situated the NBA as culturally alien, and uncouth, its players as outsiders, and hence apparently inappropriate within a UK sports context. These media interpretations demonstrate the policing of (dominant) local receptions of the NBA through the defence of the national sports space and established local hierarchies. Indeed, media reportage reveals precisely the way in which sports space is contested and defended on the grounds of the (apparent) national cultural resonance of certain sports, which are privileged over others. As noted above, this mainstream reception of the NBA must also be conceived in terms of a disjuncture between the Black (American) spectacle of the NBA, and the whiteness of UK sports space detailed by Gilroy (2001) and Carrington and MacDonald (2001).

Consequently, the NBA achieved less success in penetrating the mainstream sports market, and UK cultures more broadly, than the NFL. Such an observation suggests that NBA Commissioner David Stern's recent suggestion that 'basketball is a global language, and it's about to bloom on a global basis' (cited in Eisenberg, 2001) may be both overly optimistic and simplistic. Clearly, locals will have their say! Yet, the rise of the NFL during the 1980s and the manner in which it has receded from the UK sporting landscape during the 1990s (see Whannel, 1994) reinforces the dynamism of the local–global nexus. Furthermore, it reveals the complexity of the way in which cultural encounters can impact (and indeed reconstitute) local contexts and inform their future interdependence with global flows. Such an analysis arguably provides a more nuanced account of the diffusion of basketball to a local culture than suggestions that the Americanisation of local basketball is a 'one-way' influence (see Galily and Sheard, 2002 on the case of Israeli basketball).

As noted above, the skilfully packaged NFL TV programming impacted (and threatened) the status of established sports within the UK. As a corollary, this presence during the 1980s was significant in stimulating a corporate-media driven model of commercial sport in the UK. That is, it heightened the commercial orientation and presentation of established sports which had been threatened by the inroads of the NFL. As both Barnett (1990) and Whannel (1994) detail, the presence of the NFL was profound in influencing the commercial presentation of sports in broadcasting within the UK. For example, Barnett (1990) details how the conventions of production of English football were significantly revamped by the late 1980s, along the lines of the NFL model. This contributed to the commercial transformations of local sports, which aligned to the same corporate-media model that had underpinned the NFL presence within the UK. This heightened commercial footing, as noted above, retrenched the popularity of indigenous commercial sports including association football, rugby union and rugby league. Indeed, the downturn of the NFL in Europe during the 1990s following a dramatic rise during the 1980s, prompted NFL International Managing Director Don Garber to lament 'We've lost our strength in Europe, and it's irksome because it was the NFL who taught the European soccer clubs how to effectively market themselves' (cited in Copetas, 1997). Garber's observation sheds light on the significance of the *unintended* consequences of the operations of the powerful in patterning local contexts, which in turn reconfigure local–global dynamics. In this particular case, the presence of the NFL during the 1980s played a role in reconfiguring UK sports space in commercial terms that, in turn, was more resilient to the operations of the NBA and the NFL during the 1990s. These closing observations highlight the need for analyses to adopt long-term, developmental approaches in conceiving both the intended action and the unintended consequences of sporting transnationals.

2 'Back to the Valley'

Local responses to the changing culture of football

Joseph Maguire and Catherine Possamai

> We know that there are people who argue that they support the team and not the ground, but they miss the point. The two cannot be separated without compromising the club's identity. Do that and you lose the deep emotional bond that even today football clubs exert over their supporters.
>
> (Everitt, 1989, cited in Bale, 1992, p. 70)

These comments were written by one of the chief protagonists in the 'Back to the Valley' campaign during the seven years in which fans battled to get Charlton Athletic home to the Valley stadium in Greenwich, London. The club was forced to leave its traditional ground in 1985 due to several factors, including: the changing economics of English and global football; the closure of one terrace for safety reasons; and the interference of a former chairman of the club who still owned part of the ground. During the following seven years, the club played at the stadia of Crystal Palace and West Ham United, while some of their fans were transformed from passive spectators into political activists in their efforts to return to the Valley. How then are we to make sense of these events? What do they reveal about local responses to changes in the culture of British/English football?

Drawing on the concepts of topophilia and of *heimat*, the work of Georg Simmel (Frisby, 1992) and Norbert Elias (1996), and the wider literature on global sport, some provisional answers can be provided. This case study serves as a lens through which to see how local lives make sense of and act on the wider enabling and constraining features that structure but do not determine such lives. If, as Simmel argues, 'society is everywhere' (1992: pp. 112–113), sociologists can legitimately study the so-called serious and the mundane forms of sociation to see what they reveal about the wider local/global condition.

Here, we use the seemingly mundane local issue of a football stadium campaign to capture some wider questions of concern. Simmel's work on the sociology of urban space involved neither spatial determinism nor social constructionalism. In this way he could conclude that the city is 'not a spatial entity with sociological consequences, but a sociological entity that is formed spatially' (cited in Jarvie and Maguire, 1994). Likewise, to paraphrase Simmel, the sports stadium is not a spatial entity with sociological consequences, but is a sociological entity that is formed spatially. If the basic qualities of sociation involving a spatial dimension are borne in mind, then sport places and the role they play in establishing and maintaining a sense of identity in a rapidly changing world can be better understood. Such places can act as zones of prestige, emulation and/or resistance.

Sport, the city and globalisation

In contemporary society, as time seemingly speeds up, and space appears to shrink through the processes of globalisation, modern media technology allows people to go anywhere in the world from the comfort of their own living rooms or pubs and clubs. Given these processes, it can be argued that familiar, traditional rituals and places act as anchors of meaning in a time of increased dislocation of identity, and that people — far from being unwitting dupes manipulated by some overarching global conspiracy — can and will fight to retain these symbols of their local communities and identities. For the fans of Charlton Athletic, the Valley stadium formed a crucial part of their lives, and they battled against the local borough council, local residents, and the directors of the club itself to hold on to this important facet of their identities as football supporters.

If people in the late twentieth century were increasingly less settled and less free, due to the contradictions of modern metropolitan existence, then this may, in part, explain the growing centrality of sport and leisure adventures. One motivation for undertaking these *quests for exciting significance* was to escape the contradictions between the web of intersecting spheres that characterise city life (Maguire *et al.*, 2002). Modern city life is characterised by these entangled networks and social circles, including the division of labour, distribution, communications, money economy, commodity exchange and intellectual/cultural circles. The circulation and exchange of goods, commodities, images and practices creates a need in metropolitan people to maintain a distance between their inner selves and the kaleidoscope of impressions they are confronted with. Thus, leisure adventures allow an escape from these contradictions and overwhelming impressions by generating a mimetic sphere and a sense of social distance.

This social distance can be created by various forms of differentiation – social, physical and psychological. Clearly, leisure practices reflect these forms of spatial distantiation. The exclusion of specific groups from clubs and leisure forms, the segregation of sport practices along gender lines and the quest for novelty, adventure and excitement promised by tourism, mountaineering and seafaring, are all examples of the establishment of types of social distance. The key to understanding modern sport and leisure then appears to lie in the metropolis and the problems engendered there by modernity. A sense of belonging – *heimat* – and a love of place – *topophilia* – help people make sense of life in the metropolis.

Topophilia and the football stadium

The importance of the game of football to group collective identification has been well documented (Brown, 1998). The sport provides a potent mimetic activity to which the people who constitute a school, town, city or nation can relate. As has been detailed by the historian Richard Holt (1989), football was a crucial factor in creating a sense of civic pride and belonging among the industrial working class who constituted the large majority of new urban populations in the nineteenth century. This legacy endured into the late twentieth century. As Chuck Korr (1986, p. 19) observes: 'Even people who know little about football talk about "our club", "our lads" or what "we" did on Saturday. The phrases carry a sense of common interest and an almost proprietal view of the club'. Nick Hornby (1992, p. 187) expresses similar feelings when discussing Arsenal, the team he supports: 'The players are … our representatives … and sometimes if you look hard you can see the little poles that join them together, and the handles at the side that enable us to move them. I am a part of the club just as the club is a part of me'.

While it has become fashionable to express such sentiments, they are not new – Arthur Hopcraft had expressed them as early as 1968 in his book *The Football Man*. In the 1971 edition, incidentally with a photograph of Arsenal players on the front cover, Hopcraft concludes with these words:

> Even now, whenever I arrive at any football ground, or merely pass close to one when it is silent, I experience a unique alerting of the senses. The moment evokes my past in an instantaneous emotional rapport which is more certain, more secret, than memory.
>
> (1968/1971, p. 208)

Edgell and Jary (1973) further emphasised the importance of football to fans' sense of identity by pointing out that for many of them, the support of a football club will be their most intense emotional involvement with any abstract idea of community, thereby rendering the game a crucial and significant facet of their lives.

The stadium then should be regarded similarly, as a lived sociological experience. Bale has noted: 'The sports landscape is often integral and not merely incidental to the sport experience' (Bale, 1994, p. 130). English football clubs' stadiums such as Anfield and Old Trafford are well known names all over the world, and inspire great affection among their teams' supporters. It could be argued that this is understandable, as these stadia are magnificent edifices. However, even old, rickety, draughty and uncomfortable stadia seem to inspire the same devotion amongst fans, who regard them as 'home'. As Rick Everitt, active in the 'Back to the Valley' campaign, asks:

> Is it just because I am a Charlton fan through and through that I regard the Valley as something special? Sometimes the size and old-fashioned nature of the stands make it unique. It's not a palace, but I prefer homes to palaces.
>
> (cited in Bale, 1992, p. 70)

Hornby (1992) articulates similar sentiments with regard to Highbury, the home ground of Arsenal (at least until 2006, when the club is due to relocate!), asserting that it is 'the place I know best in the world, the one spot outside my own home where I feel I belong absolutely and unquestionably' (Hornby, 1992, p. 215).

Therefore, as Relph (1989) argues, landscapes matter. Football stadia are not simply incidental backdrops to sports contests, but provide numerous pleasures and, 'for a small number of people – the true fans – football and the stadiums within which it is played are of immense significance' (Bale, 1992, p. 64). The phenomenon of love of place is known as 'topophilia', and Bale (1992) draws on this concept and on work by Tuan (1974) in explaining the strength of resistance to locational change in football. Tuan's ideas centre around the notion of 'sacred places' that possess 'overpowering significance', and Bale argues that an interpretation of the stadium as one such sacred, quasi-religious place can aid a fuller understanding of fans' devotion to their soccer grounds. Tuan writes: 'The affection fans have for particular sports places comes very close in strength to the affection shown by those with an obsessive religious adherence to religious places or "sacred soil"' (Tuan, 1974, p. 134). These ideas are derived from and relate to work by Durkheim, who first utilised the concepts of the sacred and profane when discussing the function of religious rituals as 'collective representations' in society. Following Durkheim, it is argued that a feeling of the sacred can be, and is, evoked in the sports context. Other writers have made similar observations regarding the reification of sports – specifically football – grounds. Edgell and Jary (1973) assert that 'grounds can certainly possess the aura of a church' (p. 224). Fuelled then by quasi-religious feelings, supporters will fight to retain their stadia. There are several examples in England during the 1970s and 1980s of clubs that tried to relocate or ground share with another team for financial reasons, only to be halted by a wave of fan protests.

In 1983, for example, the late Robert Maxwell attempted to merge Oxford United with Reading and relocate the team to a new site. The plan was totally opposed by both sets of supporters and the idea was dropped. In the late 1970s, Arsenal and Spurs, Fulham and Wimbledon, and Crystal Palace and Brighton all discussed the possibilities of *sharing* new stadia. However, these proposals never got beyond preliminary discussions, and as Bale (1992) reports, opposition from fans was a significant factor. More recently, and despite the resistance by fans, Wimbledon did relocate out of London to Milton Keynes and several clubs – such as Leicester, Middlesborough, Bolton, Derby and Stoke – all developed new purpose-built stadia. Importantly, however, all remained within the town or city that the previous stadia was located. It would seem that British/English fans differ strongly from their European neighbours on this issue of ground-sharing, if not relocation within the existing city. There are several major stadia that house two football teams with no apparent problems in mainland Europe – the Olympic Stadium in Munich, which was home to bitter rivals Bayern Munich and Munich 1860 up until the end of the 2004/05 season, is a prime example.

The key question, then, is *why* fans become so attached to these stadia and *why* they fight to preserve them. Stadia are an important part of the sporting/cultural heritage of the British/English, and this is the principal reason behind the topophilic sentiments expressed by football fans. Preservation of some sports stadia may also be bound up in broader social currents concerning a nostalgic longing for a past golden age and a sense of dislocation with the present. People want a sense of *heimat* – a sense of belonging. In the case of Charlton, these elements combined with a fear of being homeless. Some local stadia – and the representatives of the local people who attend and spectate – perform this function. Research by De Biasi (1992) goes some way to explaining the peculiarly British/English nature of this phenomenon. In comparative research between English and Italian football crowds, a much greater sense of history was found to be prevalent amongst the English fans. Furthermore, English football grounds are among the oldest in the world, and of the ninety-two professional soccer clubs in England, more than three-quarters play at stadia dating from before the First World War (Duke, 1994). The notion of *heimat* sheds further light on the issue. The case study below highlights the fact that people – specifically football supporters – are not simply dupes who must bow to the will of the establishment, but are active campaigners who will fight to retain their 'badges of identity' – in this case the Valley stadium.

It is argued here that football stadia constitute important anchors of meaning for some sections of the English population at a time when their traditional identity is being challenged from a variety of directions. These challenges include: the increased cultural diversity of British/English society; impending further European political and economic integration; the nation's loss of prestige and power on the world stage over the past forty years; and the increasingly globalised nature of cultural, economic and political flows. In these times of dislocation, the local soccer stadium represents a safe relic of the past – a golden age when England was dominant in Europe and the world, in political, economic and sporting terms (Maguire, 1995). Yet, the sport of football is itself increasingly globalised. We will return to this issue in the conclusion. In what follows we seek to connect the immediate local action to wider societal and sporting change.

Leaving the Valley

Charlton Athletic Football Club was founded in 1905 and moved to the Valley ground in 1920. Except for an unsuccessful year-long move to Catford in 1923, the club played there until 1985. The stadium achieved fame during the 1920s and 1930s as the largest ground in England. In 1938, a crowd of 75,000 attended a cup tie against Aston Villa (Inglis, 1987). However, by 1985, Charlton Athletic's average gates were down to just five thousand (Inglis, 1987), and the club's financial outlook was poor. It had been rescued from almost certain liquidation the previous year by a company called Sunley Holdings, and John Fryer, a partner in that company, had become Charlton's chairman. The Valley ground itself was still owned by a former chairman, Michael Gliksten, who leased it to the club.

The first warning of trouble for the Valley came in early August 1985 when the now defunct Greater London Council applied for a summons against Charlton to stop them using their East Terrace. This came following a safety inspection of all

London football grounds, which had been prompted by the tragedies at Heysel stadium and Bradford earlier in the year. 'The GLC will not tolerate the use of any
part of a football ground where there is a risk to spectators, especially in the light of
the Brussels tragedy' stated Simon Turney, Chair of GLC Public Services and Fire
Brigade Committee (*Greenwich and Eltham Mercury*, 5 September 1985, p. 57).
The terrace ban was upheld in court and the East Terrace closed. This reduced the
Valley's capacity to ten thousand. The next blow came from Michael Gliksten,
who decided to reclaim two acres of land behind the West Stand – a condition of
the lease. This meant the loss of twenty-three turnstiles and, coupled with the closure of the East Terrace, effectively made segregation of opposing fans – and
therefore football at the Valley – impossible, or so the directors claimed. The solu-
tion reached by John Fryer and his directors was for Charlton Athletic to embark
on a ground-sharing scheme at Selhurst Park with Crystal Palace. Several question
marks surrounded this decision. However, as Inglis (1987) observed:

> They [Charlton] left in an atmosphere of bitterness, recrimination and con-
> cealment. There was an argument, but no-one seemed to speak. There were
> questions aplenty, but no-one prepared to answer. If the fans felt hard done
> by it was because no-one made the effort to explain. And if they felt swin-
> dled, it was because the protagonists' own actions were hard to comprehend.
>
> (Inglis, 1987, p. 265)

The reasons such confusion reigned about why Charlton Athletic really left the
Valley are manifold. First, the initial estimate of the cost of repairing the East
Terrace so that it satisfied safety requirements was put at £250,000 (Everitt,
1991), while *The Times* reported that Charlton and Crystal Palace were to set up
a company to handle the ground share of Selhurst Park – at a cost of £1 million
(21 September 1985). These figures suggest that Charlton were willing to spend
more money on launching the ground share at Selhurst Park than on renovating
their own stadium. Second, the *Greenwich and Eltham Mercury* ran a story headlined 'They Didn't Want To Stay' (26 September 1985, p. 68), which contained
an interview with David Chambers, the head of the GLC safety team that
inspected the Valley. He commented:

> We would have bent over backwards to keep football at the Valley, but they
> [the Charlton directors] refused to meet and discuss the problem ... We
> inspected every ground in London and in every case except Charlton we fol-
> lowed the inspection with discussions with the clubs and their own
> architects. We would have preferred to discuss the situation but we had no
> alternative but to go to court ... I can only conclude that Charlton already
> knew of the possibility of moving to Crystal Palace ... *My personal opinion is
> that this has been used as a smokescreen by Charlton while they arranged the move
> to Selhurst Park* [italics added].
>
> (*Greenwich and Eltham Mercury*, 26 September 1985, p. 68)

These comments were further evidence that the move to leave the Valley was not made for the reasons given by the directors.

Third, despite the fact that Greenwich Council had made a financial commitment to Charlton Athletic, which had helped them stay alive in 1984, their representative on the Charlton board of directors was not consulted or involved in any way in the decision to move to Selhurst Park, suggesting that the move was not agreed upon by the board as a whole. Furthermore, another crucial question being asked by many fans was 'Why Selhurst Park?' Millwall football club is Charlton's closest neighbour and, as Everitt pointed out, is not only on the same bus and train lines, but is 'also part of the same working class, South East London environment' (Everitt, 1991, p. 77). Inglis also highlighted the class differences between Charlton and Croydon: 'But the distance was more than just time or effort. Selhurst Park was in another world, as different from Charlton as Darlington is to Middlesborough, or Dumbarton to Glasgow' (Inglis, 1987, p. 268). These perceived differences render the decision to move to Selhurst Park even more open to question, particularly when Millwall, situated so close, socially and geographically, to the Valley appear not to have been asked about a ground-share option. The *Greenwich and Eltham Mercury* reported Millwall secretary Sylvia Shaw as saying: 'We were never approached by anyone at Charlton. We would have considered the matter thoroughly and not dismissed it out of hand' (12 September 1985, p. 1).

Given these circumstances surrounding Charlton's move to Selhurst Park, it would seem reasonable to conclude that there was a hidden agenda at work of which the fans and general public were unaware. One can only speculate now as to what that agenda was. Everitt (1991) postulates that John Fryer was totally unwilling to spend money on improving the Valley while it remained under Gliksten's ownership. This may well be true, but the question of 'Why Selhurst?' remains. A mutually beneficial financial deal between Fryer and Ron Noades, the Crystal Palace owner, is one possible scenario. Whatever the reasons for the upheaval, the Charlton fans were distraught, feeling that they were losing a crucial part of their identities as football supporters. As Everitt observed:

> It was just a football club leaving its ground, but to many, many people it was so much more. For the older fans it was the destruction of something that had run like a thread through their lives and for those who knew the Valley's past only at second hand it was the crushing of a dream.
>
> (Everitt, 1989, cited in Bale, 1992, p. 70)

The *Greenwich and Eltham Mercury*, which was to provide crucial support to the 'Battle for the Valley' campaign over the ensuing years, ran a front page headline of 'WHY US?' accompanied by a picture of a young fan with the caption:

> Little football fan Joe Sellick is an unusual kid in this day and age. He doesn't support Liverpool, Tottenham or Manchester United. He actually supports the team near where he lives – Charlton Athletic
>
> (12 September 1985, p. 1)

They followed this up with a telling 'What have *you* done to *our* club?' (12 September 1985, p. 1 (italics added)). This set the tone for much of what was to follow, with a them and us attitude taken by the fans towards the directors, who were seen as the outsiders, destroying a club with a strong insider community orientation (for further discussion of this, see Introduction).

Letters poured into the local newspaper, all with essentially the same message: 'A move to Selhurst will lose Charlton's identity and local interest and, most importantly, our support' (*Greenwich and Eltham Mercury*, 19 September 1985, p. 65). Considering this strength of feeling, it was surprising that there were no concerted and coordinated efforts made by the supporters to prevent Charlton leaving the Valley. There was a half-hearted attempt made at a sit-in on the pitch during the final match at the Valley, but that was the only visible expression of anger made by the fans. Everitt blames this apparent lack of protest on the official supporters' club:

> Later it would be said by some that the protests were muted, but it would be more accurate to say that they were not organised. In this respect the supporters' club failed its members lamentably, because as a body the fans might quite easily have prevented the move from taking place.
>
> (Everitt, 1991, p. 3)

In fact, the supporters' club chairman Jack Lindsell was quoted in *The Times* as saying that he fully understood the decision to move to Selhurst Park, and the reasons behind it (21 September 1985). Given the fact that the supporters' club at that time only functioned to organise coaches to away matches, perhaps this acceptance of the official club position was understandable. It was to take some forceful action from fans and the resignation of Lindsell before the supporters' club became active in the campaign to return to the Valley. Hence, the initial focus of opposition became the local press – in particular the *Greenwich and Eltham Mercury*. It had a new sports editor, Peter Cordwell, whose sympathy with the fans manifested itself as 'wave after wave of attack upon the club ... always with an inescapable tone of high moral indignation' (Everitt, 1991, p. 84). The support of this newspaper would prove crucial in the ensuing years. Thus, the departure of Charlton Athletic from the Valley in September 1985 caused confusion and distress among their fans, and outrage in the local press, but little in the way of any concerted action to prevent the directors from proceeding with their plan. This was to come later.

The beginning of fan activism (1986–1988)

Although the rumblings of discontent surrounding the co-habitation with Crystal Palace continued throughout the 1985/86 season, it was the club's promotion back to top flight football after a twenty-nine year absence that gave the campaign a fresh impetus (*Times*, 21 October 1986). After watching a match at Selhurst Park sparsely populated by spectators, the *Greenwich and Eltham*

Mercury's sports editor declared 'only an emperor with a penchant for parading around starkers would fail to see that Charlton have no real future at Selhurst Park' (cited in Everitt, 1991, p. 107). Consequently, the newspaper devoted its entire back page to a petition headed 'Our Home is The Valley', and invited readers to fill it in and send their response to the newspaper. Within two weeks, 15,000 signatures had been received. Then it was announced that the petition would be presented to the Charlton directors at the AGM of the supporters' club. This prompted hundreds of fans to turn up at the meeting to vent their frustrations. Police had to be called to control the crowds as the Valley social club became massively overcrowded. The directors were heckled by fans and could provide no satisfactory answers to pacify the supporters. Finally, they had to agree that the directors would hold a meeting with council leaders and supporters' representatives to discuss 'the next move in bringing the club back home' (*Greenwich and Eltham Mercury*, 23 October 1986, p. 1) or to explore the possibility of developing another site within Greenwich. This never actually happened.

The *Mercury* petition was presented at the meeting, prompting the observation that the 15,000 signatures represented three times the number of spectators that had been at the previous home match at Selhurst Park! The meeting did spur some fans to organise sponsored events to try to raise money to facilitate a return to the Valley. These efforts included four supporters completing a sponsored walk to an away match at Southampton. The *Greenwich and Eltham Mercury* followed up its successful petition with the launch of a trust fund for a new ground. However, only £5800 was raised, and the campaign, which had been sluggish at best, became stagnant.

In 1987, though, two significant events occurred. First, Charlton chairman John Fryer resigned due to ill health and a businessman named Roger Alwen joined the board of directors. Second, Rich Everitt, a civil service employee and Charlton fan, launched a Charlton Athletic fanzine entitled *Voice of the Valley*. In April 1988, in the third issue of the fanzine, Everitt, and his co-editor Steve Dixon argued:

> Now is the time for the supporters to take the initiative. Never again must we be relegated to the sidelines when the future of OUR club is being decided. Write to the council, sign the petition, attend the meetings. Let the voice of the Valley be heard and let there be no mistaking its message. Then, one day soon we will all join the triumphant chorus and turn our backs on this sorry chapter in the club's history with confidence. On the day Charlton Athletic return to The Valley.
>
> (*Voice of the Valley*, No. 3, April 1988, p. 3)

The establishment of the fanzine had been prompted by a row between the board of directors and the supporters' club following an attack on the board by 'Valiant's Viewpoint', the supporters' club newsletter. The ensuing dispute ended with the club having effective censorship of the newsletter, thus gagging the fans and muting opposition to the continuing tenancy at Selhurst Park. According to Everitt, this 'finally prompted me to take the plunge and launch a publication of my own' (Everitt, 1991, p. 133). Everitt's involvement in the campaign up to this point had been negligible, but his commitment to it increased following the launch of the fanzine, and he was to become one of the major players in the struggle to return Charlton to the Valley. In fact, in the summer of 1989 he resigned from his civil service job to work for the *Greenwich and Eltham Mercury* as a football reporter – allowing him a more powerful influence in the Valley campaign through the newspaper's readership. The first move by the new fanzine to gain publicity and popular support was to propose a mass boycott by the fans of the home game against Oxford United at Selhurst Park. Mercury sports editor Peter Cordwell backed this by covering the story on the back page of the local newspaper, and the idea gained much support on the terraces (Everitt, 1991). However, the boycott was soon abandoned.

Re-purchase of the Valley: decision time (1988–1989)

On 10 March 1988, the *Greenwich and Eltham Mercury* announced on its front page the re-purchase of 'The Famous Old Valley Ground'. Vice-chairman Michael Norris and director Roger Alwen had bought the ground with financial backing from Laing Homes, a building company. This allowed the club two options – either to renovate and refurbish the Valley, or to sell the ground to property developers and use the profits to finance the construction of a new stadium somewhere else within Greenwich borough. The fans and *Mercury* newspaper were jubilant at the prospect of a return to the Valley:

> Charlton fans are a rare breed in that they can show total commitment to their club without wrecking trains. But their two and a half year battle for the Valley was no less intense because of that. And Thursday's decision to return home from Selhurst Park was a victory for one of football's decent set of supporters.
>
> (*Greenwich and Eltham Mercury*, 10 March 1988, p. 30)

The Charlton Athletic historian Colin Cameron highlighted the importance of topophilia in football, saying 'people don't seem to realise that the stadium represents so much of a fan's love for a club … If the club didn't actually die at Selhurst Park, its identity would have. No doubt about that' (*Greenwich and Eltham Mercury*, 10 March 1988, p. 30).

The celebrations, however, were very premature. As *The Times* pointed out, Greenwich Council would have the final say on whether or not the club returned to the Valley with its control of planning permission (4 March 1988), and the council had already stated that it would favour a new site on the Blackwell Peninsula. Charlton Vice-Chairman Michael Norris also supported this plan, and a condition of Laing Homes offering financial backing to the re-purchase of the Valley was a two-year option on housing development of the Valley site. It was realised that more action was needed by the fans to persuade both the club and the council to support a renovation of the Valley. The supporters' club newsletter 'Valiant's Viewpoint' and Everitt and Dixon's fanzine *Voice of the Valley* cooperated in launching a petition to try to convince the council to rule in favour of the club returning to the Valley, and to discourage a move to the Blackwell Peninsula. This option was unattractive to the supporters for several reasons:

> For a start, it wasn't the Valley. A major aspect of the disenchantment with the present situation centered around *the loss of the identity the club derived from their former ground* [italics added]. A stadium which wasn't recognisably someone else's would certainly have been better than Selhurst, but it was still questionable whether they would ever call it home.
>
> (Everitt, 1991, p. 144)

Furthermore, the Blackwell Peninsula was on the 'wrong' side of the borough of Greenwich. A move there would take the team away from its traditional strong-hold, and towards Millwall's base of support. The discussions between the directors and the council went on for a year, and during that time various other sites for a new stadium were also proposed and rejected. One location favoured by the council was the Thames Polytechnic sports ground in Eltham. This was situated in a similarly middle-class neighbourhood to Selhurst Park, and as Everitt observed: 'the idea that Charlton could be transplanted into the heart of suburban and largely middle class Eltham always seemed a fantastic one' (Everitt, 1991, p. 153).

On 23 March 1989 there was a public meeting at Woolwich Town Hall at which Roger Alwen, who had just taken over as chairman of the board of directors, announced the long-awaited planned refurbishment of the Valley:

> We have had favourable indications from the council that a planning consent may shortly be given on part of the Valley and we are therefore very happy to put in hand a major refurbishment which will enable Charlton Athletic Football Club to once again play football at the Valley.
>
> (Cited in Everitt, 1991, p. 157)

Alwen was interviewed in *The Times* following the announcement, and said that 'sentimentality has been the principal fuel behind the move back to the Valley … You would have thought that the emotional ties might have been broken, but they never go away' (25 March 1989, p. 45). The announcement also included an estimated cost of renovation – £2 million – and the target date for the first football game to be played at the new improved Valley Stadium. The aim was to return by the end of the 1989/90 season. Both of these targets were to prove hopelessly optimistic. The fans' celebrations were again premature. The battle was not yet over.

Because of the Valley's prior use as a soccer stadium, it had what are known as 'user rights'. As such, the club anticipated that the only planning permission

required from the council would be for Laing Homes' proposed housing development behind the main stand, and that the club itself would need only a safety
certificate to lift the court order which had closed the East Terrace in 1985. This
was a misguided assumption. Another critical factor was the publication of the
local Greenwich Borough Plan in May 1989 (Everitt, 1991). This document
contained the strategic design for the future development of Greenwich and
within it the whole of the Valley, including the area that Laing Homes planned
to build houses on, remained designated as community open space.

A further, tragic, event which would hinder the club's renovation plans was
the Hillsborough Stadium disaster. 'As Bradford and Heysel had combined to
close the East terrace, so Hillsborough would affect the club's hopes of a return'
(Everitt, 1991, p. 164). The tragedy in Sheffield, combined with the recommendations of the Taylor Report, immediately raised the cost of redevelopment as it
rendered impossible the plans to restore the old terracing behind the goals at the
Valley. Because of this impending all-seater requirement, Alwen and Norris
decided to go for major developments on three sides of the Valley. However, 'the
scale of Charlton's new ideas also came as a surprise to Greenwich council officials' (Everitt, 1991, p. 173).

Planning permission refused: political activism during 1990

When the council learned of the grandiose scale of Norris and Alwen's plans for
the Valley, it issued the following press release:

> Charlton Athletic have been asked to compromise on plans to redevelop their
> old ground at the Valley ... At a meeting with Greenwich Council on
> December 4th, Charlton were urged to drop their controversial plans to
> include speculative office space and a banqueting suite as part of their redevel-
> opment proposals. Instead they have been asked to come up with a package of
> measures to improve the environment for those living near the ground.
>
> (Cited in Everitt, 1991, p. 178)

As well as this warning from the council, there were bitter disputes in the
weeks leading up to the decisive planning meeting over the issue of pop concerts. The Valley had staged concerts for bands like The Who during the
1970s, and the council maintained that Charlton intended to resurrect these
occasions. This naturally angered even further the local residents already
opposed to the redevelopment. However, Charlton were equally insistent that
they had never mentioned the possibility of pop concerts being held. As
Everitt observed, 'the vehemence with which both sides protested their inno-
cence in this matter made it difficult to believe that they were the victims of a
simple misunderstanding' (1991, p. 183). The suspicion was held among some
at the council that Charlton did not want planning permission at all, so had
introduced the idea of concerts (Everitt, 1991). While the council and club
squabbled before the planning meeting, the fans tried to influence the planning

committee through putting up 'YES' posters printed by the *Greenwich and Eltham Mercury* and *Voice of the Valley* around the borough, and holding them up at home matches.

The publication of the Greenwich planning officer's report on the Valley application effectively decided the issue. It began with the comment that 'it is a stadium for the 21st century but ... the fundamental issue is whether the Valley is an appropriate location for such a stadium given the overcrowded nature of the surrounding area (Greenwich Borough Planning Report, January 1990, p. 9).

The report went on to detail the several areas in which Charlton's application did not conform to the requirements of the Borough Plan, and the ways in which the club had been asked – and had failed – to modify or improve their proposals. These included the fact that for a stadium with a capacity of 18,700 spectators, the statutory car parking requirement is a minimum of 748 spaces, while Charlton's plans only allowed for 104. The proposal to construct commercial offices and a restaurant/banqueting suite also ran 'counter to the provisions of the Borough Plan'. Furthermore, the report stated 'The applicants were asked to consider providing a residents' parking compound for use on match days but no such proposal forms part of this application' (Greenwich Borough Planning Report, January 1990, p. 14). The damning conclusion was:

> No solutions have been forthcoming which ameliorate the problems of traffic, of parking, of providing accommodation for cars removed from the street, or which reduce the physical impact that the stadium would have ... The application cannot be supported as currently submitted.
>
> (Greenwich Borough Planning Report, January 1990, p. 16)

Roger Alwen's reaction to the report was predictably indignant. He dismissed it as a 'totally confused document' and said:

> We've been dealing throughout the process with people who started out on the basis that they were totally opposed to us going back to the Valley. As far as the chief planning officer is concerned, if you're a football supporter you're a hooligan.
>
> (*Greenwich and Eltham Mercury*, February 1990)

Such inflammatory remarks were obviously designed to retain the support of the fans against the council – and succeeded. The report meant that the official public meeting of the council planning committee was a foregone conclusion. Despite this, Charlton's fans turned up in huge numbers to try and sway the committee – vastly outnumbering the residents of streets near the Valley who were opposing the application. Several members of each side were allowed to speak, and Everitt was one of them: 'My speech was completely over the top, as I realised even in the process of delivering it. The threat of electoral retribution ... sounded so unlikely in practice that behind me I could hear some of the residents laughing' (Everitt, 1991, p. 195).

Everitt was to be proved right in the following months. That night marked the beginnings of the 'Valley Party', as the disenchanted fans formed their own political party to contest the forthcoming local council election. As Everitt said, 'for the supporters, that night at Woolwich Town Hall marked an important turning point ... The fans did not like being treated with such obvious contempt by their elected representatives' (1991, p. 197). However, it would appear that the fans should also have questioned the actions of the Charlton board of directors more closely. As noted earlier, some of the council believed that the club did not really want planning permission, but had to *appear* to in order to keep the fans happy. They therefore submitted an application that was so outrageous the council would inevitably fail to grant planning assent – rendering the council, instead of the directors, the 'bad guys'. The evidence would appear to support this belief. The directors must have known their application would be rejected following all the warnings and recommendations of the planning officer – which they ignored. It can be suggested that the directors lacked the necessary finance for the refurbishment of the Valley, so decided to buy time by submitting an inadequate planning application, and using the council as a scapegoat. If this is what the directors intended, they succeeded in spectacular style, with the energies of the fans now directed for several months towards contesting the local elections, instead of haranguing the directors about getting home to the Valley.

The immediate reaction to the decision of the planning committee in the local and national press was indignation that a planning proposal which fell within the guidelines of the recently published Taylor Report, which called for all-seater stadia financed by commercial development, should be summarily rejected. *The Times* headlined an article by Roger Alwen: 'Planners Conflict with the Taylor Report' (2 February 1990, p. 39), while the *Greenwich and Eltham Mercury* complained, 'What scale of development would be acceptable? Or do they expect Charlton to put up a Nissen hut by the pitch and finance their future by the re-introduction of peanut sellers?' (8 February 1990, p. 53). In the same edition, it proclaimed its support for the newly formed Valley Party with a huge back page headline saying 'Vote Valley'. As Everitt acknowledged, the free publicity given by this newspaper to the Valley Party during the three months of election campaigning was invaluable: 'without it the Valley Party might well have been marginalised' (Everitt, 1991, p. 200).

The supporters managed to contest every seat in the council elections, and erected huge billboard advertisements around Greenwich featuring famous Charlton players of the past like goalkeeper Sam Bartram. The campaign was designed to remind voters of the traditional association between the club and borough and the contribution of the soccer team to the area's identity. The fans also canvassed in Woolwich town centre and around the borough more generally in an effort to win electoral support. When polling day arrived in May, their hard work was rewarded, with many more votes cast for them than they could have hoped. In all they received 14,838 votes – which represented 10.9 per cent of those cast. This was a quarter of those polled for the Labour Party. Although not winning any seats, the Valley Party caused some Labour councillors (including the Chair of Planning Simon Oelman) to lose their seats through their vote being split. The result represented a huge endorsement by the people of Greenwich for the return of Charlton Athletic to the Valley Stadium. As the *Greenwich and Eltham Mercury* exulted, 'And now we know. There ARE thousands of Charlton fans in Greenwich. They DO think the council has got it wrong ... All we want is our ground back' (10 May 1990, p. 56, original emphasis). Almost immediately, and reflecting the new political realities, the new Chair of Planning, Norman Adams, indicated his readiness to open new negotiations to find a mutually acceptable way to refurbishing the Valley.

Permission granted: the final hurdles (1991–1992)

With a new spirit of cooperation suddenly prevalent between Greenwich Borough Council and Charlton Athletic's directors, the negotiations over a revised planning application for the Valley took just two months. This was admittedly greatly facilitated by the expiry of Laing Homes' two-year option on the land behind the West Stand, but as Everitt pointed out, it was an agreement that 'in most respects they might easily have concluded earlier' (Everitt, 1991, p. 221). The modified plans featured a reduced ground capacity, more parking spaces, a bowling alley, creche and day nursery, a smaller function room and twelve 'work-homes'. These plans kept both sides happy by still allowing Charlton potential for generating revenue, but causing less disturbance to the surrounding residential area. Charlton, now aiming for an August 1991 return to the Valley, submitted the plans in September 1990. However, the council officers went on strike, causing further delay. Meanwhile, the club was wading deeper into the financial mire. Despite receiving an income of over £1 million from the sale of players in the eight months to the end of January 1991, Charlton had still managed to make a loss of £300,000. This was due to a wage bill of £100,000 per month and the fact that the net receipts from poorly attended home games at Selhurst Park were only £10,000 per match (Everitt, 1991). Clearly, Charlton's tenancy at Selhurst Park was proving detrimental to the club both on and off the field, as the directors were forced to sell their best players to keep the club afloat financially.

The crucial planning committee meeting finally took place in early April 1991, with the result following a favourable report by the Borough Planning Officer: 'As before, the decisive meeting was an elaborate charade, with the important difference that this time the noises made by the politicians were those we wanted to hear' (Everitt, 1991, p. 237). Hundreds of fans marched from the Valley stadium to Woolwich Town Hall for the meeting, anticipating a final celebration after their five and a half years of campaigning, and on that night their wish was granted. The decision was reported in *The Times* under the headline 'Charlton's Happy Return To Valley' (3 April 1991, p. 3). The supporters' jubilation was expressed in 'spontaneous street parties' (*Times*, 3 April 1991, p. 3) as they 'sang about going home and "Bye Bye Selhurst"' (*Greenwich and Eltham Mercury*, 4 April 1991, p. 39). Roger Alwen stated that he was still optimistic that all the ground except the new West Stand would be ready for football again by the start of the 1991/92 season (*Times*, 4 April 1991). These hopes were further boosted by the promise of £1 million from the Football Trust towards the cost of redevelopment.

However, the fans were destined to be disappointed once more. The first setback was the original building contractors, Trenthams, going into receivership. Beazer, the firm that bought them out, agreed to carry on the job, but it took precious time to sort out. Then the weather took a hand. It rained nearly every day in June 1991, making construction work very difficult. In August, Charlton were forced to face the fact they would not start the new season at the Valley. Beazer announced that 'significant design changes' were needed to ensure the ground met the stringent safety standards required by the Taylor Report, and that the ground would not be ready until the New Year (*Times*, 23 August 1991, p. 36). It was therefore decided that the first few games of the season would be played at the home ground of West Ham United, at a fee of £10,000 per match, plus heavy stewarding and policing costs. Furthermore, the journey to West Ham was not an easy one, meaning that fewer fans would be likely to attend home games.

Beazer announced in August that the cost of the new refurbishment package to meet safety requirements would be £1.8 million. By September, this estimate had been increased by a further £0.5 million (*Greenwich and Eltham Mercury*, 12 September 1991). The financial outlook was not promising, with the combination of the costs of West Ham and the redevelopment placing a massive drain on Charlton's resources. In November, the directors admitted that they needed £1 million to finish the ground development (*Times*, 12 November 1991). Everitt and the fans once again responded, but there was more than a suggestion that they were reaching the end of their patience with the club:

> Let's be clear. We don't owe Charlton anything. Not after six years at Selhurst Park, we don't. Not after buying almost 3000 season tickets on the basis that we'd be back at the Valley in August. Not after winning 15,000 votes for the Valley Party ... We've paid our dues.
> (*Greenwich and Eltham Mercury*, 21 November 1991, p. 57)

Despite this, Everitt's article in the newspaper launched an appeal for fans to donate cash or raise money in any way they could to help Charlton get back to the Valley.

By March 1992, the figure needed to complete a three-sided Valley stadium had risen to £3 million. The directors had devised a plan to raise this, which again relied heavily on the commitment of the club's fans. They launched a debenture scheme, which it was hoped would raise £1.5 million to go with £1 million from the Football Trust and £600,000 from Beazer in deferred loans to pay for the ground. On launching the scheme one of the directors said:

> We have come to appreciate the efforts of our fans over recent seasons and hope that this will be something else they can get their teeth into. We like

to think we've got outside the 'them and us' situation and created just an 'us' situation.

(Greenwich and Eltham Mercury, 26 March 1992, p. 40)

The Charlton debenture scheme involved offering fans the choice of investing between £25 and £3000, to be refunded in ten years. In return for their invest-ment, fans would gain a reduction on season tickets for those ten years. For every £50 invested, a one and a quarter per cent price reduction was offered. Furthermore, the fans were offered the carrot of having a representative on the board of directors. Similar schemes launched at Arsenal and West Ham at the same time caused widespread fan anger, and failed miserably, but Charlton's pro-gramme was more modest and was very successful. By the beginning of April, over £200,000 had been pledged (Greenwich and Eltham Mercury, 2 April 1992), and in the end, the debenture scheme raised over £1 million. This extra injection of money provided the necessary impetus, and in September 1992, Roger Alwen was able to announce a definite date for the first match at the Valley in seven long years.

Return to the Valley (December 1992)

In announcing the fourth of December as the date for Charlton Athletic's return to the Valley, Alwen paid lavish tribute to the role of the fans, acknowledging their poor treatment at the hands of the directors over the years and stating: 'There can be no more loyal set of fans in the country. What they've done is quite incredible. We couldn't expect anymore' (Greenwich and Eltham Mercury, 3 September 1992, p. 55). The national newspapers also reported the story, with The Guardian taking the opportunity to comment on the importance of stadia to the sports experience: 'It is proof of the strength of emotion people feel for soccer grounds that for the past few years Charlton's success on the pitch has been overshadowed by the on–off saga of getting back to the Valley' (Guardian, 24 August 1992, p. 12).

When the day of the return arrived, the event was further emphasised by the media as a victory for the fans. The Guardian observed that: 'After all the strug-gles, Charlton are returning home. It is a rare move for a club, but rarer still because it was achieved largely by the fans; turnstile fodder turned transformers' (5 December 1992, p. 20). The Times paid similar tribute:

> Always the fans dreamed that, one day, Charlton would return home. They kept up relentless pressure on the club's directors. They formed the Valley Party and put up candidates in local elections. They stumped up more than £1 million of the £4.4 million spent on refurbishing the old ground. The stage is set and tomorrow ... the dream becomes reality.

(4 December 1992, p. 48)

The Greenwich and Eltham Mercury, exulting in its own part in the seven-year campaign with a massive 'You're Welcome' front page headline, further saluted

the fans: 'Charlton Athletic's emotional return to the Valley ... is above all a victory for ordinary people' (3 December 1992, p. 1). Everitt notes the meaning it
held for the fans themselves:

> In the end, the battle for the Valley transcended football. It was about the
> way people's lives are manipulated by money and politics. The remarkable
> endurance of the supporters was only possible because they were fighting to
> preserve part of themselves.
>
> (Everitt, 1991, p. 261)

Over a decade after returning to the Valley, Charlton Athletic are arguably at the
most successful point in their history, both on and off the pitch. During the
2004/05 season the club have vied for a place in the top group of the clubs of the
Premier League and sought qualification to European competition. The legacy of
the seven years of campaigning by the fans to return the club 'home' has created
an atmosphere of cooperation between them and the club's directors, which is
arguably unparalleled in English football. In a rapidly changing football culture,
Charlton is one of the few British clubs with a sense of stability and continuity in
coaching staff and club ownership.

Conclusion

The Charlton Athletic fans' 'Battle for the Valley' highlights several issues surrounding the academic debates concerning both sports stadia and local reactions
to the changing nature of football culture. While the foci for the struggles were
local, such spaces and places are interconnected with wider societal changes.
The cut and thrust of the campaign reflected local politics, but this needs to be
placed on a broader canvas of what was happening in British/English soccer.
This, in turn, needs to be considered in the light of the changing nature of football across the globe. The fans' struggle to return to their home ground was
prompted by a fear of 'homelessness' and an intense feeling of attachment to the
Valley stadium. The latter was linked to a recognition that the team and the
ground were inextricably linked facets of their identities as football supporters.

Considered in the light of what Tuan (1974) and others have argued with regard
to stadia, the Valley was a sacred place for Charlton supporters, and thus its preservation was worthy of a vast investment of time, money and emotion. Furthermore,
stadia such as the Valley are relics of the past, and thereby generate feelings of nostalgic attachment. They act as anchors of meaning, an unchanging aspect of
people's lives that remain constant while other local and national factors are irrev-
ocably altered through the processes of globalisation, which have been dominant
in the late twentieth century and remain so in the early part of the twenty-first.
When their space was threatened, the fans' love for the stadium manifested itself in
a campaign which spanned an incredible seven years. They harangued the club and
the borough council, stood in local elections, and raised over £1 million towards
the renovation of the Valley. Charlton Athletic's supporters proved that football

fans are not just 'turnstile fodder', but are capable of united action to protect their interests, despite seemingly impossible opposition.

The Battle for the Valley was concluded in 1992. Since then, several clubs have relocated their grounds and major changes have taken place to virtually all English stadia as the recommendations of the Taylor Report have been implemented. Seats have replaced terracing in the attempt to prevent a repeat of the Hillsborough stadium disaster. This has been accepted as inevitable by most fans and the changes have gone largely unopposed. However, ticket prices have been raised as clubs compensate for the reduced capacity that the increase in seats has brought. This change has been fought by fans (Brown, 1998), yet thus far unsuccessfully. As Brown observes:

> One of the key problems in confronting democracy in modern football is the justification of the issue itself. Why should a multi-million pound industry which increasingly sees itself as part of an 'integrated leisure sector' be concerned with football supporters beyond being customers in their market?
>
> (1998, p. 63)

Charlton Athletic may be one of the exceptions to this situation. Their supporters proved that challenging the establishment could be successful, and as a result of the Valley campaign, club and fans now enjoy a largely harmonious and mutually beneficial relationship. 'Fan-power', such as was wielded by the Charlton supporters, and reflected in the growth of fanzine culture in football more generally, may well come to be regarded as a twentieth-century phenomenon. With the ongoing global and European restructuring of soccer, such supporters will be replaced by 'satisfied customers' and consumers of media–sport products.

In understanding the local–global figuration, questions concerning the interactions and disjunctures between and within global flows and local cultural identities must be addressed. TNC actions are now a pronounced feature of the local–global interplay which surrounds the structure, organisation and meaning of global sport. The creation of corporate alliances, international media synergies and corporate and state sponsorship are part of the sports–industrial complex (Maguire, 2004) and have emerged as a 'significant feature of the global sport system' (Maguire, 1999, p. 128). The activities of the groups involved in the sports–industrial complex have a range of implications for local cultures and identities. We view the dynamics of the local–global nexus as powered by multi-causal processes that flow multidirectionally. Notwithstanding this, questions of power balances, 'disjunctures', knowledgeability of the consumer, and unintended dimensions must all figure as part of the conceptual framework. That is, the analysis needs to examine the interplay between transnational brands and images, and how these influence and are influenced by local identities and experiences. As Falcous and Maguire observe:

At the centre of the analysis must be multidirectional processes, marked by power struggles of different kinds which are contoured by unintended consequences stemming from the disjunctures between local–global flows and an uneven power geometry. On this basis, researchers are better able to grasp that in making sense of the local–global equation we must also grapple with a model of local cultures and local knowledgeability.

(2005, p. 16)

Insights of this kind lead us to reject a simple homogenisation thesis. TNC activities embrace 'global marketing strategies of difference and individuality' (Maguire, 1999, p. 213) and are involved, along with the nation-state and other stakeholders such as non-governmental organisations, in the re-imagining and reconstitution of local cultural identities. There is a danger that this approach will be seen as a return to a version of pluralism. This is not what we are about. There are clear winners and losers in global sport. Observations of this kind tend to be somewhat speculative – hence the empirical work undertaken here has shown how power balances struggled over in everyday life, and how the meanings and outcomes of local/global sport remain highly contested.

Part II

Lived experiences

3 'Cricketers of the empire'

Cash crops, mercenaries and symbols of sporting emancipation?

Joseph Maguire and David Stead

England has long been cricket's global cultural, political and economic core, with the game's traditions and rules diffusing out around the world, mainly on the back of British colonial expansion (Guha, 2002; James, 1963; Manley, 1990; Stoddart, 1979, 1988). One factor in the establishment of England's world status has been the role English cricket has played as a global 'finishing school' for the former colonies' best talent. Here, we highlight how English cricket has used such talent as a 'cash crop', but also that increasingly such labour can be viewed as symbolic of the changing relationship with the former imperial master. This labour migration has been controversial since its inception and, ironically, the developmental role that it has offered to other nation's players has helped fuel the increasing challenges to England's centrality in global cricket affairs.

Cricket's experience has to be seen in a wider labour migration context. For centuries, people have moved from country to country selling their physical, intellectual and artistic labour. This has proliferated on a European stage and – as the wider world has become more reachable (emotionally and physically) – labour migration has become a global phenomenon. In more recent times, sports labour migrants have appeared on the scene. They have taken their athletic talent and moved, not only within their home country but also across national and, frequently, continental boundaries. Here, we want to reconsider both the question of labour migration in general, but also a case study of international cricket in the early 1990s. In doing so, we will briefly compare this period with the position in the present day.

Sport labour migration research revisited

Research into sport labour migration is in its relative infancy. If we are to match the progress made in other areas of enquiry in the sociology of sport then much more work needs to be done, both at a conceptual level and with regard to empirical enquiry. The work so far conducted, whatever its merits, has only 'scratched the surface' and should be seen as a symptom of a beginning – and here work by Maguire and joint work conducted with colleagues is included. Given the need to build a solid social scientific stock of knowledge, new research conducted in this area must be welcomed. Thus, the works on association football labour migration by Jeanrenaud and Kesenne (1999), Lanfranchi and Taylor (2001), Maguire and Pearton (2000a; 2000b), Maguire et al. (2002), McGovern (2000, 2002), Moorhouse (1996), and Szymanski (1999) have proved useful additions to our understanding of the processes involved. In addition, labour migration research is gaining attention in Japan (Chiba, 2001; Kudo et al., 2003). This area of study has also proved increasingly attractive to journalists. While they have not added a great deal to what we already know, some of their anecdotal evidence offers glimpses into the lives of particular migrants (Reng, 2003).

Considered in this light, the publication by Magee and Sugden (2002) is also helpful. The world system theory approach which they use to provide a 'basic understanding of the political economy of world football' (2002, p. 427) is one that brings with it a global perspective – this is arguably one of the building blocks for understanding how the local and global intersect in migration processes. Of course, the relative merits of such an approach have been hotly contested within the broader globalisation literature (Held et al., 1999; Held and McGrew 2000, Therborn, 2000). Bale and Maguire (1994) highlighted its potential contribution, and in Global Sport (1999), Maguire argued that this approach alerts us to the extent to which hegemonic powers exploit other nations in their search for new markets to sell sport forms, leisure products, equipment and cultural merchandise. In addition, world system theory, in the context of sports and arts labour migration, could fruitfully focus on how hegemonic states search for new sources of skilled labour whose early development was resourced by these former colonial countries (1999, p. 19).

There are some conceptual links between a process-sociological perspective – and that of world system theory, though they differ in their relative emphasis on the economic dimension of global processes. Nevertheless, it is necessary to draw into any broader analysis the insights from world system theory that highlight that the core states dominate and control the exploitation of resources and production. A deskilling of semi-peripheral and peripheral states occurs on the terms and conditions set by core states. The most talented workers, in which peripheral or semi-peripheral states have invested time and resources, are lured away to the core states whose wealth derives from their control over athletic and artistic labour and the media–sport/leisure production complex (Maguire, 1999, p. 19; Maguire and Pearton, 2000a). Work of the kind conducted by Magee and Sugden reinforces this case.

Where we are forced to part company with Magee and Sugden is over the way in which they develop their typology of association football labour migration. The paper suggests that the typology by Maguire has 'contextual use for this article but is only a starting point for an assessment of sports labor migration' (2002, p. 429). However, we would suggest that this research – on which their typology rests – is both misrepresented in the paper, and also more central than simply a 'starting point' for their work. Furthermore, a critique of the field as it presently stands should be comprehensive and thus cite the existing work such Maguire and Stead (1996); Maguire and Pearton (2000a, 2000b); Stead and Maguire (1998a, 1998b, 2000a, 2000b); Lanfranchi and Taylor (2001) and McGovern

(2000, 2002). The field of research on sport labour migration has much to gain from such a dialogue, as we all, from various perspectives, work to clarify our findings and theoretically informed explanations. Indeed, such work needs to be more fully engaged with work on migration in general (Brettell and Hollifield, 2000; Castles and Miller, 2003).

Magee and Sugden argue that the typology developed by Maguire is 'based on secondary interpretation and conjecture and lacks grounded and interpretative substance' and claim that 'by having no primary data to support the classifications, the explanatory power of Maguire's model is weakened' (2002, p. 429). On the contrary, the typology comes out of research conducted by Maguire, and in conjunction with others, on association football and other sports, and research on migration (Dezalay, 1990). This research includes primary data – interviews with players, data gathered at FIFA, and interviews with people such as the then FIFA Law officer and subsequent General Secretary Michel Zen Ruffinen and PFA Secretary Gordon Taylor (Stead and Maguire, 1998a, 2000a). The original research also involved interviews with basketball players, cricketers and rugby players (Maguire, 1994b; Maguire and Stead, 1996; Stead and Maguire, 1998a; Maguire and Tuck, 1999). Magee and Sugden are correct that empirical work is crucial for the construction of adequate typologies, although we cannot agree with their assessment that such empirical evidence is lacking in the case of the typology that colleagues have used. Indeed, in 2000, Stead and Maguire (2000b) focus on precisely the issue of labour migration and association football, presenting primary data from interviews with a range of English Premiership players as part of a discussion of the labour migration typology.

With regard to the typology used in their article, Magee and Sugden state that it is based on the 'lived experiences of the foreign players interviewed' (2002, p. 429). It is important that typologies continue to be checked against new data to ensure their adequacy. As such, it bears mention that three of the six categories are the same as those in the typology previously used by Stead and Maguire, suggesting the continuing usefulness and adequacy of some of the categories, such as the 'nomadic cosmopolitan', for which Magee and Sugden offer the same examples as those given in Stead and Maguire (2000b) and Maguire et al. (2002).

The writers also argue that their 'typology identifies a combination of overlapping categories surrounding a central sphere – the foreign migrant in English league football. This is in preference to Maguire's approach, which tends to pigeonhole migrants into one or other exclusive category' (Magee and Sugden, 2002, p. 429). By way of reply, let us cite a passage from our article (2000b) where, having reviewed the primary data from interviews with Premier League soccer players, we write:

> The typology does sensitize us to the kind of emphasis that can characterize the motivation of sports migrants. However, the complex motivation of soccer players in this study would suggest that it would be inappropriate to assign this particular group of athletes to any one of the ideal types.
>
> (2000b, pp. 54–55)

Far from pigeonholing, this is an attempt to provide a more adequate, nuanced and sophisticated understanding of the processes involved. Furthermore, we go on to connect the specific question of soccer migrants to wider sociological issues – something that research on sport labour migration must do if it is to provide an adequate understanding of such complex social, and global, processes.

Magee and Sugden claim that their study 'is in a stronger position to comment on the experiential dimensions of sports labor migration because of the methodology employed to attain grounded information' (2002, p. 429). However, the methodology – 'focusing on a single sport using primary data' (2002, p. 429) – is the same methodology used in Stead and Maguire (2000b) and focuses on the same sport. This is the also the same grounded approach deployed to interview basketball players, cricketers and rugby players over the past decade (Maguire, 1994a, 1994b; Maguire and Stead, 1996; Stead and Maguire, 1998b; Maguire and Tuck, 1999). What seems important to note, then, is the strength of this particular approach, which has served researchers working from different theoretical perspectives.

Finally, Magee and Sugden write: 'Maguire draws on a wide range of sports on which to base his classifications of pioneer, settler, returnee, mercenary, and nomadic cosmopolitan, which, in themselves, provide inconsistencies and inaccuracies' (2002, p. 429). It is not clear if Magee and Sugden regard the typology per se as inconsistent and inaccurate, or the data on which it is based. We would argue that typologies are ideal type representations of the 'real world' and that it would be foolish to see their categories as either mutually exclusive or set in stone – hence why in diagrammatic form they are represented in an overlapping fashion. Sociologists have long debated the relative merits of typologies, and we would not suggest that this typology is any different in its limitations. As noted above, such work is but a symptom of a beginning.

It is appropriate and potentially productive to critique and refine work, and the typology developed should certainly not be seen as the final word. The new categories which Magee and Sugden offer – ambitionist, exile and expelled – have some merit. Indeed, further investigation would help to flesh out the distinctions between the overlapping exile and expelled categories. In studies on basketball, cricket, association football and rugby union, we and colleagues have probed the motivations of players in a series of interviews (Falcous and Maguire, 2005; Maguire and Stead, 1996; Stead and Maguire, 1998a, 1998b; Maguire and Tuck, 1999). The ambition to play at the highest level was one of several themes to emerge in their explanation for migrating. However, this was not included as part of the typology, because we found that such ambition cut across several of the categories. Nevertheless, this is something on which to further reflect. Sport labour migration research certainly needs further conceptual and empirical development, and could benefit from dialogue with the wider migration literature (Maguire et al., 2002; Stalker, 2000; Zimbalist, 2001). In doing so, however, it will also be important to sustain the craft of good sociological enquiry (Maguire and Young, 2002). Let us now turn our attention to a case study of cricket that demonstrates some of the points outlined above.

Cricket, cash crops, mercenaries and emancipation

In order to discuss the nature, complexity and significance of sport-based migration, and address the motivation issue, we will focus on male English elite cricket. Initially, attention will be given to the historical development of cricket migration. Consideration will then be given to the extent, form and experience of such migration during the 1980s and early 1990s. Cricket offers a particularly revealing case study for other sports. The importation of the overseas cricketer into England represents, arguably, the longest established example of the phenomenon of sport labour migration. It has been a controversial practice from its earliest days (Lemmon, 1987; McLellan 1994). At the time of this study, the impact of migrant players was a central element in heated and linked debates about the shortage of international class indigenous talent coming through in county cricket and the failings of the England team. Questions were being raised not only about the employment of foreign nationals but also with regard to a growing influx of overseas developed players who were using various qualifying routes to become eligible to play for England.

In addition, misgivings had surfaced about the level of commitment to England by players from an immigrant, particularly Black West Indian, background. Such sentiments burst on the public scene following an article by Robert Henderson (*Wisden Cricket Monthly*, July 1995). His comments were perceived as racist, and prominent Black England players such as Philip De Freitas and Devon Malcolm reacted angrily and sought legal redress. The debate ignited by Henderson's article echoed that which ensued in 1990 when Norman Tebbit, a prominent right-wing politician, used allegiance to England's cricket team as a litmus test by which the 'Englishness' of citizens of the United Kingdom would be judged. His remarks were made in the context of matches between England and countries of the Indian sub-continent and implied strong reservations about the general level of commitment and loyalty to their adopted country found in the UK's Asian immigrant population (Maguire, 1993a). The importance of the overseas recruit was emphasised in 1994 by the Warwickshire county club's enormously successful importation of the West Indian Brian Lara. In his brief, one-season sojourn, Lara was instrumental in Warwickshire winning all but one of the competitions contested and securing major increases in public and sponsorship support. Lara's dramatic incursion into the county game represented a watershed moment in the part played by overseas players.

The appearance of the overseas cricketer in England dates back to the end of the last century and some charting of the subsequent key developments is necessary to ground an appreciation of the contemporary situation. The actual extent and form of involvement of migrant players in county cricket is outlined for the 1993 season. The principal source for this data has been a range of annual player directories. Central to our analysis in this chapter are the hopes and concerns of the key individuals and organisations that network together to fuel and structure the flow of cricketing talent. Reference is made to the frequently conflicting attitudes found in England, the host country, and in Australia, the West Indies and the other major donor countries. The motives of the overseas cricketers themselves, and how these have been developed, have been examined through a series of player interviews. In fact, the questions about personal and professional objectives and motivations represented but one element of what were wide-ranging interviews.

Other topics raised included players' employment negotiations and conditions, personal and professional adjustments, reception in England, reaction in their home country and effects on their national and cultural identity. This agenda is illustrative of the complicated nature of migration experience for athletes, many of whom may be young and inexperienced in the demanding worlds of both professional sport and international travel. Our contention is that such concerns and experiences are common across sports (Maguire et al., 2002).

The development of labour migration in English county cricket

In the early 1870s, just as overseas players started to appear in England, so too did regulations to govern their participation in county cricket. The complex development of such regulations is central to the story of how England became the focus of professional employment ambitions of cricketers across the world. Three factors have dominated as they have in other areas of sport labour migration. First, there is the imposition of quotas – rules stipulating the number of overseas players any club/team can have. Second, there is the use of place of birth, parentage or residential qualifications to permit or restrict migration. Third, there are requirements laid down with regard to the quality and status of a prospective migrant player.

An additional factor of specific relevance to the English cricket migration situation has been the question of a player's eligibility to play for England. Overseas born and/or developed players have come to England and through their length of residence, UK birth or parental background have become eligible to represent their host country on the international stage. An overseas quota place in the player's county club is thus released. This switch of national allegiance is controversial for many reasons. In particular, concerns regarding cricket player migration have typically focused on the reduction in opportunities for indigenous players, the donor country's lost investment in the migrant player, and the doubts about the migrants' sincere emotional commitment to England's cause.

The early pioneers of migration into English cricket were mainly Australian professional players, who took on the challenge of living so far away from home and family. Some had been born in the UK and used their place of birth to qualify whilst others gained qualification through length of residence. From the beginning of the twentieth century, fears were aroused in domestic cricket, particularly about the threat to jobs resulting from the introduction of the overseas professional (Lemmon, 1987). The latter's true allegiances and level of commitment were also questioned. These kinds of concerns came to a head around 1909, with the exploits of the Middlesex player, Frank Tarrant, when back in his native Australia, and led to a rule that prohibited any prospective commuter cricketer from playing alternate seasons in the northern and southern hemispheres. No player could represent more than one county in a calendar year – with a British colony, dependency or state being treated as a county (Lemmon, 1987).

Some West Indians appeared on the county scene in the early part of the century, aided by the cricketing 'missionary work' of such prominent English players and administrators as Sir Pelham Warner and Lord Hawke. These imports started to put the Caribbean firmly on the cricketing map and were the vanguard of the influx of top West Indian talent that was evident in the last three decades of English cricket. Nevertheless, as C. L. R. James's work makes clear, such missionary work entailed a form of dependent development (James, 1963). The imperial master was still supreme.

The tight qualification rules in force from the First World War until the 1950s tended to inhibit significant overseas player participation in county cricket. The exception was the amateur cricketer, who was exempt from the more draconian restrictions, and positively encouraged. Despite the barriers to county cricket, the lure of England was still strong and it was with the good money and large inter-war crowds of the northern leagues, particularly the Lancashire League, that the overseas professional was to be found. Richly talented players, such as the West Indian Sir Learie Constantine, brought with them a certain glamour and provided a new dimension to the leagues.

Since the Second World War, the employment of overseas players has increased significantly, although the process has been characterised by both facilitation and restriction. A batch of rule changes in the 1960s was the key catalyst for the most significant expansion in importation; however, a crucial step was taken in 1945 with the introduction of the 'special registration' provisions. This term referred to all those players who had moved to counties and claimed qualification to play on the grounds of place of birth or length of residence. In 1953, fuelled by officials of the Marylebone Cricket Club (MCC) who feared a soccer style transfer market developing in cricket, a rule was introduced allowing county teams only ten such special registrations. The sting in the tail was that only two players could be registered under the length of residence category. Thus English cricket was formally accepting that the overseas professional was part of the county scene but at the same time instituting tight and clear restrictions.

In the 1960s, acceptance started to turn to recognition of the possible benefits from importing players. The background to this shift was that English domestic cricket was in decline. County attendances had fallen dramatically from the pre-war levels. A culture shift was also taking place with winning becoming crucial. Playing success became equated with attracting vital sponsorship. Radical thinking was called for and one frequent suggestion made was to enhance the attractiveness of the game by increasing the numbers and, more importantly, the quality of the overseas players (McLellan, 1994). Despite many misgivings, the gateway into English cricket gradually widened. In 1963, the requirement of being resident in an employing county was relaxed from two years to one, if the registered overseas player had lived in England for five consecutive years. Significantly, a registered player was no longer barred from playing first-class cricket overseas, if his county approved. These were still tentative steps as the residential requirement remained a major deterrent to an overseas player.

However, the reforming zeal of officials in the 1960s proved relentless. Major cup competitions and one-day cricket emerged in this period. The role of television coverage and the need to entertain became prominent. Some county clubs became increasingly enthusiastic about the value of the world's superstars being able to play in county cricket. The Nottinghamshire club proposed the introduction of immediate registration, i.e. the waiving of a residential qualification. The Test and County Cricket Board (TCCB), which had taken over control of county cricket from the MCC, reflecting the growing desire of the clubs to control their own affairs, eventually agreed. From the 1968 season, one immediate registration player was to be permitted per county.

Although the quota of two overseas players was retained, immediate registration was a landmark in the development of England as the focal point for the international cricketer. Professional and geographic mobility was made easier and the top players and talent flowed in. The vast majority of the world's most famous cricketers of the last thirty years have played English county cricket. An international player market has opened up with the best players eagerly sought by the county clubs. This has placed the top foreign imports in an increasingly strong bargaining position, particularly in relation to the indigenous English professional.

The first prominent immediate registration was Nottinghamshire's capture of the West Indian captain, Sir Garfield Sobers. He was a 'standard bearer for an illustrious parade of global talent over the ensuing years' (Midwinter, 1992, p. 72). Initially, many other counties were slow or reluctant to get involved. However, by the 1990s, all had taken up their quota, including Yorkshire which had long resisted recruiting players born outside the county. Another rule change allowed players born abroad to be qualified for England if they had lived in the country for four consecutive years before their fourteenth birthday. This enabled the sons of immigrants to play county cricket without them having to take up an overseas player quota place. Counties have grasped this opportunity and a number of such players, particularly those of West Indian parentage, have gone on to distinguished careers representing England.

England, therefore, has been the global core for the development and realisation of professional cricket career aspirations. It has been a position fuelled in part by a lack of cricketing employment opportunities in other countries. However, it was not until the regulation changes of the 1960s that England's finishing school role became truly formalised. Alongside the hopes arising from importing players came the fears. Over the last twenty years, there has seen a growing unease over the perceived pervasive presence and dominance of the overseas recruit. This has led to steps to close access. From 1982, only one registered overseas player was permitted to play in a county championship match; effectively a move towards a quota of one player per county squad, this became the regulation from the 1991 season. Such tightening has led to counties having to be more careful about recruitment decisions. The more developed world star, often a match-winning fast bowler, has become the norm. Even for these often very experienced performers, English cricket provides a graduation function, where skills, reputation and visibility can be enhanced. Such benefits are also being sought by many other lesser-known or particularly young overseas players who, denied access to the county game by the various regulations, are to be found gaining their English cricket experience at lower levels of competition, i.e. with local league teams all around the country (Osborn and Greenfield, 1995).

As entry to the county game has become more restricted, so further regulation loopholes have been identified and used. In the 1980s there was a rush to take advantage of a rule giving eligibility to play for England to those overseas players who had a parent born in the UK and had lived in the country for four consecutive years. A number of well-known England players have emerged through this rule and their counties have thus been able to release an overseas quota place. Around the same time, Mortensen, a Danish player with Derbyshire, successfully invoked EU/Treaty of Rome employment laws, to rid himself of the overseas player tag: an early pre-Bosman example of the European labour mobility question encroaching into cricket. Players from Holland and Ireland have subsequently followed suit. Although the opposition to their presence is vocal and, in some instances, tinged with racist overtones, migrant players remain active at various levels of English cricket. The basic characteristics of the group at the top – the county cricketers, particularly the registered overseas players – require specific attention. It is to this that we now turn.

The structure of international labour migration in English county cricket

In the 1990s, each of the 18 county clubs was allowed one registered overseas player. In 1993, at the time of our earlier study, every club had taken up this opportunity. A total of 416 players were registered to play in county cricket, of which 18 were overseas players and a further 4 held an EU qualification. However, as we noted, the evidence of migration extended far beyond these two categories. Table 3.1 outlines the range of qualification routes and highlights the complex nature of migration into the English county game.

The 'born overseas/qualified' or 'qualifying as English' category included those players who have eligibility status derived from their period of residence or parental places of birth or the age when first resident in England. It also included students or players with special dispensations. Many of the players in the category may have spent most of their lives in England but all had been involved in the migration experience and brought with them exposure to another country's culture, sense of identity and cricketing traditions. These players represented over 10 per cent of the total county cricket workforce and the significance of this in terms of quality and impact is reinforced by the fact that fifteen – more than one-third – of the players represented England in Test matches in or before 1993. These findings are reflective of wider migration issues, including the cultural attachment to cricket of West Indian communities in England, and the return of

Table 3.1 The migration dimension in English cricket

| | Seasons | | | | | |
| | 1987 | | 1993 | | 1996 | |
Qualification	Nos	%	Nos	%	Nos	%
Born overseas/qualified or qualifying as 'English'	39	10.6	44	10.6	42	9.5
Registered overseas players	29	7.8	18	4.3	18	4.1
European Union qualified, incl. Irish	4	1.1	4	1.0	3	0.7
Born UK/educated abroad	6	1.6	12	2.9	14	3.2
Subtotal of 'overseas migrants'	78		78		77	
Born UK excluding England	14	3.8	17	4.1	17	3.9
The non-migrant English players	277	75.1	321	77.1	346	78.6
Total county cricketers	369	100	416	100	440	100

former migrants or their sons to British colonies whose class and recreational biases leaned towards an interest in cricket. The extensive and selective recruitment policies of county clubs may also be in evidence, as would their enthusiasm for players to become qualified as English.

Continuing to focus on 1993, similar observations also apply to the 'born UK/educated abroad' category. For these players, home in a cricketing sense may have always been England. Of the twelve players, two played in the England Test side. The county clubs' recruitment practices are again indicated, as are their links with former UK citizens and institutions, such as schools, abroad. The 'EU qualified' category includes one player born in the Irish Republic. The 'born UK excluding England' group is composed of seventeen players and includes ten who are Welsh and with the Glamorgan (Welsh) county club. The non-migrant English players, effectively the indigenous players, are those whose available biographical details indicate birth in England and no significant education or residence abroad, especially during their formative cricketing years. The eighteen registered overseas players are at the top of the inward migration tree and it is important to look more closely at the particular characteristics of this group (see Table 3.2).

In the 1993 season, two-thirds of overseas players came from the Caribbean. This underlines both the impact of West Indian cricket and culture on the English game and the continued exploitation of Caribbean human resources that has been such a dominant factor in English life since the 1960s. It also reflects British colonial ties and the way in which migration to the UK has been viewed traditionally in many colonies as the desired route to employment and betterment. The next highest overseas donor country is Pakistan. Two or three Australians may well have been involved but their participation was excluded by their involvement in Australia's 1993 tour to England. The average age of the

Table 3.2 Registered overseas and European Union qualified players in England county cricket 1993

Player	Country	Age	Specialism	Seasons in county cricket
1	Pakistan	22	SB	1
2	Pakistan	26	FB	5
3	West Indies	29	FB	4
4	West Indies	26	FB	1
5	West Indies	28	FM	7
6	West Indies	25	FB	5
7	New Zealand	22	FM	4
8	West Indies	26	FM	1
9	South Africa	26	FB	7
10	West Indies	37	B	4
11	West Indies	26	AR	2
12	Pakistan	30	B	2
13	West Indies	35	FB	11
14	West Indies	41	B	13
15	West Indies	31	B	1
16	West Indies	34	AR	8
17	West Indies	30	FB	7
18	Pakistan	21	FB	3
19	Holland	31	FM	4
20	Denmark	35	FM	11
21	Holland	20	FM	3

AR – all-rounder; B – batsman; FB – fast bowler; FM – fast medium bowler; SB – spin bowler.

registered overseas players is 28 years, with a span of 20 to 41 years. This average is relatively high due to the presence of three veterans of West Indian cricket. In general, the ages and length of time in county cricket suggest a period of some maturing of the migrant workforce, with players recruited when young and staying with their counties for a significant number of seasons.

This observation is confirmed when consideration is given to the length of player service to the county. The group has 104 seasons of county cricket within its ranks, with an average of 5 and a span of 1 to 13 seasons. The evidence suggests some long-term commitment and loyalty on the part of both employer and employee. There has also been some intra-England movement with four of the players moving between first-class counties, in one case on two occasions. Player specialisms, based on directory classification and performance data, reflect a move towards quick bowlers as match winners. The importers of this form of sporting athletic talent want a rich guaranteed dividend on their investment. With only one registered overseas player allowed, the counties have concentrated their attention on fast and fast-medium bowlers and together they make up two-thirds of the imports. More than half of this category are West Indian. The large number of overseas tours undertaken by national teams also empha- sises the international globetrotting undertaken by these and other cricketers. Such recruitment strategies also reflect broader cultural/sporting stereotypes regarding the presence, or absence, of specific qualities in different ethnic groups. These observations provide some indication of the extent and complexity of overseas involvement in contemporary English county cricket and an outline of some of its key characteristics. This is clearly a significant sport labour migration process but why has it happened, and just how stable is the position of the English game as cricket's global finishing school?

Host and donor country attitudes to migration into county cricket

In England there has been a certain consistency regarding the arguments for and against the importation of overseas players. At different times one or the other lobby has been in the ascendancy. Today, those observers who see problems with county cricket's role as the principal employment host to the world's cricketers are again flexing their muscles. The way in which the dominant view of migra- tion can change, and the kinds of arguments put by both proponents and opponents, are frequently evident in other sport labour migration situations. The large influx of foreign players into English soccer in the mid-1990s started to arouse much debate, as does the possible impact of the overseas recruit in the emergence of English professional rugby union. Observers of such developments would do well to reflect on cricket's experience.

Supportive views in England about the importation of overseas cricketing tal- ent have been motivated by the following kinds of potential benefits:

- a revitalisation of the English game
- personalities, excitement and new ideas
- regular opportunities for the English cricket public to see the world's best
- increased club memberships and attendances
- more sponsorship and media attention
- role models, teachers and challenges for indigenous players
- playing success and greater recognition for the employing counties
- the availability of talent when it is absent in indigenous players

These hopes, often fuelled by deeply felt fears about the health of the game, have tended to be held by club managers, sponsors and a wide range of observers. For example, Geoffrey Boycott (1990), an ex-England player noted for his outspoken views about the strengths and weaknesses of English cricket, has argued strongly for quality in county cricket and championed the value of indigenous players rubbing shoulders with the world's very best. England is seen as a finishing school not just for the overseas migrant but also for the indigenous player who, by association with the best international talent in a hot house of sporting excellence, gains a crucial professional education experience.

Confronted by the strength of the above case, the opposition within England to the presence of migrant players in county cricket has concentrated on four main lines of attack:

- Damage is done to the development opportunities and commitment of indigenous players, particularly young cricketers and players in certain specialist positions, e.g. fast bowlers.
- The quality of the England team and its leadership is negatively affected because key county positions, including captaincies, are held by players not qualified to play for England.
- It is not proven that all the players coming in are necessarily better than available indigenous talent.
- The migration represents an erosion of the spirit, ethos and ethics of the English game.

The latter point is worth expanding. The issue appears to involve somewhat more than straightforward insularity or jingoism. To encourage migration, or more specifically to resort to deliberate importation, has been seen to be a lowering of the standards of acceptable behaviour. In many ways it reflects the amateur ethos of the game, strong in the early years and still prevalent in some quarters today. Amateur visitors were always more welcome than the professionals. Sewell, writing in the 1930s about an Australian professional from earlier in the century, took a particular exception: 'Trott had no more right to play for Middlesex at cricket than Stalin has to lead the Guards Brigade into action' (cited in Lemmon, 1987, p. 21). Somehow, it was not English, or cricket, to have these players come in.

Antagonism towards the overseas migrants has also been linked to fears about a transfer market developing, often with unflattering references to soccer, and with concern over the increasing intrusion of commercialism into the sport. The pursuit of money and, with particular regard to the migration topic, the buying of results, has been seen as weakening the purity of the game (Lemmon, 1987). The traditionalists, former players and others who have held these views have done so with some vigour. They have highlighted the failures and often questioned the motivation and commitment of the overseas players. Their arguments have led to the periodic tightening of the qualification rules, as in 1991.

In 1993, as in the past, critics turned on migrant players, like the Zimbabwean Graeme Hick and the New Zealander Andrew Caddick, who had qualified as English and were thus eligible to play for the national side. Many of the same arguments against the registered overseas players again came to the fore. Former England captain and now TV presenter, Tony Lewis, whilst speaking about the two players mentioned above, suggested that 'importing overseas players camouflages over weaknesses in the English system in the schools' (BBC Radio 5, 30 July 1993). Clearly then, very strident positions are taken over England's role as the global focal point for cricket employment and development.

Experiences of the host country's reception of the individual migrant player have been mixed. Acceptance can take time, and personality and personal performance factors are important. Team colleagues might welcome an overseas player as a potential saviour of the county's and, by association, their fortunes. On the other hand, players may be worried about the loss of opportunities and indeed jobs arising from the appointment. Overseas players do take key specialist positions and cost significant money. Numerous writers (Martin-Jenkins, 1984; Lemmon, 1987) have alluded to the loss of first-class and potential England careers through the arrival of an overseas player. Jealousy over the level of money paid to the newcomer could also affect team-mates' reactions. As Vic Marks wrote in 1986, 'professional cricket is a precarious, cut-throat means of earning a living' (cited in Sissons, 1988, p. 317). Despite such comments, many players have blended in and been well received:

> We don't tolerate stars in the Lancashire team, Clive [Lloyd] has filled in excellently and he's a great team man. Jack Bond [the captain] delighted to have acquired a star must be equally relieved that he resolutely refuses to behave like one.
>
> (Stevenson, cited in Hayter, 1981, p. 96)

Those players who have tried hard to get close to the community, and the long-serving players, are most likely to receive a positive reaction.

When the focus shifts from the host to the donor country, attitudes and motives can vary widely. In general, donor country opinion has tended to reflect a positive approach towards their players venturing into English cricket (McLellan, 1994, pp. 115–125). However, this may be changing, as overexposure of talent to possible international adversaries and too much cricket leading to injury and loss of enthusiasm are being seen to outweigh the developmental benefits to players and, by association, their national side. Such voicing of concerns is not new. Previously, when residential and travel issues restricted a player's availability for domestic and representative cricket, donor countries took some exception to the lure offered by English cricket. Around the turn of the century Australian players were given money and jobs not to go to England whilst in the case of George Headley, in the 1940s, public subscriptions were raised to fund his return home to play for the West Indies (Goodwin, 1986). West Indian people have a history of migration and when the region's players started to be in demand, particularly but not exclusively in England, and with little cricketing employment available locally, it was not surprising that there was a general acceptance of players going overseas.

Whilst historically countries like Pakistan and India have supported their players' migration, some other donors have been somewhat less enthusiastic. Australia, a heavy exporter in the early years, lost nearly half a Test side just after the war when key players moved permanently to England. Perhaps this was an unplanned consequence of wartime service abroad. Since then, Australians have been more qualified in the support of their experienced players entering county cricket. Restrictions on the eligibility of returning migrants to play State cricket have been implemented. The perception of England as a cricketing finishing school, or the need for it in the context of what their own game offers, would appear to be different in Australia. The influx of young Australians and New Zealanders into the local English leagues is another matter as the personal and professional experience gained there would be seen as constructive.

As we have pointed out, it is important to consider migration into county cricket as being potentially beneficial not only to the individual but also to the donor country's cricket, national side, and even international status as a nation and people. The visibility and exploits of the registered overseas players have helped put the likes of the West Indies, Pakistan and New Zealand on the cricketing map and helped them achieve Test status. Players have developed skills and experience which have helped improve the quality of both their country's domestic and its representative cricket. For West Indians, the time spent in England has assisted in what Goodwin calls 'the evolution from talented amateurs, entertaining but fragile to fully fledged professionals' (1986, p. 115).

High-profile successful migrant players from countries like Pakistan and the West Indies have become role models and sometimes coaches for young people in their home countries. On the other hand, success in England may not always impress donor country opinion. The New Zealander Glen Turner, for example, found he had to prove himself again every time he returned home (Lemmon, 1987). Pakistan, with its players increasingly evident on the county scene, represents a revealing case study of the donor country experience. As with the West Indies, there has been little consistent money in Pakistani domestic cricket. To travel to England, the home of professional cricket, is acknowledged as a wise developmental move for a player. The experience gained is also considered of potential benefit to the nation's cricket. Indeed, Crace, with reference to Imran Khan's early 1990s attempt to arrange a county placement for his protégé, Waqar Younis, suggests that the Sussex club 'were probably wary of being used as a finishing school for one of Imran's Pakistani colts' (Crace, 1993, p. 118). In Pakistan the top players are put on a pedestal. Their exploits, cricketing and otherwise, in England are noted eagerly. The success of Imran and Wasim Akram is viewed as helping put not only Pakistani cricket but the country itself on the map, thereby suggesting how a former colony and a Third World country can use sport to state its case for international respect and attention.

Today, it is the risks arising from playing too much cricket that are central to donor country concerns about players going to England. High pressure international representative cricket is being played throughout the year. This is compounded by an English county game that is highly demanding in terms of the frequency of matches, the travel and personal upheaval involved and the continuous high expectations placed on the overseas player. The Pakistani cricket authorities were prominent in recognising potential problems and placed restrictions on their senior players. There were also reports in the mid-1990s of the West Indian cricket authorities threatening to pull their Test stars out of county cricket, a move fuelled, to a large degree, by their captain, Richie Richardson, leaving his contract with Yorkshire midway through the 1994 season because of physical and emotional fatigue. The West Indian authorities considered offering winter contracts that would negate the financial need to go to England and thus keep players sharp for Test cricket and protected from burn-out (*Mail on Sunday*, 14 August 1994). None of this proved successful and the long-term decline of the team is signalled by the back-to-back series defeats to the English in 2004.

A further concern for donors relates to the overexposure of key players. To participate in the English county cricket finishing school is to give, as well as to receive, but the price paid may be too high. Damage to a donor country's inter-national competitive prospects could come through the loss of surprise, arising from potential opponents becoming acquainted with the skills of its players through playing each other in county cricket. Allan Border, the then Australian Test captain, speaking about the likelihood of Shane Warne, his match-winning spinner, joining a county, expressed concern that to allow English players to gain experience against the bowler would not be in his country's best interests (BBC Radio 5, 23 August 1993).

Another sensitive issue for Australia has been the steady flow of their young players who have used the experience of English cricket as a stepping stone to defect to the England Test team. In the 1990s, players like Martin McCague (Kent), Alan Mullally (Leicestershire) and Craig White (Yorkshire), in whom Australian cricket had made a considerable investment, utilised a UK birth qual-ification to switch allegiance. Despite the reservations and controversy outlined, considerable enthusiasm still exists for the annual migration into English cricket both in the donor countries and in England. But what of the principal figures involved, the migrant players themselves? Through interviews with a sample of registered overseas and EU qualified players, and an examination of biographical material about such cricketers, we sought to establish their motivations.

The motivations and experience of migrant players

An overriding motivation evident amongst the migrant players is the desire to have a professional career in cricket. In most of the major cricketing nations there now exists sponsorship or some cricket-related employment possibilities for, in particular, the top players. Whilst professional playing opportunities do exist else-where, it is England that is the home of the fully developed professional game. From the early years of the migration this basic fact of cricket's global political economy has been the key. The first pioneers made big sacrifices and came, by sea, all the way from Australia to earn a living as cricketers. Today, the migrant player will expect to gain appropriate remuneration for his efforts. Indeed, whilst county cricketers cannot be classed as particularly well-paid sportsmen, the overseas recruits are in an advantageous bargaining position and some large salaries and attractive fringe benefits are received. The attractiveness of some of these employ-ment packages was suggested by reports that in England the tax authorities launched a 'probe into cash plans for cricket stars' with special emphasis on past and current overseas players (*Mail on Sunday*, 7 August 1994, p. 95). Allegations have also been made about the use of offshore bank accounts into which sponsors have paid money (*Sunday Times*, 10 July 1994).

Despite all these developments it remains a central question to what degree financial gain is the prime inducement to go into county cricket. To read of the lucrative packages negotiated by Brian Lara and others, and to note the high-profile jet-set lifestyle of some of the top migrants, might suggest that money is the main attraction. Whilst not wishing to underestimate the fact that the migrant cricketers want their financial reward from the greater commercialisation of cricket, we would argue that other motivating factors are also at work. These factors underpin the concept of England as the finishing school where overseas players come to develop personally and professionally, gain skills and knowledge, and seek status and recognition – such developments that will, of course, also enhance their future earning potential.

Questions asked of the overseas players sought to substantiate this wider appreciation of the motivations involved. We set out to delve into the genesis and attraction of the migration, the significance of England as the preferred destination and the knowledge base on which the decision to migrate was made. All are crucial to the understanding of sport migration, in particular the development of the athlete's motivation to make the move. To what degree was the decision taken freely and in pursuit of what ends? Examination of the history of overseas player migration into county cricket suggested that a strong and consistent motivation has been the personal challenge, the opportunity to test and improve oneself in the English game. Two of the interviewed players put this particularly firmly and succinctly. One player observed that: 'If you can play county cricket and prove yourself then you can make it. I wanted to do that, I wanted to make it'. In addition, another player commented: 'There's a lot of cricket here so when you play a lot of cricket you improve your lot … professional improvements'. For one EU qualified player, the challenge motive was compounded by the very limited opportunities for cricketing development in his home country:

> In Holland there comes a time when you can't go any further … the opportunity came to go to England. I said to myself what if when I'm 35 or so and haven't gone and look back on the opportunities passed. So I thought go for it and see what happens. I wanted to see if I could make it.

To a degree, the impression gained is one of athletes identifying migration as a means for the exploration of the boundaries of their ability, to discover things about themselves as players. Extrinsic, more mercenary motives, tended to be much less prominent than might be imagined, at least in their initial decision making. Reflecting on his time in England, one long-term migrant commented: 'Cricket was the main thing. I wanted to play at the highest level I could. It certainly wasn't a money thing at the start. I suppose it is a bit now."

This point was reinforced by several players. Pakistani Waqar Younis noted: 'I'd have probably signed for almost nothing, just to have the chance of playing county cricket' (Crace, 1993, p. 120), while the West Indian Vivian Richards observed: 'I didn't stop to worry about meagre rewards, after all I was getting such a kick from playing and I was being paid at least something for playing the game I loved, the thing I could do best in life' (cited in Richards and Foot, 1979, pp. 61–62).

The overall notion of migration being an act of personal investment loomed large with many of the players. It could have been to improve as a professional cricketer or to increase market value. For some it was also clearly a desire to make their mark as a top international cricketer. As the Pakistani captain and Lancashire recruit, Wasim Akram, observed: 'If a player does well in England, he is recognised all over the world' (Crace, 1993, p. 37). This view was shared by Richards who saw England as a 'necessary shop window' which had enabled him to be noticed by the West Indian selectors (Richards and Foot, 1979, p. 157).

For at least one, albeit much-travelled and long-serving migrant, another motive was present. He acknowledged the developmental benefits of his time in England and indicated a wish to reciprocate. As he put it: 'One of my biggest motivations is that people come to watch you and they want something to remember. They come to be entertained and that's what you aim at.' Interestingly, this same player also alluded to another motivational emphasis that perhaps equated the provision of entertainment with the receipt of financial gain. He stated that: 'one of the big benefits is the money that I'm earning but I'm actually putting a lot into the game, of this I'm sure'.

The selection of English county cricket as the migrant cricketer's preferred destination links strongly with the challenge and professional development objectives. As we have underlined, England is perceived as where the professional game has its home, where a cricketing career means something. The players were often very clear on this as this comment would confirm:

> Opportunities. If you want to make it as a professional England is the only place because in other countries, Australia, South Africa, you can play but there's no money. Basically people spend six months there as part of a holiday and getting fit, that kind of thing. You don't get a lot of money there to survive.

Similar sentiments were expressed by another player who said that 'I got the appetite from a pretty early age that England would be the place for me if I wanted to further my cricketing career'. For many, the possibility of a move into English cricket was dependent on approaches made by representatives of county or league clubs. Their ability, or perhaps their potential, had been spotted. What might have been a flight of fancy now took on a different dimension and required serious consideration. The historical evidence of developing recruitment practices, more international exposure at all levels and the existence of an international player market place were all substantiated by the experience of three players from quite different parts of the world. One of the Caribbean migrants reflected on how he 'actually came first with the West Indian youth team and then moved to play for a team in the Central Lancashire League'. For a

Pakistani player, international exposure was also important for he observed: 'I had played them last year with Pakistan and played very well. They obviously liked me and thought me OK. They made me an offer'. A similar situation had arisen for one of the European players who said: 'I was playing for Holland against England when I was fifteen, my county's manager saw me and invited me over, that's why I'm in England now.'

Some experience of England through participation in senior or youth tours or some experience of playing league cricket characterised the way many of the migrants learned about England and the English game prior to joining a county club. Frequently, there had been a former migrant cricketer on hand back home to offer advice. Generally the players felt reasonably aware and confident that their motives were realistic. This point was emphasised by the three Europeans whose exposure to English cricket had come in many forms, not least via the coverage on British television.

But for one player, like so many of the West Indian cricket migrants of the days before the ease of international communication and travel, the move was more of a leap into the dark. When asked how informed was his decision, he stated:

> Not much, as a matter of fact I was told some ridiculous stories. I was told if you get a bucket of water and leave it outside it would turn to ice by morning. Basically I was more or less willing to see it for myself. I believe in seeing things first-hand.

Despite such vivid imagery, the overall picture was one of cricket's migrant players having informed motives, definitive about the potential role of an English cricket experience in their lives and with a sincere interest in testing out and discovering more about themselves rather than just a preoccupation with mercenary objectives. Interestingly, although committed to finding out about both cricket and themselves, the players interviewed showed little interest in working abroad as a way of experiencing the wider culture.

Migration and English county cricket in the twenty-first century

Ten years on from the original study and English cricket continues to have a love–hate relationship with regard to the importation of overseas players. Cricketers from all over the world are still attracted to the idea of plying their trade in England. Their motives remain difficult to establish, but these are likely to be varied and, therefore, reflective of the wide range of experience and seniority to be found across the players involved. The eighteen employing county clubs have seen the benefits of this pool of able, and willing, recruits and have invested significantly in employing them. Today, their presence in England is at one of its highest ever levels. Changes in English cricket's quota regulations, and the increasing impact of pan-governmental legal decisions, such as the Kolpak ruling (2003), challenging sporting quota systems, are just two of several key factors that underpin this increase. As has been the case in previous eras, this greater presence of the overseas player has brought to the surface distinct divisions within the sport. Familiar issues and calls for the total or partial banning of overseas recruitment are again being heard.

A brief examination of the 2004 season is instructive with regard to the picture outlined above. The season started with some indications of English cricket being in good health. The national side returned from the West Indies with an historic Test series win. This success continued with a series victory over a highly rated New Zealand team, and again against the West Indies. New younger players were emerging and playing central parts in these victories. The establishment of the English Cricket Board's National Academy at Loughborough University in 2003, the growth of local academies, and a general restructuring of support to representative squads at all age levels, indicated that the prospects for the development of indigenous talent were very promising indeed. However, whilst this may be the case, over forty official registered overseas players (ROPs) were participating in the English cricket season of 2004. In addition, the county clubs continue to exploit the various other regulative or legal devices to bring in even more non-indigenous/non-England qualified players.

From the 2003 season, each of the eighteen clubs could field two ROPs and all took advantage. Rulings had also been eased to permit these players to be replaced during the season if, for example, international commitments took them away from their counties. After some years of greater restriction, the move to the two-player quota and increased flexibility reflected a number of factors, some quite familiar. The overseas players were seen to provide something extra for the spectators and sponsors, as well as offering experience and skill in what had become an increasingly competitive county scene. A two-leagues structure had been introduced to heighten interest and competition. A new feature was that the English cricket authorities had copied the successful Australian system of giving central contracts to those players likely to be selected by England. In effect, these players, the best of the indigenous talent, were now being protected from having to play more than a handful of matches for their counties. This left the county squads short of not only talent, but also their star performers. This gap is one that the overseas players are there to fill.

The ROP category has been a feature of the game for many decades, as has the use of other means of making non-indigenous talent eligible to play professionally in England. Place of birth, parental background, and period of residence have all been used extensively, and continue to be so. In 2004, the Derbyshire club was able to register seven non-England qualified players through various means. These kinds of eligibility situations greatly increase the degree to which migration is impacting on English cricket. Indeed, the two new 'young' stars to emerge in the England side in 2004 do not fully support the idea that indigenous talent is coming to the fore. Andrew Strauss (Middlesex) and Geraint Jones (Kent), both aged 27 at the start of the 2004 season, were born in South Africa and Papua New Guinea respectively. Strauss came to England at an early age, whilst Jones grew up and was educated in Australia.

Both utilised British ancestry and/or residence in order to gain eligibility. Another device enlisted from the 1980s onwards has been the European Union labour mobility laws/rulings. These have been used by, for example, Scandinavian and Irish cricketers with European passports, as the way to become eligible to work in English cricket. The Bosman ruling of 1995 has had an extensive impact in such sports as football, but the lack of cricketers in most European countries has tempered the impact of the Bosman ruling on English cricket. However, players from cricketing nations such as Australia, who have a European family background, have used this as a means of qualifying. Bearing in mind the history of Eastern European immigration to places like Australia, the 2004 expansion of the EU may be of some significance to English cricket. The year 2004 also saw attention focused on yet another European legal development, the Kolpak ruling (2003), which may have direct consequences for migration into English cricket. It is a ruling of similar significance to Bosman, and is of growing concern to English rugby union, a new and fast expanding area of sport labour migration.

Maras Kolpak, a Slovakian handball player, won his restraint of trade case at the European Court of Justice after being prevented from playing in Germany by a quota system. The relevant ruling deems that the imposition of quotas is illegal if the individual migrant has a work permit and is a national of a country that has associate status with the European Union. The significance for English cricket is that prominent cricketing nations such as South Africa and a number of Caribbean countries also have such status. Indirectly, it is a challenge to the two-ROPs quota, and will become even more so if other key cricketing countries, like Australia, also attain EU associate status.

A country's international cricketing success continues to affect the make-up of the group of registered overseas players in English cricket. Australia has been the dominant world force in cricket since the late 1990s and it is Australian players who constituted nearly half of the overseas players in England in 2004. There are particular enclaves of such ROPs in certain counties, reinforced by other players of an Australian background eligible through other routes. The two next largest groups of ROPs are Pakistanis and South Africans, and they have sometimes also been recruited as a national pair by one county. The playing status of the overseas players does vary considerably. A few counties like Hampshire and Somerset have invested heavily by employing the Australian superstars Shane Warne and Ricky Ponting respectively. Many of the other imports are far less experienced and not as well known, yet the employing counties are still using up vital financial resources in having to pay for wages, accommodation, airfares and so forth. The mix of migrants suggests that whilst economic motives may well be present, the idea of England as world cricket's 'finishing school' may also have some credence. It is this role in helping opponents to gain experience of English cricket playing conditions that also features in the criticisms levied against the importation of overseas players.

Negative feelings about the growth in the number of overseas imports were clearly evident in 2004. Questioning the quality of these players, and linking this with the issue of England's central contracts scheme, the journalist Mike Dickson has written about spectators having 'more chance of watching foreign nobodies than England's heroes from the Caribbean' (*Daily Mail*, 16 April 2004, p. 88). The broadcaster and former England captain, Bob Willis, has pointed to the negative impact on the development of international standard English players, and highlighted what he views as inappropriate use of vital money that could be allocated for such purposes. Willis has gone so far as to say: 'I would like to see a total ban on overseas players given a try' (*Daily Mail*, 16 April 2004, p. 88). Another influential voice, Duncan Fletcher, the England coach, himself a Zimbabwean cricketing migrant, has tempered the Willis stance by speaking in favour of banning players in certain specific positions, such as captains, spinners and wicketkeepers (*Daily Mail*, 16 April 2004, p. 88). The English players' union, the Professional Cricketers' Association (PCA), has been another influential group drawing attention to overseas imports and such developments as Kolpak, and, in doing so, has pointed to the potentially harmful impact on the indigenous professional, and the ambitions of young English players.

The PCA's Report on the Overseas Player in Domestic Professional Cricket (2 October 2003) came out strongly for greater regulation including going back to the one ROP per county situation and offering increased incentives for counties to develop and play indigenous cricketers. However, the county clubs are still arguing for the freedom to recruit from wherever they are able. James Whitaker, Leicestershire's Director of Cricket, when defending the use of the Kolpak ruling to sign a South African bowler for 2004, said: 'It is a competitive market and we are a small club. I do not see much wrong with having three non-England qualified players. There are still eight out on the field who can play for England' (*Daily Mail*, 16 April 2004, p. 89). Clearly, the migration debates evident over past decades are set to continue.

Conclusion

Migration into English cricket has a long and involved history. Britain's colonial past and role as originator of cricket's practices and traditions have been instrumental in fuelling the development of migration knowledge and aspirations amongst cricketers worldwide and providing the necessary routes and supportive networks. English county cricket, as the global centre for professional cricket employment, has attracted the very best of the world's talent. There has been a two-way flow of rewards. The overseas players have brought glamour, variety and great skill to the English game. They, and by association their home nations, have also reaped benefits. Careers and reputations have been made or enhanced and national cricketing identities developed. England has willingly, but also sometimes reluctantly, provided cricket with its world academy.

However, as we move further into the twenty-first century, the role of county cricket as the global finishing school is again coming under close scrutiny. The ever present dissenting voices in England are still vocal. To some, the two player per county quota is still too high. Temporary and even total bans on importing players have been placed on the agenda. The importation of players continues to be a major issue in arguments over the health of English cricket. Not least are the ever present fears expressed about the drying up of England's production line of elite-level talent in general and in specific playing positions.

In response to the opposition came calls throughout the 1990s for greater sensitivity to the needs of the county clubs. When, as noted above, James Whitaker referred to the entertainment value of the overseas players, he was echoing the sentiments expressed by one of his predecessors, Jack Birkenshaw, a decade earlier (Radio Leicester, 17 August 1994). Whatever the ebb and flow of opinion, the high profile match winner is still in demand. The reluctance of donor countries to support their players' involvement in county cricket may restrict the supply line of top overseas talent. It could be said that having got what they want out of county cricket, and with England no longer all-powerful in world cricket politics, donor countries are now in a better position to dictate events. Professional opportunities for elite cricketers have also increased in these countries. In addition to which, the empire has also struck back against the 'Mother Country' (Maguire, 1993a). Despite a resurgence in 2004, England's frequent defeats on the field of play have been mirrored by the waning of English control of global cricket. At an earlier stage in cricket migration, the players may have been exploited as cash crops; today, they may also serve as role models and symbols of sporting emancipation.

But what of the enthusiasm and motivation of overseas cricketers in England and, indeed, sports migrants in general? Out of our work on a range of sports has come the typology of sports migrants referred to earlier. Monetary motives figure highly with such migrants, but financial ambitions for many existing or would-be migrant cricketers are likely to be answered increasingly in their home countries and through rewards from the much expanded global circus of international representative cricket. Our previous studies revealed that challenge and self-development motives appear to take precedence over monetary gain for the migrant cricketer. It follows, therefore, that some sense of frustration may arise if any further discouragement and restriction of participation in county cricket occurs. That said, the amount of international cricket being played now may well satiate the migrant's hunger for the developmental experience that comes from being tested against the best.

English county cricket has provided a cricketing academy for other countries. Ironically, these countries have been able to utilise the experience, as noted, to help defeat their former colonial masters on the field of play. Is the UK providing such a developmental opportunity to competitor nations in other sports? Should international migration experiences be seen as a deliberate ploy in the preparation of British talent? Today, the sports labour migrant has become a central figure in the emergence of the global sporting village. Our cricket case study illustrates how the international migration of athletes can play a fundamental part in the national and global development (and under-development) of a sport. Wider political, economic and cultural considerations are also involved. Migration brings with it questions of labour rights, and can therefore put social and sport policy considerations on a collision course. This has clearly been the case in European sport following on from the Bosman and Kolpak rulings. Actions and attitudes can vary considerably over time and place with the migrant likely to encounter both resistance and assistance. Their presence in or loss to a country may have contradictory aspects in connection with the development of indigenous athletic talent as part of the sports–industrial complex.

meanings until it is out of step with the dominant sport culture. It is then transformed and incorporated by it.

Until the Super League deal with Rupert Murdoch's News Corporation, the game had remained relatively less affected by the increasing commercialisation of its competitor sports in Britain, particularly soccer, but also basketball and ice hockey (Maguire, 1988, 1996). Several factors, including this lack of commercialisation, put the game in a parlous financial state by 1995, when Murdoch made his offer to rugby league officials. The situation was summed up by Kelner's observations: 'The implementation of the directives of the Taylor Report into the Hillsborough disaster, spiralling wage bills and the deepening recession left even those clubs established in the first division in a state of penury' (1996, p. 97). Rugby League was therefore keen both to expand its base of support and participation through the establishment of a European Super League, and to increase its income with the television revenues on offer.

However, the move away from its traditional roots to a new 'global' presence held certain implications for people's identities, both at a local 'community' level, and at a local 'national' level. This is because the structure, organisation and meaning of the game would be altered by the processes inherent in the globalisation of many sports, particularly with regard to global flows surrounding people, finance, media coverage and ideological meanings (Appadurai, 1990; Maguire, 1999). As Arundel and Roche argue: 'The media sport industry ... tends to promote local identities in a way which transforms them from the unreflected 'ways of life' and traditions of local people, into reflexive and organised cultural productions and stagings for outsiders' (1998, p. 84). However, it is necessary to examine to what extent the media–sport production complex achieved this in the case of rugby league.

The transformation of rugby league provides a powerful case study that enables us to assess how the processes of globalisation reach either the core of the culture or merely the ephemeral aspects of local identities. Equally, this case study allows us to consider the response of those cultures. Global media–sport products such as rugby's Super League may be resisted or recycled, and subjected to a process of hybridisation. The power and richness of local identities should not be underestimated. Equally, it should not be assumed, a priori, that a simple process of homogenisation is at work. This chapter aims to assess these issues through an analysis of the changes in the structure, organisation and meaning of rugby league that occurred as a direct result of the advent of Super League. We will trace and analyse these changes from a process-sociological perspective and connect them to the interwoven sportisation and globalisation processes (Maguire et al., 2002). In this connection, a broader discussion of global media sport issues and questions is appropriate.

Sport, the media, and global cultural flows

In exploring global media–sport, the nature and extent of the interdependencies involved must be traced and located within wider global developments. The

4 'In league together'?

Global rugby league and local identities

Joseph Maguire and Catherine Possamai

In the bitter struggle between two Australian media moguls for the exclusive television rights for rugby league in the southern hemisphere in the 1990s, the impact was not to be confined to Australia (Rowe and Lawrence, 1996). In an increasingly interdependent and globalised sport system, developments in Australian rugby league were to cause significant upheavals in the British version of the sport, which had remained largely unchanged since its inception in 1895. This chapter is concerned with the initial launch and development of the northern hemisphere's European Super League, and the consequences that this attempt to globalise a traditionally parochial sport has had for local British identities. We focus on the decisive phases of the early 1990s; more recent developments lie outside the scope of this chapter. Here, we conduct a review of national broadsheet coverage of rugby league in order to trace the turbulent development of Super League. Local responses to these broader processes are explored through regional press coverage. In so doing, we seek to contribute to the debate regarding local/global issues surrounding transformations of sport (see Andrews, 1997; Maguire, 1999; Maguire *et al.*, 2002; Miller *et al.*, 2001, 2003).

Though it is the second largest spectator sport in Britain, rugby league has been largely neglected as an area of enquiry largely due to it being seen as a 'local' rather than 'national' sport (Arundel and Roche, 1998). In fact, it is so localised that in 1994, 60 per cent of all those who attended professional games came from just four postal districts in the motorway corridor of the M62 (Kelner, 1996). The sport engenders fierce local allegiances, and rivalries between towns sometimes no more than a few miles apart. Thus, rugby league was known in Britain as a northern working-class sport, associated with the origins of the industrial revolution and a subculture that values a tough masculine style. This cultural identity was crucially manifested in its media representation (Arundel and Roche, 1998; Falcous, 1998), particularly the working-class image perpetuated by the BBC coverage of the sport. Many people within the game felt this coverage was both of a poor quality and 'patronising and haphazard' (Kelner, 1996, p. 82). Such media representation was perceived to have hindered the game's expansion from its northern home. In many ways, rugby league is an example of what Donnelly (1993) – with regard to rugby union – terms a 'resilient' sport subculture: one that holds on to traditional ways and media flow is a part of an interdependent global sport system (Maguire *et al.*, 2002). Other global flows that structure this system include technology, capital, migrant labour, and national symbols and ideologies. This system involves what Sklair (1991) terms transnational practices which take a variety of cultural forms, and gain a degree of relative autonomy on a global level. These transnational processes sustain the exchange and flow of goods, people, information, knowledge and images. By utilising terms such as 'transnational', this chapter moves beyond the nation-state as the sole reference point for understanding the growing integration of the world. The media–sport production complex is an integral part of this general process (Jhally, 1989). Think of the technological advances involved in the media coverage of the modern Olympics, and how satellites now relay powerful images across the globe in an instant. For Real (1989), these images reflect and help sustain the emergence of a global culture, however briefly and superficially.

The relative autonomy of these transnational practices needs to be linked to what Appadurai (1990) has termed the disjunctures that occur as global flows weave together. These disjunctures are part of the figurational dynamics that lead to a whole series of unintended features of the global sports system, which possesses a relatively autonomous dynamic that is not dominated by any one group. Notwithstanding this, it is important not to overlook a related point concerning global media sport. Transnational practices are prone to attempts to control and regulate them. This can involve the actions of transnational agencies or individuals from the transnational capitalist class (Harvey, Law and Cantelon, 2001; Sklair, 1991). Such interventions cause cultural struggles of various kinds, and at different levels.

An analysis of global media sport has then to examine both the intended and the unintended aspects of its development (Maguire, 1999). The intended acts of representatives of transnational agencies or the transnational capitalist class are potentially more significant in the short term. Over the long term, however, the unintended, relatively autonomous transnational practices may predominate. These practices structure the subsequent plans and actions of transnational agencies and the transnational capitalist class. Globalisation processes involve a blend between intended and unintended practices (Maguire *et al.*, 2002).

The impact that global media sport practices have on the global sports system should not be underestimated. Though such transnational practices cannot be explained solely by reference to nation-states, the global media complex is influenced by American practice in sports such as American football, basketball and baseball (Gruneau and Whitson, 2001; Jackson and Andrews, 1996; see also Chapter 1). Such practices have forced a range of sports, such as soccer and rugby, to align themselves to this model; to do otherwise would place in question their survival in the global media marketplace. Despite pointing to the influence of American media models, it would be unwise to suggest that such practices are all-pervasive and not resisted, and that the consumption of the products that flow from this media–sport complex is accomplished in an uncritical manner that does not reflect local culture and circumstances. Research rightly reminds us of how meaning is produced in and through particular expressive forms and how it is continually negotiated and deconstructed through the practices of everyday life (Golding and Murdock, 1991/2000).

On this basis, research concerning global media–sport has to focus on both an analysis of cultural texts and the way that people in different societies interpret media products and incorporate them into their world-view and lifestyles. While there is a political economy of media–sport, global audiences are composed of knowledgeable, creative active agents. Consumption involves an active process of interpretation and, at times, of resistance and rejection. Hence, zones of prestige are also marked by these processes (see Introduction). The reception of global media products relates to how local circumstances allow people to make sense of and give meaning to their particular situation. At issue, therefore, is the role of popular culture both in the reproduction of global capitalist social relations and in resistance to those relations. These themes surface repeatedly in studies of sport and popular culture (Rowe, 1999) and, in this specific case, rugby league.

In highlighting how people across the globe are engaged in the practice of winning meaning and creating space from and within global media–sport consumption, a further point regarding these processes can be made. There is a danger in over-emphasising the sovereignty of the consumer. At times the romantic celebration of resistance appears at odds with examining the way the mass media operate ideologically to sustain and support the prevailing relations of domination (Alt, 1983; Bourdieu, 1999). Attention also needs to be paid to how the global media–sport complex operates as an industry. By focusing on the meaning of consumption, the transnational practices that impinge on the production and circulation of meaning and the ways in which people's consumption choices are structured by their position in the wider global formation should not be neglected. These links are important in studying globalisation and the media–sport complex (Jhally, 1989; Tomlinson, 1996; Wenner, 1989). A sensitivity to local responses to global flows has to be stressed (VanWynsberghe and Ritchie, 1998). Given these points of departure, attention can now be paid to the specific features involved in the globalising tendencies evident in the development of rugby league in the 1990s.

Australia: the background to the creation of European Super League

The European Super League came into existence following the development of a schism within rugby league in Australia – the nation where the game is most firmly established and where, in some areas, rugby league is the most popular sport. The disagreements in Australia which were to have such far-reaching consequences for British rugby league concerned the television rights to screen the Australian rugby league (ARL) club competition (Rowe and Lawrence, 1996). The exclusive rights had been held by Channel Nine television, owned by media mogul Kerry Packer, through his company Optus Vision. However, Rupert Murdoch also wanted a degree of involvement in the sport, and in

February 1995 announced he was planning a massive investment into the creation of a 'Star League' in Australia, to be screened on his television network Star TV. To this end, players and existing clubs were signed by Murdoch's News Corporation company which also launched two new teams. The ARL responded by attempting to hang on to its players backed by the vast financial resources of Packer and Optus Vision. The result was that many players were offered huge sums of money as the two opposing media networks battled to secure enough players to run their respective leagues. The situation was in fact rather ironic, given Kerry Packer's instigation of the Cricket World Series in the late 1970s. As *The Guardian* noted: 'Reports of Packer stomping around Sydney, moaning about this bounder Murdoch stitching up the sport and buying up his players, will tickle anyone with a half-decent memory' (1 May 1995, p. 22). Murdoch's greatest coup, however, was to achieve the effective international isolation of the ARL by signing first Great Britain and New Zealand, and later Western Samoa, Papua New Guinea, Tonga and Fiji, to his Super League. This meant that players who remained loyal to the ARL would be unable to compete in international competition, and thus Murdoch's position was further strengthened. The battle between Murdoch and the ARL/Packer moved to the courtroom and was to persist for the next eighteen months, causing uncertainty and concern throughout the rugby league world.

Figure 4.1 shows the networks of interdependencies that formed across the globe as a result of the instigation of Super League in the southern hemisphere. It includes a blend of links and outcomes, some of which were intended by Murdoch when he established Super League, and others which were completely unintended and which flowed from the disjunctures between the different flows involved (Appadurai, 1990). This diagram therefore demonstrates both the unpredictable nature of globalisation processes, and the fact that although the transnational capitalist class may seek to dictate the course of events, people are active in interpreting and resisting change in their lives. For example, it is unlikely that Murdoch, at the genesis of his plans for a Super League in Australia, could have foreseen that his actions would result in newspaper headlines in a small town like Featherstone, in Yorkshire, England. Similarly, the actions of people from towns such as Featherstone and Castleford in the furore surrounding the Super League shows the potential that local communities possess to become involved in – and disrupt – wider global processes. The network of interdependencies highlighted in Figure 4.1 contours and reflects developments in both hemispheres. For our purposes, we wish to emphasise how this global network reinforced and reflected developments taking place in Europe and especially in northern England.

Plans, negotiations and unintended outcomes

The negotiations which led to the formation of the European Super League took place in the space of just a few days in early April 1995. Murdoch's News Corporation approached the RFL Chief Executive Maurice Lindsay with the idea

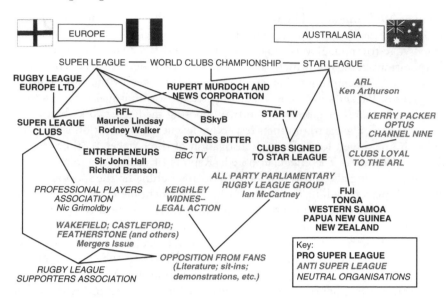

Figure 4.1 Network of interdependencies involved in the remaking of 'global–local' rugby league

of creating a Super League in Europe, which could then compete in a World Club Championship against the Antipodean sides. It would be screened on Murdoch's television networks around the world, including Fox TV in the US. This would give rugby league the opportunity to be seen for the first time on a world stage. Furthermore, the £75 million figure which was initially proposed as News Corporation's investment over five years was a huge windfall, given the game's financial situation of the time. As a reporter in *The Times* (owned by Rupert Murdoch) stated: 'After years promoting the thirteen-man code as the 'greatest game' and nobody listening, to have the world placed at its feet is like a light piercing a century of pitch black' (7 April 1995, p. 39). It is perhaps understandable that Lindsay and the RFL Chairman, Rodney Walker, agreed to the deal so readily, for as well as the incentive of the apparent benefits there was the threat of what would result from non-involvement. As the *Daily Telegraph* observed: 'The choice was either to go with the tide and the huge financial rewards or face financial ruin with top players moving on and the possibility of rival clubs being set up' (10 April 1995).

Although it was widely believed that it was Murdoch's company that had dictated the way in which the League was to be restructured, including the controversial mergers, it was in fact Maurice Lindsay and Rodney Walker who formulated the plans, including the decision to switch the playing season to the summer to coincide with the Australian system. They developed a plan, in the space of a few hours, to launch a fourteen-team Super League which would include two sides from France, one from London and one from Wales. It would also entail fifteen of the existing clubs merging to make five new teams. These were Hull and Hull Kingston Rovers, which would become Humberside; Salford and Oldham would form a Manchester team; Widnes and Warrington were to be Cheshire; Workington Town, Whitehaven, Barrow and Carlisle would constitute Cumbria; Sheffield Eagles and Doncaster would become South Yorkshire; and Featherstone Rovers, Castleford and Wakefield would merge to form Calder (named after a nearby river). Only five of the existing major clubs were given Super League status in their own right. These were Wigan, St Helens, Bradford Northern, Halifax and Leeds.

Having come up with this proposal in a matter of hours, without any consultation with club administrators, players or supporters, Lindsay and Walker presented it as a fait accompli to the clubs involved at a meeting on the evening of 7 April 1995. Clubs were told that a decision had to be reached quickly, or the offer from News Corporation would be withdrawn. This effectively restricted the club chairmen from making any consultations with their boards, players or supporters. The following morning, the rest of the clubs' chairmen were told of the deal, and that they had to vote on the matter that day, or the offer of £75 million would be withdrawn. There was much unease from the club chairmen – particularly those whose clubs would be merged, and from Keighley rugby club, who were due to be promoted to the top flight at the end of the 1995 season, but instead found themselves consigned to a First Division from which there would be no promotion or relegation for two years. Despite their misgivings, the chairmen all voted for the proposal, bar one abstention from Chorley club. This apparent approval, however, was not necessarily because the chairmen felt the Super League was a wholly good thing. As Kelner observed:

> While most representatives agreed that the game's dire financial state needed root-and-branch treatment, and that this was a once-in-a-lifetime offer that should not be rejected out of hand, there was a widespread belief among those present that voting against the plan would mean exclusion from further meetings.
>
> (1996, p. 115)

Among the national press, there was a mixed initial reaction to the announcement of the Super League. The Murdoch-owned *Times* was predictably enthusiastic. As one writer observed: 'The Super League is a boldly attractive concept, which, by incorporating clubs from other countries in a grand finale, will give a global perspective to a sport that encompasses only a small base of participation' (15 April 1995, p. 33). *The Guardian* called it: 'The most momentous decision in the game since northern clubs left rugby union almost exactly 100 years ago' (9 April 1995, p. 24). Reporters in both *The Independent* and the *Daily Telegraph* were more sceptical. One reporter noted: 'Why the haste? Has there been a hidden agenda, and if so, for how long? What happens if Murdoch goes after the five year deal?' (*Daily Telegraph*, 11 April 1995). Reinforcing this more critical tone, an *Independent* reporter concluded: 'The idea that 35 club chairmen should make these decisions after two hours talks and no opportunity to consult with their boards, players, or ... supporters, looks precipitate in the extreme' (*Independent* (*Sport*), 9 April 1995, p. 6). Little or no local consultation was sought or received. Decisions were made by a small group of chairman which would result in the transformation of the game's structures, organisation and meaning.

The subsequent restructuring of the original Super League plans, and the controversy and setbacks which surrounded it during the following two and a half years were to prove *The Independent's* assessment prophetic. In what follows we trace these developments. In so doing we highlight both the plans by particular elites and the reaction of local communities to these globalising trends. The period from April 1995 to December 1997 in the fortunes of the Super League can be broadly divided into five phases, with arguably a sixth phase emerging during the early part of 1998.

Phase one: April 1995 – shock, horror and resistance

The reaction and response throughout all sections of the rugby league fraternity to the announcement of the Super League deal was one of shock and disbelief, particularly at the speed with which it had happened. What followed was outspoken opposition to both the deal itself and the way in which it had been made. The Rugby League Professional Players' Association expressed 'outrage that the decision was taken without consultation and that hundreds of professional players learnt of the decision from television news' (*Independent*, 11 April 1995, p. 32). Among the clubs which opposed the deal, Keighley were the most vocal, and issued a writ against the RFL, although this was due in greater part to their exclusion from the Super League rather than any more fundamental reservations about the League itself.

The administrators and fans of the clubs scheduled to merge provided the most passionate opposition, particularly in the area designated to become 'Calder', which involved the implacable rivals Featherstone Rovers, Wakefield and Castleford. Local resistance focused less on the concept per se and more on the costs associated with this move for *their* club. Yet it must also be remembered that there was considerable strength of feeling regarding the proposed mergers in other areas. As one fan pointed out: 'Salford and Oldham have been asked to merge to become Manchester. Salford is a city in its own right and Oldham is a town. We're not Mancunians. They even talk different to us' (Clayton, Daley and Lewis, 1995, p. 41).

Just a few days after the Super League deal was made public, *The Guardian's* report reinforced this sense of local hostility: 'Passions are at boiling point in Wakefield, Castleford and especially Featherstone ... the prospect of clubs losing their identities clearly appals many supporters and bringing about the proposed mergers could prove an impossible task for Lindsay' (12 April 1995, p. 19). The importance of rugby league for community identity was highlighted by the national broadsheets and linked closely to the decline of the mining industry during the 1980s in the same areas now threatened by the loss of their local rugby league team. *The Independent* stated: 'Rupert Murdoch does to many of these northern communities what Margaret Thatcher failed to do. She closed their pits; he will destroy the most potent badge of their identity' (16 April 1995, p. 9). *The Guardian* went further: 'Call it Super Pit or Super League, it's still a small core of selfish individuals getting rich at the expense of the wider community' (30 April 1995, p. 4). *The Times* was predictably more restrained, yet its reporter still observed in a somewhat ironic tone: 'In the metropolitan district of Wakefield, the proposals have achieved something no Government has in recent times, by opening up a minefield' (18 April 1995, p. 23). The local papers from the Wakefield area gave further testament to the anger and dismay felt by the fans of Castleford, Featherstone and Wakefield.

The two papers which cover the area – the *Pontefract and Castleford Express* and the *Wakefield Express* – both carried front-page headlines about the intended mergers: 'Calderdash' proclaimed the *Pontefract and Castleford Express* (13 April 1995, p. 1). This strong headline was surrounded by photographs of fans demonstrating against the merger. The *Wakefield Express* articulated similar sentiments with: 'Angry Fans Reject Murdoch Millions' (14 April 1995, p. 1). A telephone poll of the *Pontefract and Castleford Express* readership had 344 respondents, of which 92 per cent were against the merger. Large amounts of column space were devoted to canvassing the opinions of local people. A Featherstone councillor argued: 'It's an assassination of the game and they have pulled the plug on the Featherstone community again. They closed the pit and now they propose to close our Rugby League Club' (*Pontefract and Castleford Express*, 13 April 1995, p. 1). In similar fashion the *Wakefield Trinity* fanzine argued: 'Not only have the men in shiny suits seen fit to strip the area of its Industry, taking away thousands of jobs, destroying communities and robbing the younger generations of a future, they now want to take away our sport' (*Wakefield Express*, 14 April 1995, p. 3). This local criticism was not confined to newspaper columns. Fans marched through their respective towns waving banners, and organised sit-ins at games.

The fierce local opposition prompted a book, *Merging on the Ridiculous*, which contained further arguments against the merger from mainly Castleford, Wakefield and Featherstone supporters, and was published within a couple of weeks of the Super League announcement. Drawing on local supporters' vociferous criticisms, it was observed:

> After all the hardships this area has suffered – a long and costly pit strike, the loss of thousands of jobs, a bleak future for the young folk – we took all the Tory Government could throw at us and we came through it because we all had an identity … and now we are threatened
>
> (Clayton *et al.*, 1995, p. 16)

The usage of personal pronouns such as 'we', 'they' and 'our' in the above statements is indicative of a strong 'we' identity evident within the communities concerned (Maguire, 1999). It conveys the impression of an 'us' – the insiders – against an unspecified 'them' – the outsiders – mentality. As well as linking the loss of the rugby league team to the loss of the pits, a further connection was made by some supporters: 'Nobody did more than Murdoch and his lackeys to con the nation into re-electing Thatcher in 1983 and 1987, and the coal industry was butchered as a result' (letter to *Pontefract and Castleford Express*, 13 April 1995, p. 10). Continuing in the same vein one fan observed:

> Often speakers called upon our communities to rally round in the same way as we did in the 84/85 Miners' Strike. We were reminded that it was the likes of Murdoch and the millionaire-owned-and-controlled press and media who had labelled the striking miners as the 'enemy within'. We all know what Murdoch thinks of the working class.
>
> (cited in Clayton *et al.*, 1995, p. 14)

This connection was also recognised by Maurice Lindsay, the RFL supremo: 'With the name Rupert Murdoch attached to … the offer, it brought up images in peoples' minds of Wapping and the Miners' Strike, and everything they felt they had been battling against' (cited in Kelner, 1996, p. 122). Other opposition to the deal focused not on the mergers themselves, but on the concept of rugby league as a global televised sport. *The Independent* argued:

> Featherstone folk want to see the representatives of their community engaged in what is still one of the purest, most honest and most thrilling of professional sports; what they do not crave is 'top class action beamed live and exclusive to your living room'.
>
> (16 April 1995, p. 9)

A fan offered the following observation:

> Spectators are active participants in the fate of their club, their game and their community. There is the feel of virtual unreality about thousands of people, each in his or her own little box, pressing the remote control at a pre-ordained time to watch the game on Sky.
>
> (Clayton *et al.*, 1995, p. 50)

Fans demonstrated at a match in Featherstone. Banners from both Castleford and Featherstone fans shared a common message – testament to the fact that although the teams may be implacable rivals, the threat to their existence brought forth a show of solidarity from both sets of supporters.

Some supporters were clearly sensitive to the likely impact on the meaning of the game flowing from its global restructuring and reorganisation. These fears are also testament to the perceived power that satellite television possesses to erode people's sense of place and stability by transporting the consumer across space, enabling him/her to be at any venue in the world at the push of a button. Yet we should be careful in reaching such a bleak conclusion too quickly.

Criticism of the restructuring of the game was not confined to supporters or reporters. Some of the main objections to the Super League concept came from the All Party Parliamentary Rugby League Group. Ian McCartney, MP for Makerfield and Chairman of the group, stated: 'Murdoch says he is giving Rugby League a world-wide audience but what's the point of showing the game in Beijing when people in Bolton, Barrow and Blackpool can't watch because they haven't got a Sky dish?' (*Guardian*, 17 April 1995, p. 12). The initial opposition from the strong community-based support of rugby league to the Super League therefore centred on the proposed changes to the organisation of the game in terms of the merger plans, which held important implications for the sport's meaning.

The opposition to Murdoch's plans for Rugby League was vehement amongst the (mainly Labour) MPs who constituted the Parliamentary Rugby League Group. In a House of Commons debate on the issue, calls were made for a variety of bodies to carry out inquiries into the matter. These bodies included the Monopolies and Mergers Commission and the National Heritage Committee. In the end, no such inquiries happened. According to David Hinchcliffe, MP for Wakefield and secretary of the Rugby League Group, this was due to the fact that the Monopolies and Mergers Commission was powerless to intervene due to the multinational nature of BSkyB, and that the National Heritage Committee could not affect a decision already taken by an individual sport.

The MPs' concerns centred around the mergers, which many, reflecting the feelings of their constituents, felt would be a crippling blow to some northern communities that had been in decline since the pit closures of the 1980s. There was, according to Hinchcliffe, anger that 'a battle between two Australian media magnates should result in my constituents losing something very important which we have had for 122 years – Wakefield Trinity Rugby League Club' (Hansard, Proceedings of the House of Commons, 26 April 1995). There was also concern at this further extension of Murdoch's empire. Another Labour MP, Ian McCartney, observed:

> There are serious implications for the United Kingdom outside Rugby League. The House must consider whether it is right that Mr Murdoch or any other media mogul can decide the shape, size and rights of *any* [italics added] sport.
>
> (Hansard, Proceedings of the House of Commons, 26 April 1995)

McCartney's observation clearly has relevance to the wider debate regarding British society and global sport development (Maguire, 1999). McCartney also warned that the consequences of the Super League could be a small number of players making huge sums of money, while the sport at the grass roots withers away and clubs are left to go bankrupt. As it turned out, this was an astute prediction. A further allegation made by Hinchcliffe in the same Commons debate was that 'certain writers and broadcasters are no longer free to report the facts about the Super League' (Hansard, Proceedings of the House of Commons, 26 April 1995). Although he did not specify to which writers and broadcasters he was referring, it is evident that he was speaking about those working for the newspapers and television networks owned by Rupert Murdoch. The fact that News Corporation journalists were (allegedly) being censored with regard to this issue provides evidence of the close synthesis between the various sections of Murdoch's media empire, and raises questions about the degree to which one organisation should be permitted control over such a potent social, economic and political weapon as the media, and global media–sport in particular.

While Lindsay and the RFL were facing widespread fierce opposition to their merger plans, they were also confronted with the problem of the ARL, which was attempting to sign many of the elite British players as a part of its battle against Murdoch's News Corporation in Australia. Large sums of money had to be spent by the RFL on tying players to loyalty contracts in order to prevent this pillaging of talent. Further discussion of this lies outside the scope of this chapter but highlights broader questions concerning global labour migration (Maguire et al., 2002). Though not foreseen at the time, these contracts were to cause controversy months later. Furthermore, as the month of April progressed, it became evident that with the exception of Sheffield Eagles and Doncaster, the clubs told to merge were determined not to do so. They were generally willing to take their chances in a First Division outside the Super League rather than put aside hundred-year-old rivalries and merge with their neighbours. It became obvious that an alternative proposition was required. In that sense local responses had achieved what they thought was a significant victory over the global reach of media moguls and entrepreneurs.

Phase two: May–October 1995 – adaptation and consolidation

Towards the end of April 1995, there were media-inspired rumours that the Super League would be expanded to accommodate 16 or even 18 teams. These rumours were soon dashed. At the beginning of May it was announced that the league would in fact be limited to 12 teams instead of the originally proposed 14. The 12 teams would be the top 10 finishers in the 1994/95 Championship season, plus teams from London and Paris. There would be two lower divisions, and promotion and relegation would happen from the first season. This meant that no clubs would be forced to merge and to lose their identity. The £75 million was to be divided according to which division a team was in. The new structure was a complete change from the original format, and although inevitably making some unhappy, it placated the fans who had been so appalled at the prospect of merging with their local rivals. It also prompted Keighley to abandon their legal action against the RFL. The club most distressed by the revamped League was Widnes, who were excluded after being included in the original plans. They claimed they had spent £350,000 on players on the strength of a Super League place and took the case to the courts. Their law case was unsuccessful.

The restructured Super League again provoked a mixed reaction from the national press. *The Times* adopted a pro-Murdoch line and argued: 'The moral high tone taken over Rugby League's deal with News Corporation, the parent company of *The Times*, ignored the sport's dilemma. Without two brass farthings to rub together, it was going nowhere and is now heading somewhere' (2 May 1995, p. 48). *The Independent* was far more circumspect, pointing out that the disadvantage of the new format, with no mergers, meant that Wigan's dominance of the game was now unlikely to be challenged (2 May 1995). It also observed that: 'there is a danger that Rugby League's chief benefit from the Murdoch–Packer skirmish will be one generation of exceptionally well-paid players' (20 August 1995, p. 23). The *Daily Telegraph* was particularly disparaging: 'Rugby League players are foot soldiers in a war of billionaires' egos and corporate business strategies. Its administrators are pawns in a geopolitical game of chess, dictated by the profit margins of the communications industry' (27 October 1995). These press observations were reinforcing comments made by officials within the game.

The director of Leeds rugby league club was one disappointed by the re-negotiated structure of the League:

> I feel we pussyfooted into the Super League. We had a chance to create a truly national sport but because of the outcry of a few thousand–and that's all they were–the dream was eroded and the money was spread more widely.
>
> (cited in Kelner, 1996, p. 125)

Despite these rather gloomy assessments, this was a period when the future of the Super League looked financially bright. Bass, the brewing corporation and owner of Stones Bitter, signed a deal to sponsor the Super League for three years from March 1996, and there was optimistic talk of staging the World Club Championship Finals in San Francisco, Tokyo or Hong Kong. There was also interest from the entrepreneur Sir John Hall, owner of Newcastle Rugby Union and Association Football clubs, in establishing a Super League team in the north-east. Furthermore, the position of the ARL was looking increasingly untenable, as the other major Rugby League nations all signed up with Murdoch, thus achieving the international isolation of the ARL and a global network for Murdoch's own Super Leagues. The significance which this development was perceived to have is testament to the importance of international competition in today's interdependent sports world.

The English teams began to enter into the spirit of razzmatazz perceived necessary for selling their sport as a worldwide commercial venture by adding American-style suffixes to their names. Although this was not unheard of in the English game (Sheffield had been the 'Eagles' and Keighley were known as the 'Cougars' for some time), it had never been previously envisaged on such a scale. Thus Bradford Northern became Bradford 'Bulls', Leeds reinvented themselves as the 'Rhinos' and Halifax became the 'Blue Sox'. These name changes were further signifiers of the process of change in the meaning of the sport, which could arguably have more far-reaching effects than changes in the game's organisation.

The development of new nicknames removed the need to mention the name of the town when talking about a team, thereby having a dislocating effect of sport from place. As Arundel and Roche (1998) pointed out.

> There is a suspicion in the game that the name changes are part of a process aimed at the elimination of place identities in order ... to enable Super League team locations to be more determined along American sport business lines, by the auctioning of franchises rather than by tradition.
>
> (p. 78)

As the first Super League season in March 1996 drew closer, doubts about the venture began to emerge as problems and criticisms mounted.

Phase three: November 1995–October 1996 – honeymoon over

The loyalty contracts that the RFL had signed with several elite British players in April 1995 came back to haunt Maurice Lindsay in December of that year. It was claimed by some national newspapers that the contracts would be used to control the movement of these players between clubs. Thus this would artificially influence the strength of some clubs and ensure an even competition. Such a system would operate on similar lines to the NFL draft system in America. These allegations were emphatically denied by Lindsay and by News Corporation, but suspicion persisted nevertheless. This controversy was followed by a disastrous blow for Super League worldwide as Murdoch lost his legal battle against the ARL in Australia and a court ruled that the Super League in the southern hemisphere could not begin until 2000. This meant that the planned, and extensively hyped, World Club Championships would not take place, and as Murdoch had only originally invested in a European Super League to support his Australian venture, it also threw his commitment to the deal in doubt.

Although Lindsay maintained that the Super League in Europe would go ahead regardless, the outlook was bleak. Lindsay admitted: 'If News Limited and its immense ability to invest is lost to us, I honestly believe we will see the end of Rugby League globally' (*Daily Telegraph*, 11 March 1995). This statement from Lindsay betrays the degree of dependency which Rugby League already had on Murdoch and his capital investment. This is a factor identified by Donnelly (1993) as one of the conditions associated with the transformation of resilient subcultures as they are incorporated into the dominant sport culture. *The Independent*, which had consistently been one of Super League's harshest critics, argued:

> Without the World Play-Offs and without international tours, the European Super League will be hollow, its vision and viability chronically impaired. It no longer makes sense; certainly not enough sense to justify jettisoning Ashes Tours, switching seasons and generally standing the game on its head.
>
> (24 February 1996, p. 27)

Despite this setback, the launch of the Super League took place in Paris at the end of March 1996 with a match between Paris Saint Germain (the link with the famous soccer club crucial for its credibility in France) and Sheffield Eagles. It was imperative that Paris did well in the League in order to maintain 'the rather threadbare European dimension of the Super League' (*Independent*, 24 March 1996, p. 26), and they did manage to win this first game. However, as even *The Times* wryly observed: 'launching Super League in Paris was the equivalent of Wigan staging a Boule tournament' (30 March 1996, p. 48). Parisians reacted with indifference to this Anglo-Saxon import.

Criticism soon began to mount surrounding the changes to the game's rules and structure – a reaction against the perceived Americanisation of the sport. *The Times* stated: 'The money that the sport craved, and received almost overnight, meant that it could afford the vision. The danger is that communities that have supported it for 101 years can see little more than a blur' (29 March 1996, p. 46). In a similar vein, a reporter in *The Guardian* wrote: 'The game's destiny is in the hands of people who neither know nor care about its traditions … This is, or was, the people's game. Now it is just a product; one only hopes it proves as durable' (21 January 1996, p. 7). Media concerns centred on not only the 'jazzing up' of the game with name changes and pre-match entertainment, but also the rule changes which had made it easier to score tries, in the belief that this is what people wanted to see. These were the greatest changes made to the actual structure of the game as a result of Super League, and confirm how the commodification of sports leads to a specific type of rule change designed to increase spectacle. These rule changes are generally intended to speed up the action, increase scoring, promote uncertainty of outcome, and provide commercial breaks in the action to maximise potential advertising revenue (Coakley, 1994). *The Guardian* argued that the rule changes devalued the 'try' and made the game into a scoring orgy – similar to basketball. Suggestions made that the game should be divided into quarters instead of halves, and allow unlimited substitutions caused consternation in one journalist:

> Led by the archetypal Aussie-American Murdoch himself, there appears to be emerging a determination to reduce our grand old code to a kind of gridiron-basketball hybrid, a chocolate-box, tin-soldier prance about, played out in short, jerky periods to afford the mulch-minded millions time to grab their new tinnies from the fridge.
>
> (*Guardian*, 19 November 1996, p. 10)

This media reaction had not been anticipated. Equally, there were signs that the American razzmatazz that had been introduced to rugby league was not as effective as Murdoch and the RFL had hoped. The pre-match entertainments, a further example of structural changes, were generally poor – a few cheerleaders or something similar – and although attendance at most clubs reached a twenty-year high, there were still not as many people coming through the turnstiles as had been hoped. One letter to *The Times* was indicative of the expressed opinions of many fans: 'The administrators should be told we have watched the experiment, it didn't work and could we please have our game back' (9 September 1996, p. 35). It appeared that the fans had rejected the changes to the structure and therefore to the meaning of their sport.

It began to become clear that too much of Murdoch's £75 million was going to the players, as many commentators had predicted when the deal was first announced. Peter Tukes, the Chief Executive of Wakefield Trinity, argued:

> I can't see how you can regard the money over here as anything other than a great opportunity. If Rugby League is ever going to kick on in the northern hemisphere, it has to do it on this News Limited vehicle. But at the moment the money is being wasted, mostly on paying the players more than the game can afford.
>
> (*Guardian*, 16 July 1996, p. 22)

As well as worrying that players were being paid too much, there was also concern that too great a gulf was developing between the Super League teams and those in Divisions One and Two, in terms of both playing standards and financial status: 'One of the dangers of Super League is that the clubs outside it will wither into obscurity' (*Independent*, 24 March 1996, p. 26). This problem intensified when, in September 1996, the Super League clubs created their own company 'Super League Europe Ltd' to look after their interests and maximise the marketing and commercial potential of the League for the clubs. This made the clubs in lower divisions feel even more vulnerable, and they briefly threatened a breakaway to avoid financial disaster. There was even renewed talk of mergers by some of the clubs, who saw it as the only way to escape economic ruin, suggesting perhaps that such organisational changes were rendered inevitable by Murdoch's investment in the sport, and the associated globalisation process. The initial successful rejection of the mergers by fans was seemingly merely a stay of execution for some clubs. Yet, perhaps, the most embarrassing incident for the RFL in the first year of Super League happened at the end of the season, as Great Britain toured its fellow Super League aligned country – New Zealand. The players who were surplus to requirements for the last Test match were sent home early so the RFL could save money on the hotel bill! This debacle generated further questions about just where Murdoch's money had gone. It had to be concluded that the first season of the Super League was not the resounding success that Lindsay and the RFL had hoped. Indeed, *The Guardian's* headline went further with: 'Super League is a Flop' (7 July 1996, p. 8).

Phase four: October 1996–May 1997 – hope and revival

The beleaguered European Super League got a much needed boost in October when the appeals court in Australia ruled that the Super League could operate freely in Australia. This meant that international matches and the World Clubs Championship could now take place between the northern and southern hemisphere. This was essential for Murdoch's global vision for rugby league, and gave the financial input of more high-profile games, which would mean increased gate revenues. The verdict was particularly crucial for the game in the northern hemisphere, as had it gone in favour of the ARL, Murdoch would arguably have given up on rugby league in the Antipodes and concentrated on his rugby union project (*Guardian*, 6 October 1996).

The financial situation for the clubs began to look more promising as Sheffield Eagles took the initiative and floated on the stock market. Billionaire entrepreneur Richard Branson showed his interest by buying a 15 per cent stake in the London Broncos, which he increased to a controlling percentage some months later. Furthermore, the RFL took the positive step of trying to market the League in a more professional manner by employing M & C Saatchi as advertisers. This showed just how far the meaning of the game in Britain had altered – to administrators as well as fans. As the 1997 season began, the prospects for the Super League were looking better, and attendances were on course for a twenty-year high. However, the optimism proved to be misplaced, as the Super League hit another trough.

Phase five: June–December 1997 – defeat, despair and receivership

The World Clubs Championship was not the great spectacle and advert for Rugby League that the clubs and RFL had hoped. Instead, it was an embarrassing farce as there were 27 defeats in the opening 30 games for the northern hemisphere clubs. No British team made the semi-finals, and the championships provoked widespread criticism of the British game: 'One-sided World Championship matches leave weaknesses in British game cruelly exposed' (*Times*, 16 June 1997, p. 38). The setbacks on the field were surpassed by those off it, as Bass, owners of Stones Bitter, withdrew its sponsorship support of the League. It was realised as the year drew to a close that the financial position of many of the clubs was increasingly untenable. There was renewed talk of mergers, and calls for a salary cap to be introduced. As *The Times* observed: 'Players cannot escape blame. They have swallowed up the first £35 million of the £87 million invested in the domestic game by News Corporation … facilities, youth schemes and marketing have remained moribund' (3 November 1997, p. 36). Thus, although the globalisation process produced organisational changes within the game, they were not necessarily fundamental, or for the better. The fact that players were absorbing too great a percentage of clubs' incomes had been a major factor in the weak financial state of the game, which had allowed Murdoch's easy takeover in 1995. The problem had been predicted by many since the inception of the Super League, yet it still took the RFL until December 1997 to decide to introduce a salary cap to restrict clubs' spending on players. The cap involves a limit of 50 per cent of clubs' projected turnover for the following year, which was still very vague, and continued to allow scope for the clubs to find a way around the regulations.

Also, towards the end of 1997, the 'Européan' dimension of Super League was eradicated in one step, when the Paris Saint-Germain club was disbanded. This left the RFL running a European Super League without a single representative from outside England. The Rugby League Supporters Association fanzine commented: 'For anyone who ever believed that Rugby League had a future beyond the English counties of its birth, the symbolism is depressing' (Rugby League Supporters Association, Winter 1997/98, p. 3). The Oldham club folded due to bankruptcy in late 1997, and it appeared that some other clubs were not far behind when KPMG published its report on the financial status of Super League clubs (*Times*, 3 December 1997). It found that only two Super League clubs were in profit, and several were technically insolvent. The elite level of the game was revealed as having collective debts of £13 million. The report again advocated mergers as a means to partially solve the problem, stating: 'The time has come when local rivalries have to be set aside if the game itself is to survive' (*Times*, 3 December 1997, p. 40).

The case of Keighley is particularly illuminating. The club had a remarkable rise in fortunes during the early 1990s, with attendances increasing from an average of 445 in 1986/87 to an average of 4,119 during 1994/95. It was thriving, with well-established community links, youth and education programmes. It was about to be promoted to the top flight in 1995 when the Super League was announced and destroyed their hopes. By December 1997, the financial situation of the club had become so dire that it was nearly expelled from the League by the RFL. The following observation by *The Times* would seem both to summarise these two and a half turbulent years in the history of rugby league, and to serve as a warning to others: 'Television income, initially regarded as a panacea, merely accelerates the cycle of boom and bust' (3 November 1997, p. 36). It would appear that not only had the vision of rugby league as a global sport faded, but also the money for which the game in Britain had sold out 100 years of tradition failed to magically cure the sport's ills. In the transformation of rugby league from sport to spectacle, the best laid plans of the entrepreneurs involved in the changes had gone awry.

Phase six: January 1998 – another new beginning?

The reconciliation between the ARL and News Corporation in Australia that took place in December 1997 might have created a sense of stability in Australia, but it did not help the financial situation of the British clubs. The decision was taken to run the Super League in 1998 on a no-relegation basis, in order to allow clubs to prepare their franchise applications for the 1999 season, when clubs had to compete for places in the League, in a similar way to the American cartel system of sporting franchises (Sage, 1990). The RFL was seemingly hoping for strong applications from a rejuvenated Paris side, and possibly teams in other areas of Great Britain. This, they hoped, would revive the proselytised ideal with which the Super League was born in April 1995. By the mid to late 1990s, the signs were not promising and despite the marketing hype of agents, media personnel and promoters, rugby league was no more secure than when it tried to globalise. The costs seem to have been paid by local supporters and communities.

Through the late 1990s to the early part of the twenty-first century, further changes have taken place. The game is now also played in the summer months, there has been an increase of southern hemisphere players playing for English clubs, and television contracts have been renewed. Yet, an air of instability remains. Symptomatic of the globalisation of the game was the announcement that a Tri-Nations match between Australia and New Zealand would take place in London in late October 2004. Appealing less to those English communities who supported the game, Gary Tasker, spokesman for the Rugby Football League, stated that the game was being played in the capital because 'it has proved a popular venue with Antipodean fans in London' (BBC, 12 May 2004, online).

Conclusion

From this account of the launch and development of the Super League, several changes to the structure, organisation and meaning of rugby league can be identified. In terms of the structure of the game itself, the regulative rules (those governing how the game is played) were altered in order to improve its attractiveness to the spectator. This included making try scoring easier, on the premise that people want to see high-scoring games. The structure of a match day was also changed to encompass pre-match entertainment such as music, cheerleaders and parachutists. The administrative organisation of the sport was fairly radically changed with a switch of season to the summer, a move towards American-style team nicknames, and the initial inclusion of teams like London and Paris in the top flight.

These structural and organisational changes to rugby league were intended to have the effect of altering the meaning of the sport to many people, at both a local community level and on a wider local national stage. The metamorphosis of rugby league from sport to spectacle was intended to dislodge it from its strict association with northern working-class masculinity, as the game's promoters attempted to attract a more middle-class, family-oriented audience, from a wider geographical area. However, it is arguable to what degree News Corporation and the RFL achieved their aims. The penetration of commercialisation and spectacularisation into the game's culture of support was resisted by the fans and produced outcomes certainly not intended by Murdoch and Lindsay. This forced them to reconsider their original plans.

One of the major organisational changes intended for rugby league was the merger of several long-established clubs. The active and successful resistance of fans to this scheme proved that the local is capable of reciprocally influencing global processes orchestrated by the transnational capitalist class. There were further unintended outcomes to the Super League project, which forced a reaction from the RFL and News Corporation. These included the apparent inability of clubs to run as financially viable enterprises and the failure of the Paris Saint-Germain team. These factors meant that, at the end of 1997, rugby league seemed to have come full circle back to its situation in 1995, when the Super League deal was first proposed.

Changes have occurred, both organisationally and structurally – a new season, a Super League, and changes in the rules of the game. However, a fundamental alteration in the game's economic fortunes is not evident. The sport is still in a poor economic condition and relatively confined to its traditional northern England home. By the 2004 season, only the London Broncos were outside this area. Localism has continued to restrict the sport from advancing, both economically and geographically. Supporters managed to prevent some mergers and retain their rugby league clubs as badges of their identity (though names have been modified, e.g. Warrington Wolves, Widnes Vikings, Wakefield Trinity Wildcats), but they have not been successful in preventing the development of the game from being increasingly influenced by media and corporate interests. The advent of competition at club level between the southern and northern hemisheres has been matched by a rekindling of the Ashes series between Great Britain and Australia. These changes have also been linked to the development of new marketing initiatives such as the introduction of end-of-season play-off matches and, in 2001, of the 'Origin' concept – involving matches between Lancashire and Yorkshire – again echoing ideas drawn from Australia.

The game's political economy is closely interconnected to the plans of News Corporation, media companies and marketing concerns. Yet, to date, Super League (currently sponsored by Tetley's) has failed as a commercial venture. Given Murdoch's increasing control over media coverage of both rugby league and rugby union interests, media speculation continues that there will be an attempt to synthesise the two rugby codes. It is doubtful that this would occur, and if it did, even less likely that this new version would emerge as a global sport. Though we have pointed to an elaborate political economy attached to rugby league, the case of the Super League demonstrates that the global activities of the transnational capitalist class are subject to both reinterpretation and resistance from groups within local cultures and communities, and are hemmed in by the effects stemming from the disjunctures that characterise global sport systems.

Part III
Identity politics

5 'A world in union'?

Rugby, globalisation and Irish identity

Joseph Maguire and Jason Tuck

Globalisation processes accelerated markedly during the twentieth century. It has become increasingly difficult to comprehend events at the local or national level without reference to these processes – this case study is no exception. Developments in the world of sport, such as increases in transnational player migration and 'global' sports events, all indicate a more interconnected world with nation-states situated in a closer and more intense network of interdependencies. Sport is an aspect of popular culture which has the power to both reinforce and challenge the concept of globalisation (Maguire, 1999; Miller *et al.*, 2001). Sport provides an important arena for the construction, maintenance and challenging of identities and has the capacity to bind together individuals, local communities, nations and the world – but also to fragment them (Billig, 1995; Blain, Boyle, and O'Donnell, 1993; Bloom, 1990). Modern sport provides a complex cultural location for the coming together of the individual, the nation and the global, and, through this commingling the nation can appear more than what Anderson (1983) terms an 'imagined community'. In making this case we draw on a process-sociological approach to the study of national identity (Elias, 1996).

This approach to sport, globalisation and national identity seeks to make sense of these interdependencies by considering a series of key 'processual' dynamics (such as the simultaneously enabling and constraining features of globalisation processes). These dynamics can be studied in order to uncover the long-term relationships between sport, globalisation and national identity and the ways in which individuals are enmeshed into these networks of interdependency. A case study of rugby union in Ireland since 1945 will be used to highlight the relationship between a particular sport and a specific nation. Rugby union (as a sport organised on a 32-county basis and a global team sport now with a recognised World Cup) is one of most significant sporting arenas whereby the imagined community of Ireland can become more real. This union of two politically distinct entities through sport provides an interesting context for the researcher of national identity. This context will be explored by considering official historical accounts of Irish rugby, how the media portray Irish rugby union, and the views of contemporary international Irish rugby players (for discussion of the Celtic vision of Irish sport, see Bairner, 1999). An additional question is also raised in this context. While rugby union has clearly exhibited accelerated global diffusion in recent decades, to what degree has it contributed to the development of a 'world in union'?

National identity and issues of habitus

The principal roots of the figurational approach to national identity lie in the work of Norbert Elias (1991, 1994, 1996). Several key tenets of Eliasian thought help to explain the interconnection between national identity, globalisation and sport, including the multiple characteristics of personal identity; the balance between invented traditions and habitus construction; the formation and employment of 'I-', 'we-' and 'they-images', and the emergence of wilful nostalgia (Maguire, 1999). The development of this framework also allows for a more critical review of research on nationalism which has been carried out by, amongst others, Anderson (1983), Gellner (1983), Hobsbawm and Ranger (1983), McCrone (1998) and Smith (1995, 1991). Contrary to Hargreaves' (2002) view, this approach does not rely on Anderson's idea of the nation as being merely an 'imagined community' or in Hobsbawm and Ranger's term, an 'invented tradition'. In fact, in specific ways, it is quite critical of aspects of them. In addition, far from adopting the narrow modernist view of these writers, a process-sociological approach seeks to trace the deeply rooted traditions that Hargreaves (2002) also wishes to explore. Seeing the debate as one of emphasising the role of the nation-state, or of global processes, is simply a false dichotomy.

To understand national identity in an Eliasian sense, it is necessary to consider the long-term social processes underpinning the formation of states: namely, the development of culture and civilisation (Fletcher, 1997). This 'civilising process' has been extensively explored in the context of state formation in Western Europe (Elias, 1939/1994) and, whilst it is not the intention here to explicitly examine all the complexities of Elias's work on the civilising process, many underlying themes of this approach prove useful tools for conceptualising the nation and the development of national character.

The quickening of civilising processes in the modern era has been exemplified by the gradual shifting of societal power from male aristocratic (dynastic) social groups to middle-class elites. This changing power ratio ensured both a social transformation (sociogenesis), and an associated psychological transformation (psychogenesis) which have promoted the growth of a national consciousness within the individual and generated a wider perception, and significance, of national character. This development can be explained through an increased correspondence between the individual and social (national) 'superego'. In other words, as a consequence of a long-term civilising process, there has been an unplanned and gradual change in personal identification networks whereby the individual and the nation are bound more closely together. The promulgation of an idealised national self-image rooted in history (as advocated by Anderson, 1983; Hobsbawm and Ranger, 1983; Smith, 1991) made the modern nation the primary frame of reference for comments about 'us' and 'them' (over other identifications such as gender and class). The nation thus became the principal survival unit for individuals to look towards as a secure source of identity.

Thinking processually, the use of the term habitus can aid in the understanding of these complex inter-related socio-psychological transformations. Whilst Bourdieu popularised the term, Elias (1991) argued that habitus was one of the conceptual keys to the dissolving of the false dichotomy between the individual and society within the social sciences. Habitus can be explained as a complex, multi-layered interlocking 'container' for the balance of tensions within the sub-conscious. Habitus refers to the modes of conduct, taste and feeling which predominate among members of particular groups, and highlights the shared traits of people who may be largely unconscious of them. In sum, they form 'sleeping memories' or, as Elias remarked, a 'second nature' (Mennell, 1994, p. 176). The complexities of habitus can be grasped with an appreciation of the concept being constructed of both individual and social elements (Elias, 1991). At the individual level, there are a series of learned behavioural dispositions which are unique to the person. At the social level, there reside a collection of personality characteristics which individuals share with other members of their group. The social habitus of people forms a foundation from which more individual feelings can develop.

Collective identifications (such as national identity) can thus be described in terms of sets of behaviour, or habitus codes, which work to bind individuals together. The multi-layered qualities of habitus, and the intertwining of the individual and society, can be more clearly understood by thinking in terms of what Elias (1991) called the 'we-I balance'. Put simply, there can be no 'I' without the presence of a 'we', and the individual is always located within shifting networks of identification which move from, between and within the 'I' and the 'we'. For Elias (1991, p. 182), 'the individual bears in himself or herself the habitus of a group, and it is this habitus that he or she individualises to a greater or lesser extent'.

At the level of the nation there exists a semi-sacred and privileged we-ideal whose strength is drawn from a set of 'impersonal symbols of a hallowed collectivity' (Elias, 1996, p. 148). The strength of this we-identity is closely linked to the development of a national ethos that reflects, and is reflected by, the individual. This 'double-code' of nationalism, binding individual and national character in a 'knot of interwoven part-processes' (Elias, 1996, p. 2) thus provides a continuous source for self-perpetuating beliefs about the nation.

Habitus needs to be understood as a complex and dynamic construct, neither biologically nor temporally fixed. At a national level, the fortunes of the nation (as this case study reveals) continually influence and shape national habitus by forming linkages with the 'we-layer' of personal identity. This layer can become hardened or softened through a variety of processes, most notably with fluctuations in the power ratios between social groups, and in times of external threat. National character can therefore be perceived as being grounded in the dynamics of a series of 'habitus networks' which act both between, across and within the individual and society to produce dominant, or hegemonic, codes of behaviour. Within national culture, these habitus codes are diffused, concretised and flagged up by institutions such as the national mass media and were evident in coverage of the Euro 96 soccer championships and the 1999 rugby union World Cup (Maguire and Poulton, 1999; Tuck, 2003).

National we-identity is clearly founded on an ideal that privileges the nation as culturally and politically superior (although it can embody inferiority feelings as well). Elias' s concept of established-outsider relations is essential to explaining the processes at work here. Developed as a model for investigating power differentials between groups, the concept furthers our understanding of the interdependence of social groups and the ways in which individuals are located in these interlinking chains. National identity 'works' by contrasting the best elements of 'us' (the established) with the worst elements of 'them' (the outsiders). Elias conceptualises this form of distorted identity politics as the development of a power balance in which a 'minority of the best' is juxtaposed against a 'minority of the worst' (Mennell, 1994). This permanently shifting juxtaposition, grounded in collective mythology and real lived experiences, becomes active through habitus codes which serve to stigmatise the other. However, this process is not unilinear. Due to the double-bind between established and outsider groups, this may in turn lead to counter-stigmatisation by the outsiders, if the power ratio evens out and they become more established (see also the Introduction).

Elias (1991) identifies globalisation processes as a new stage of worldwide integration, which decreases the social distances between groups, while simultaneously increasing the scope of identification by offering a variety of identities for individuals to enbrace. In this more global era, it is tempting to explain away the greater interdependencies between nations, and the changing power ratios between them, as reducing the significance of national identity. However, such rationalisation of the nation would fail to appreciate the powerful emotional attachment the nation still holds as an inner circle of identification (De Swaan, 1995, p. 36). Elias (1991) explains this enduring power of the nation in terms of a drag effect, whereby the power of the nation to resist global processes, at least in the short term, makes them appear as 'islands of nationalism' in a sea of lengthening and deepening chains of interdependence. These issues were also addressed in the Introduction – thus it suffices to just remind us of the point that Elias made in this connection: 'The [national] we-image trails far behind the reality of global interdependence' (1991, p. 227).

Elias explains the often taken for granted, deeply embodied nature of national habitus as a result of its overwhelming presence as a we-identity. The traits of national group identity are a layer of the social habitus sedimented very deeply into the personality structure of the individual. Like Bourdieu, Elias is keen to avoid the charge of appearing to view habitus as immutable and too determining of social action. The social habitus, and therefore the layer of habitus forming the national character, is 'like a language, both hard and tough, but also flexible and far from immutable. It is, in fact, always in flux' (Elias, 1991, p. 209). In this sense, when national habitus codes are stimulated (usually in response to a threat from outsiders), it is possible to see a reflexive process at work which hardens the we-identity of the national collective by bringing the nation closer to an individual's I-identity, and vice versa. The individual can thus *become* the embodiment of the nation, and the social group represented by the nation, *becomes* that individual. These deep-rooted, historical foundations of national habitus, anchored in the memory of a continuous collective culture, are what make national identity so particularly resistant to more integrated, or global, we-identities. This resistance is also central to the maintenance of the nation as a credible survival unit and the continuance of national identity being played as the 'trump card' against other identities (Calhoun, 1995).

Sport, identity politics and national habitus codes

Identity politics are described by Calhoun as being located 'not only in ideological and cultural changes but in transformations of social structure and societal integration' (1995, p. 205). The pursuits labelled identity politics have several dimensions. They are collective, not merely individual, and public as well as private. In addition, identity politics involve seeking recognition, legitimacy, expression or autonomy. In turn, and in reaction to such actions, other people, groups, and organisations (including states) are called upon to respond. In this sense, identity politics movements are 'political because they involve refusing, diminishing, or displacing identities others wish to recognise in individuals' (Calhoun, 1995, p. 214). This interpretation of identity politics dovetails with Elias's (1991, 1996) work on habitus by endorsing the notion of identification as a complex, tension-laden, dynamic and multi-layered process. The acknowledgement of such pursuits proves useful in further interpreting both the real and imagined interconnection between individual and nation.

The political dynamics of identity are also useful in demonstrating how identities are constructed socially and can change across space and time. Maguire and Poulton (1999), in their work on football's European Championships, discuss the notion of dominant, emergent and residual views of identities. These represent the multi-layered nature of habitus that is contoured by more or less dense social networks of interdependencies over time. Personal identities are therefore constructed and transformed through a process of cultural representation, which encompasses a form of political exchange (or power struggle) within and between these habitus layers (see also Maguire, 1993a, 1994a, 1999; Maguire and Poulton, 1999; Maguire, Poulton and Possamai, 1999; Maguire and Tuck, 1998; Tuck, 2003).

Mennell (1994) views the formation of identity (or I/we-images) as a social process through which various categories of people come to share a collective cultural consciousness. This 'consciousness' is built up over time both within and between increasingly interdependent social groupings. However, individuals do not simply find themselves shackled to one consciousness. Each individual possesses multiple and complex identities that are continually developed and shaped, through time, by social networks of interdependencies (Maguire, 1993a). The dominant, or hegemonic, notion of identity tends to invent traditions, recall common events and stress those who belong and those who do not (see Hobsbawm and Ranger, 1983). Central to identity politics are questions such as 'who am I?' and 'where am I?'. Exploring the use of personal pronouns can thus aid the researcher in understanding these exchanges.

These issues can be developed further with reference to Elias's work on established-outsider relations. This approach can provide a valuable lens through which to view 'the nation' as a prominent we-identity. Writing about a range of European countries, including Spain, the Netherlands and Great Britain, Elias observes that 'the we-image and we-ideal of [these] once-powerful nations ... has declined'. As a consequence of their power superiority being lost, 'the radiance of their collective life as a nation has gone' (Elias, 1939/1994, p. xliii). Despite this:

> The dream of their special charisma is kept alive in a variety of ways – through the teaching of history, the old buildings, masterpieces of the nation in the time of its glory, or through new achievements which seemingly confirm the greatness of the past.
>
> (Elias, 1939/1994, p. xliii)

How is this possible? For Elias, the fantasy shield of their imagined charisma as a leading established group buttresses the self-worth of the citizens of a declining nation. However, the discrepancy between the actual and the imagined position of one's group among others can also entail a mistaken assessment of one's resources. As a consequence, group strategies, in pursuit of a fantasy image of one's own greatness, are adopted that may lead to self-destruction. As such, for Elias 'the dreams of nations ... are dangerous' (Elias, 1939/1994, p. xliii).

In contrast, it is possible to speculate that citizens of a former colonised country, such as Ireland, have to shake off the collective group disgrace stemming from the stigmatisation and shaming processes enacted by the colonial power – in this case the established English/British. From the Irish Free State, on through Eire, and into the Republic of Ireland, Irish people experienced a series of struggles, material and symbolic, in forging a new state, and in widening the circle of identification away from the former coloniser's culture. Despite the contradictions inherent within a people with multiple identities, the domination of the Irish we-image with a sense of group disgrace was subverted by a growing sense of a more confident group charisma. In spite of this, the stereotyping of the former English/British rulers remained. These processes were acted across the cultural spectrum – sport, as we will demonstrate, was no exception.

International sports operate to perform the functions of nations and constitute a form of patriot games. The individuals representing their countries therein become highly visible embodiments of these nations – they are patriots at play. These patriots at play are significant actors who both define and reflect the special charisma of nations writ large and, through their practices, sport becomes one of the fantasy shields whereby imagined (and real) charisma is both fuelled and protected (Maguire and Poulton, 1999). International sport, imbued with national symbols, therefore provides an environment rich in collective identifications and identity politics.

It could be argued that sport forms one of the most significant arenas by which nations become more real. Particular sports often come to symbolise the nation – a process which dates back to the third phase of sportisation in the late nineteenth century (Maguire, 1999; see also Chapter 8). The close bind of sport with national identifications has made it an important conduit for a sense of collective resentment and popular (male) consciousness. For example, the health of Wales as a nation is constructed as inseparable from the success/failure of the national rugby team. Sports can also become metaphors for national character; for example, cricket is portrayed by some as the embodiment of a quintessential Englishness, imparting meaning to the nation (O'Donnell, 1994; Schwarz, 1992; Tudor, 1992).

Making sense of sport in the 'British' context is a habitus problem par excellence. Though politically the United Kingdom is a single state, even post-devolution, at many international sporting events, and within the domestic sports context, it has several national identities (Moorhouse, 1996; for discussion of the UK identity politics more broadly see Crick, 1991; Nairn, 1977). This situation is made more complex by the position of the Republic of Ireland and Northern Ireland. For example, at the Olympic Games, athletes from the 'British Isles' compete for either Great Britain or Ireland (see Cronin, 1997). On the soccer pitch there are teams representing England, Scotland, Wales, Northern Ireland and the Republic of Ireland (for further discussion see Bairner, 2001). In rugby union, it is significant that the Irish (essentially two divided nations) compete as a united sporting nation-state against the English, Scottish and Welsh – and with the formation of the World Cup, on a global stage. The 'southern Irish' are also eligible to represent what the British press tend to term the 'British Lions' touring team; however, this team is more correctly named the 'Great British and Irish Lions' (Coughlan, 1983; Thomas, 1996).

Within the British Isles, the 'Celtic fringe' (Ireland, Scotland and Wales) has employed sport in various ways as a means of asserting its own identities. The Welsh and the Scottish have used traditional British sports to challenge the political and economic dominance of England by trying to beat them at their own games (albeit by employing a different approach or 'style' to the way the game is played). For example, in rugby union the Calcutta Cup is played annually between Scotland and the 'auld enemy'. Indeed, rugby union also provides one of the main sources of I/we identity politics by which the English identify the Welsh, and the Welsh identify themselves. In contrast, in the late nineteenth century, Irish cultural nationalists, eager to reclaim their cultural identity and forge a new Irish nation, rejected British sports and established their own Gaelic games under the auspices of the Gaelic Athletic Association (formed in 1884).

Rugby union in the British Isles thus represents a unique arena for investigating the construction, reproduction and contestation of national identities. The sport provides a series of national cultural paradoxes, including the juxtaposition of the Anglo-Saxon English against the Celtic nations, and European rivals, in the annual Six Nations Championship and the World Cup competition, whilst also uniting the best players from the 'Home Unions' as the British and Irish 'Lions' when on tour to the old commonwealth countries of Australia, New Zealand and South Africa. In addition, the sport can also operate by giving the appearance of uniting the people of the politically divided nation of Ireland.

Rugby union, national identity and Ireland

In examining sport in Ireland, one must consider that this seemingly imaginary Celtic nation of Ireland is in fact composed of two politically separate entities: Northern Ireland (part of the United Kingdom) and the Republic of Ireland (for discussion of Irish nationalism and identity politics more broadly see Bradshaw, 1994; Fennell, 1989; Graham, 2001; O'Mahony and Delanty, 1998). Whilst it is not possible to review all the arguments and counter-arguments about the island of Ireland here, it is necessary to briefly contextualise the nation(s) that are being explored in this chapter, and endorse Cronin's (1999) view that there are several dynamic Irish national identities in existence on the island (and beyond within the Irish diaspora) at any one moment in time. Ireland was partitioned in 1921 when the Irish Free State was created in the 'south' (now known as the Republic of Ireland) and divided from Northern Ireland (made up of six of the nine counties of the province of Ulster and a political constituent of the United Kingdom). Northern Ireland, a culturally and politically divided society, is largely characterised through sectarianism and nationalism which have contributed to, at times violent, civil unrest (the so-called 'Troubles') ever since its creation.

Here, collective identifications are strengthened (and complicated) by a series of we/they groupings (Catholic–Protestant, Nationalist–Unionist). Despite continuing attempts to find peace in Northern Ireland, the insights of Sugden and Bairner (1993) and Bairner (2003) on sport remain relevant today in their discussions of a society of two separate communities deeply divided along sectarian lines. This complexity is compounded by the divisions within Unionism and how this is acted out in the sport world (Bairner, 2003). Indeed, the competing identities at play in the North neatly demonstrate the complexities of Irishness. Irish nationalism, in its various guises, has to be appreciated in terms of the long (and often fractious) relationship between the Irish and the British. As Cronin (1999) argues, it is Anglo-Irish relations that shape the oppositional character of Irishness by juxtaposing the provinces of Ireland against the dominant 'other' in the shape of Britain (and, in particular, England).

Irish cultural nationalists established their own Gaelic games under the auspices of the Cumann Lúthcleas Gael (GAA). The GAA was seen by its founders as a defender of Irish culture against the penetration of foreign English imperialist culture (and sports) into Ireland (a far more detailed analysis of the GAA can be found in Bairner, 2001; Cronin, 1999). Religion and sport, as well as neighbourhood affiliation and educational background, play a significant part in community identity and divisions between communities in Northern Ireland (Sugden and Bairner, 1993). Irrespective of what form

Irishness takes, sport appears to play a role in articulating key aspects of it. Cronin (1999) states that:

> sport and nationalism are inextricably linked and play a key role in defining Irish nationalism and notions of Irish national identity. This role, as with the very nature of Irishness, is constantly in a state of flux as sport is an ever changing vehicle for the transmission of both ideology and identity.
>
> (p. 23)

The remainder of this chapter investigates these issues in terms of the relationship between rugby union and Irishness. The evidence used here has been collected from the official archives of the Irish Rugby Football Union, newspaper coverage of rugby union in Britain since 1945 (Maguire and Tuck, 1998) media coverage of recent rugby World Cups and interviews with international rugby players (Tuck and Maguire, 1999).

History and tradition in Irish rugby

The history of Irish rugby, and how it allegedly developed from a Celtic ball-carrying game called cad, has been extensively documented in the past, most notably by Diffley (1973) and Van Esbeck (1974, 1986, 1999). In attempting to uncover the links between rugby union and national identity in Ireland, it is useful to begin by revisiting the prefatory remarks of Van Esbeck (1974), who, drawing on stereotypical views of Irish habitus, states that: 'the essential physical character of the game is certainly compatible with the essential character of the Irish temperament' (p. 2) and observes that rugby was starting to gain in popularity across Ireland by the late 1860s. It is interesting to note that the formal organisation of Irish rugby began with a division between Belfast (in the north) and Dublin (in the south). After the Irish Football Union had been formed by Dubliners in 1874, overlooking those from Belfast, the Northern Football Union was formed in Belfast in response (Diffley, 1973). Although these were separate organisations, an agreement was made to support the Irish nation in the first international match (against England) the following year. These bodies eventually amalgamated in 1879 to form the single governing body for Irish rugby, the Irish Rugby Football Union (IRFU). This organisation, along with but a few other sport associations, spans the two separate nations and continues to promote rugby across the 32 counties. This manipulation of Irish identity politics within rugby union was to fuel a particular national habitus by creating a sporting dimension to an Irish group charisma.

The accelerated diffusion of rugby in Ireland was underpinned by the expansion of the sporting influence of the English public schools, and particularly their former pupils who went on to attend Trinity College Dublin in the second half of the nineteenth century (Diffley, 1973). From then, rugby spread throughout the provinces of Ireland in spite of strong competition from Gaelic sports (football and hurling) and association football. The connections between rugby union, the individual and the Irish nation can be initially appreciated by considering the perceived culture and playing style of Irish rugby. Diffley (1973) contends that:

> The [Irish] players may ... play as intensely as teams from any other country but always bubbling close to the surface is the saving grace of gaiety which makes sure that matters seldom become too dour. Even in the hottest and most serious matches one can expect the odd shaft of Celtic wit to keep matters in their proper perspective ... Of the eight major rugby-playing countries the Irish have the least number of players involved in the game which tends to make them the eternal underdogs – and ... the Irish never seem to lack for popular support even among the ranks of their opponents' supporters. And a dashing, devil-may-care manner of play ensures that the world-wide popularity remains.
>
> (p. 11)

The official archives of the IRFU contain a variety of recent evidence which also reinforces these stereotypical we-identity images of the Irish. The connection between rugby and the Irish nation, for example, is captured by an article written by Jim Tucker in the official programme to the match between New South Wales and Ireland played on 5 June 1979. He writes:

> Ireland, like all of the world's great rugby playing nations, has a fierce record steeped in tradition. The Shamrocks play a brand of football that is as uncertain as it is brilliant. The Irish have always been known for their fierce determination to come out on top; their fighting qualities when the chips are down; and players who possess that unique brand of magic ... Rugby football has had a huge influence in Ireland itself. Officials proudly claim it is the only sport which has united athletes from Northern Ireland and Eire.
>
> (New South Wales v Ireland, Official Match Programme, 5 June 1979, p. 25)

In addition to such reports emphasising the 'traditional' qualities of the Irish, the cultural bond between the Scots and the Irish is explored by John Beattie (a former Scottish international and British and Irish Lion) in the official programme to the Ireland – Scotland game of 1990. In an article entitled 'You Hit Your Friends the Hardest', he writes:

> Any Scotsman playing against Ireland has two very mixed emotions. Because the game is bound to be physical and open there's the dreadful anticipation of the battle to come, and the fear that the game might be lost, but alongside that is the unsettling knowledge that in a strange way you are playing against your mates, even if you don't know all of them. Our two countries are so similar in many ways, not least in ... our rugby ... Murrayfield and Lansdowne Road seldom see the slow pace of the English pack ... Instead it's breakneck rugby, played for possession and for keeps.
>
> (Ireland v Scotland, Official Match Programme, 3 February 1990, p. 59)

The existence of such a bond is substantiated in various official IRFU documents in the post-Second World War period. For example, it was noted that: 'we defeated our Scottish friends' who were also referred to as 'our good friends north of the Tweed' (IRFU Report of the Committee, 1952/53, p. 2). In addition, Scotland were also recorded as being 'our Auld and friendly rivals' (IRFU Report of the Committee, 1954/55, p. 3); and 'our brothers' (IRFU Report of the Committee, 1954/55, p. 6). Such views implicitly depict a Celtic we-identity, linking the Scots and Irish together and in opposition to the Anglo-Saxon English, through the context of rugby. A widening of the circle of identification is evident. Considered in this light it is interesting to note that since the first international against England in 1875, beating the English has 'always been an Irish priority' (Diffley, 1973, p. 51). This was again demonstrated in the media coverage of Ireland's recent victory over world champions, England, at Twickenham in March 2004. Making reference to Bjorn Minge's famous description of the England football team's loss to Norway in 1981, Gerry Thornley, Rugby Correspondent for the *Irish Times*, began his report with 'Tony Blair, Clive Woodward, Prince Charles, Maggie Thatcher, David Beckham, Martin Johnson, Winston Churchill … Your boys took one hell of a beating' (*Irish Times*, 8 March 2004). Throwing off the shackles of colonial shame clearly features strongly in such sentiments (see also Guha, 2002 and James, 1963 on Indian and West Indian cricket).

Rugby, Irish identity politics, and the representatives of the nation

Although there have been few direct and explicit connections made between rugby and politics for the majority of the post-Second World War period, the importance of rugby union to politics in Ireland was exemplified in a significant article entitled 'De Valera Comes Out for Rugby' (*Times*, 30 April 1957, p. 5). This neatly juxtaposed sport and politics, and showed that the nation's Premier (*Taoiseach*) may have valued rugby union above traditional Gaelic sports – indeed, he played rugby to a fairly high standard. It was reported that:

> Mr De Valera, Prime Minister of Eire, took sides for the first time on the controversial issue of Gaelic football versus Rugby football when he told a surprised audience last night: 'There is no football to compare with Rugby. If all sporting young Irishmen played Rugby we would have a team which would beat not only England and Wales but also France and the whole of them together . . . I have not seen a Rugby game since 1913, because I do not want it being raised as a political matter and having rows kicked up about it, but I will not deny that I listen in to Rugby matches'.
>
> (*Times*, 30 April 1957, p. 5)

Rugby union is thus perceived to have a unique ability in Ireland to transcend political, religious and social class divisions. Take, for example, the observations by Diffley:

Wars and rumours of wars, social upheavals, the situation peculiar to Ireland of two political entities, none have made much dent in the united progress of rugby in Ireland ... The recent troubles in Northern Ireland created their own problems and it was not always easy to preserve the social and sporting *bonhomie* of rugby football. However rugby has been disrupted much less than many would suppose. Fixtures between northern and southern clubs have been scrupulously honoured by teams, and all the interprovincials have been played. And in all those hundreds of matches not a single unsavoury or embarrassing incident has occurred ... What rugby football has done for Ireland is to provide a different definition of Irishman from the acrimonious political one. Politics, too often, have tended to divide the Irish. Rugby football has worked to widen friendships and unite.

(Diffley, 1973, p. 14)

Rugby union is thus projected as one of the few sports in which a united 'All-Ireland' can compete on a world stage against other nations. This is important as the 'traditional' Gaelic sports, whilst still very popular in the Republic, do not give the Irish this opportunity to compete internationally on a regular basis.

How do the players involved in these international matches view such sentiments? Conducting interviews with then current international players, some of whom have subsequently retired from the game, we sought to capture how those who embody the nation felt about the part they play in the remaking of the group charisma of the nation. As one player, Patrick, stated:

Everybody looks to national teams ... One of the few team sports [in which] you can compete at the world level is rugby football and we are competing in a World Cup as a national team in an international arena. It's very important to do well ... it helps to keep Ireland in world focus ... [and] any successful sporting team gives the nation ... a sense of pride.

Another player, Brendan, made reference to the tremendous support for the Irish national team evident at Lansdowne Road, and though acknowledging the existence of 'two different nations', he remarked that perhaps rugby does not therefore mirror the divisions in Irish society. In similar vein, Nigel, commented:

Rugby's one of the only sports in Ireland where you have guys from the North and South playing under the same title with the same colour jersey ... So having a successful rugby team is important, not only for rugby, but for the country as a whole.

When victorious, the Irish team was seen by the players to generate a sense of national pride in both Northern Ireland and the Republic. Additionally, even during the darkest moments in North–South relations, the players could not recall the troubles ever materialising in a rugby context. As Patrick, from Northern Ireland, observed:

I'm playing with my friends here, guys that I've played with for years. I don't know how they feel towards us but there's never been any problem – even in the worst times during the political situation. There's never been any problem in a rugby arena that I can ever remember.

At the end of the interview, when probed about the effect of the political situation on rugby in Ireland, he remarked that:

I don't want to get too controversial about the Northern Ireland – Republic of Ireland thing. It's a funny situation ... for someone outside Ireland ... [who] don't really understand it. We have just got to accept that there are two different countries – but in rugby terms we are one country ... Nobody has ever made a political issue out of it and they never will because rugby is bigger than that. In terms of the way rugby was set up, it was always ... on a provincial basis; i.e. Ulster, Munster, Leinster, Connacht ... So ... with the provincial set up there could be a division but it didn't have the same effect because we played for Ulster, even though Ulster *is* Northern Ireland. But it is not, never has, and never will be an issue – not in sport.

These observations imply that rugby union does indeed serve at one level to bring the two Irelands together but, in contrast, the players did not make too many references towards a truly united Ireland. Indeed, Patrick restated the common assumption that Ulster *is* Northern Ireland. Ulster is in fact made up of nine counties, six of which form Northern Ireland (three of Ulster's predominantly Catholic counties – Cavan, Donegal, and Monaghan – were ceded to the Irish Free State in 1922, to create a Protestant majority in Northern Ireland). On closer inspection, it is also evident that there is still a degree of 'them and us' feeling between the Northern Irish (or Ulstermen) and those from the Republic. This division in the island is perhaps most apparent in terms of language (those from the Republic having available a Gaelic language, whilst the majority Protestant North speak English). In rugby union, this manifests itself in issues surrounding the choice of anthem played at Ireland's international matches.

National symbols, flags, and anthems

The connection between Irish politics and sport is perhaps most evident when one considers issues relating to national symbols such as flags and anthems. Since the formation of the Irish Free State, the IRFU has been involved in a series of debates over national flags and whether the Irish Tricolour or the Union Flag should be flown at international matches at Lansdowne Road. It would appear, from the evidence to hand, that the Union Flag may have flown over the ground, post-partition. The IRFU committee were soon embroiled in controversy that centred on what flag should be flown at international matches, as Ireland played both in Belfast (at Ravenhill), which was politically part of the United Kingdom, and in Dublin (at Lansdowne Road), the capital of the Free State. The question was resolved in 1925 by the IRFU designing a special flag of its own (which incorporated the arms of the four provinces (Van Esbeck, 1986: pp. 97–98)). Despite this, calls were also made to play under the new national flag. Such requests were not met with approval by the IRFU committee. Whatever the reasons for their decision, this would not remain a decision taken solely by the rugby community.

Pressure for the flying of the national flag was taken up by the press and by many of the clubs. And, as Van Esbeck (1986) notes:

> More important, the minister of External Affairs in the Free State government asked to meet the President on the matter. That meeting ... on 5 February 1932 [resolved] ... that in future the national flag would be flown alongside the [Irish Rugby Football] Union flag at all international matches at Lansdowne Road.
>
> (p. 98)

While this event is of significance in signalling the gradual assertion of a more confident we-identity and a co-relative waning of a sense of group disgrace, arguably the more important debate over national flags in Irish rugby occurred in 1954. Diffley (1973) refers to the players' strike in 1954 before the match against Scotland to be played at Ravenhill in Belfast as 'perhaps the most closely guarded secret of all in Irish rugby' (p. 49). Diffley (1973) goes on to explain that:

> It was a time of rather simplistic attitudes in Irish politics and some of the Southern players held a meeting on the morning of the match and decided that they were not prepared to stand to attention before the game for the British national anthem unless the Irish anthem was also played and the Irish tricolour flown, both of which were illegal north of the border.
>
> (p. 49)

The compromise by the IRFU was that all further internationals would be played in Dublin at Lansdowne Road (a decision also coloured by financial factors: this was a larger stadium in a more populous location).

These actions of the IRFU have successfully minimised the risk of (political) disruption to Irish rugby. Yet, the existence of two Irish entities, with two different languages spoken in various parts of Ireland, has also created problems in both the selection and rendition of the 'Irish' national anthem. Up until the 1995 World Cup, the official anthem sung by the Irish rugby team was, in most instances, 'The Soldier's Song'. Sung in Gaelic, this was the anthem of the Republic of Ireland, and was adopted because 'home' international rugby matches were played in Dublin, the Republic's capital. However, the national anthem for players from Northern Ireland, themselves Unionists, from predominantly Protestant backgrounds, would be 'God Save The Queen'. This is suggestive that those from the North have more outsider status within the established group. Commenting on these issues, a player from the North, Jimmy, stated that

I can't sing the Anthem because I don't know the words ... Me being from the North, it's not my Anthem so I don't sing it. I respect it, I stand still for it ... but it's in Gaelic ... so I don't know it.

Some of the Ulster players spoke of the coaching they had received in the past from players from the other provinces who had attempted to teach them suitable replacement lyrics in English so that they could sing along (albeit in meaningless terms) to 'The Soldier's Song', and thus keep their mouths in time with the others. Although the Ulstermen did not understand the specific meaning of the words of the anthem, they all admitted that it did move them, and put them, as Jimmy expressed it, 'in the mood'.

The potential conflicts and contradictions surrounding the anthem prompted the Irish Rugby Football Union to select a new 'sporting' anthem, 'Ireland's Call', to be sung in English. The introduction of this anthem would clearly reconfigure established-outsider relations based on language. Sean, another Ulsterman, declared that:

The Anthem is officially played because the game is played in Dublin, not because it's the team anthem ... But they've brought the new song 'Ireland's Call' out ... to give the team a sense of identity so that all the members of the team could associate themselves with this song, with Ireland, with Irish pride.

This new Irish sporting anthem, sung for the first time during the 1995 Rugby World Cup, has a particularly relevant chorus: 'Ireland, Ireland, Together standing tall, Shoulder to shoulder, We'll answer Ireland's call.' This anthem seeks to promote a unified we-identity and an Irish group charisma with members from both Irish political entities rallying as one, 'shoulder to shoulder', on the rugby field 'for the four proud provinces of Ireland'. Written by a Northern Catholic with no rugby background, these lyrics mirror the ways in which the players themselves perceive rugby union as an 'All-Ireland' game. Indeed, one of the Ulster players, Brendan, stated that he was playing for his country and that he had always supported Ireland as a 'whole nation'. However, an Ulsterman who plays for his country is technically representing either Northern Ireland or the United Kingdom, whereas clearly Brendan perceives that he is playing for Ireland, which he perceives as a single nation. Such contradictions were manifest in the language of many of the Irish players and these provide a valuable illustration of the complex duality of Irishness, and the slow forging of a collective shared we-identity.

As a response to the delicate political situation in Ireland, a mutual agreement was made between the Rugby Football Unions of the Irish and English not to play any Irish anthem when Ireland play England at Twickenham. Even with a more 'neutral' anthem, 'Ireland's Call', this practice remains the case. The issues surrounding the playing of the Irish Anthem were commented on in personal correspondence from the Administrative Officer of the Irish Rugby Football Union, Martin Murphy: it is worthy of quoting at some length:

The Irish Rugby Football Union is the governing body for the game of Rugby Football throughout the four Provinces of Ireland. Thus, its activities span two political jurisdictions on the island and the Irish team is selected from both. This obviously creates difficulties in relation to the Anthem to be played at international matches in which Ireland is playing. To meet these difficulties, the Irish Rugby Football Union decided some years ago that the Anthem played at international rugby matches under its control would relate directly to the jurisdiction of the ground in which the match is played. Thus, at Lansdowne Road only the Irish anthem is played whereas at venues such as Twickenham no Irish anthem is played. This practice is in accordance with an agreement of some years' standing between the countries involved.

This official response illustrates how contemporary Irish identity politics is sometimes writ large in a sporting context. It also highlights the complexities of 'Irishness' and the problem of national symbolism which had been an issue in Irish rugby since the founding of the Irish Free State in 1922 (Sugden and Bairner, 1993; Bairner, 2001). Although 'Ireland's Call' (presumably as it is deemed less 'political') is now played when Ireland visit Twickenham, the only flag/emblem officially displayed alongside the team when the anthem is played is that of the IRFU. Despite the development of a more confident Irish group charisma, the national rugby union team still encounters a series of stereotypes – some of which the players and officials appear to still internalise about themselves.

National stereotyping and playing styles

Between 1948 and 1951, Irish rugby experienced its so-called 'Golden Years', where only four matches were lost, During this time there developed a new style of play, in which the Irish, borrowing the South African tactic of forwards working in close support of each other, employed hard, fast, tough, 'devil-may-care' forwards as attacking spearheads (Diffley, 1973, p. 97). Of course, the 'hustling and harrying' qualities of Irish forward play are also connected with other tactical developments in the game, such as 'the Garryowen' (named after the Irish club), where the ball is kicked high and deep giving the forwards time to charge up to the catcher at full tilt. These invented traditions have remained at the core of the Irish style of play until relatively recently.

Throughout the post-war period, the Irish were characterised by their 'swashbuckling', 'rollicking', 'whirlwind' style of play (Diffley, 1973, p. 94). However, the over-exuberance and lack of control that this style breeds have been long-standing concerns for national coaches. Indeed, these concerns were still with the Irish until relatively recently. They were both a part of how Irish rugby players viewed themselves and how others viewed them, and are also regularly highlighted by the media. Diffley (1973) provided a useful summary of the (somewhat invented) history and tradition of the Irish style of play when he observed: 'the fiery Irish had the opposition completely rattled but could not take advantage of the disruption they wrought in the ranks of their opponents. The chances were created but the over-exuberance ensured that they were never seized upon' (pp. 130–131). These stereotypes have persisted through to recent years.

The post-Second World War Irish style of play was commented on officially by the IRFU in their annual reports. The IRFU have consistently characterised their national team in relation to the dynamism and intensity of the players, especially the forwards. For example, it was reported that through their dynamic approach, Ireland 'practically blew up Scotland' in their encounter in 1950 (IRFU Report of the Committee, 1949/50, p. 2). Similarly, the Irish forwards who are usually lighter than their opposition, were also described as producing 'the traditional fire of [their] forefathers ... showing much more fire in the loose' (IRFU Report of the Committee, 1957/58, pp. 2–4), and were characterised by 'their battering assaults' (IRFU Report of the Committee, 1959/60, p. 4) and their 'fury and enthusiasm' (IRFU Report of the Committee, 1964/65, p. 15). Such sentiments were also in evidence during the match against England in 1993. Officials recorded: 'the pace, ferocity and concentration of the Irish players together with outstanding play in the loose left the much vaunted England team bewildered' (IRFU Report of the Committee, 1992/93, p. 45). The IRFU also recognised the tendency for Ireland to 'run out of steam'. Ireland's decline after winning the Championship in 1974 was explained by Ireland's ability 'to let the opposition "off the hook" with monotonous regularity' (IRFU Report of the Committee, 1977/78, p. 24). Against England in 1981, the following report was made: 'it was very much a case of the same old story, with Ireland taking an early lead, putting the opposition under pressure but then appearing either to relax or be reluctant to stretch the lead too much!' (IRFU Report of the Committee, 1980/81, p. 30). Such comments reflect a less positive we-image and appears to confirm a lack of confidence.

In a series of interviews with international rugby players it was illuminating to discover that many of these 'qualities' were also mentioned (Tuck and Maguire, 1999). All the Irish players interviewed characterised their style as fast, aggressive hustle and bustle. Brendan described the players as 'chasers and scavengers'. The Irish game was described by Sean as 'purposeful chaos' and the situation was neatly condensed by Nigel who spoke of the indefatigable Irish fighting spirit:

> We may not have tremendous flair but the team has great spirit and when you put on an Irish jersey you'd die for each other on the pitch. You realise when you come up against the likes of England and France that you can't outplay them, the only way you can really take it to them is to test them out, see if they have the same sort of spirit you have.

These sentiments betray a degree of the colonial legacy of group disgrace, or at the very least the internalised stereotyping developed in the shadow of the former colonial power. Whatever the merits of this analysis, it is also the placement of stereotypes in the media which provides the greater framing and representing of national habitus codes. The exploration and collation of national stereotypes employed by the media (such as those relating to playing styles and national character) can shed important light on the relationship between sport and national identity (Beard, 1998). Such descriptions provide exemplars of national habitus codes which may trigger the double-bind between the individual (in this case either a player, a spectator or a member of the media audience) and the nation. Post-war newspaper reports in the British media have tended to stereotype Celtic teams by employing tribal signifiers (and thus contrasting them with the Anglo-Saxon English). A study carried out by Maguire and Tuck (1998) of the reporting of rugby union in *The Times* since 1945 reveals that, on the rugby pitch, the Irish are consistently characterised as war-like tribesmen and 'marauding green devils' creating 'emerald commotion'. The Irish, with their 'native flair', were typically seen as the wildest and most tigerish of the Celts. For example, a reference was made comparing the Irish to Kipling's 'Fuzzy Wuzzy', in which it was noted that, for both '... 'e's all 'ot sand an' ginger when alive an 'e's generally shammin' when he's dead' (*Times*, 13 March 1961, p. 18).

Some of the most frequently used sporting metaphors are those related to warfare (Beard, 1998). This deeply embedded discourse of sport, recreating a sporting battlefield, is thus frequently used to stereotype the 'battling qualities' of a nation. In relation to national identity, sport and war both provide ideal environments for the awakening of the national consciousness. The stereotypical war-like nature of the Irish was exemplified in a newspaper report that commented: 'Perhaps inspired by "The Minstrel Boy" on the pipes during the interval, Ireland girded on their fathers' swords and went to war' (*Times*, 16 March 1970, p. 9). During the 1995 Rugby World Cup, the media continually fuelled these codes of Irishness. ITV's television coverage (on their programme *Rugby World Cup* hereafter *RWC*) of the 'rampaging madmen' of Ireland reinforced stereotypes about Irish spirit, fervour and passion. The Irish were rarely described as anything less than dynamic. Traditionally dubbed as underdogs, the Irish were portrayed as a team who sought to disrupt the opposition through 'tremendous heart and tremendous tackling' (*RWC*, 10 June 1995) and one which started games with passion and commitment. This peculiarly Irish style was labelled 'the green onslaught ... seeking to fight, tackle and contest every ball' (*RWC*, 10 June 1995). The coaching staff of the Irish rugby team have also played on this war-like discourse, perhaps as a deliberate motivational tool. For example, Warren Gatland (the New Zealand-born coach of Ireland between 1997 and 1998) stated: 'I keep telling the boys – you're going into battle; it's nation versus nation ... and if you're not prepared to fight to the death then you don't deserve to wear your country's jersey' (BBC *Grandstand*, 21 March 1998).

This 'mad dog' style of the Irish was also encapsulated in the print media after the loss to the French during the 1995 Rugby World Cup. The *Independent on Sunday* reported: 'Ireland stuck firmly to their familiar battle plan of launching an early blitzkrieg of Garryowens and piling in with determination and spirit only to successfully achieve ... glorious Irish failure' (11 June 1995, p. 3). Stephen Jones in the *Sunday Times* commented:

You had to feel ambivalent about Ireland at the end. They resisted reason-ably well. But all that stuff about giving it a lash and about being brave in defeat, that they take losing so well because they get plenty of practice, and about cheerfully downing the black stuff, is becoming a numbingly boring cliché. The brutal truth is that, like their football team, they may play with Irish spirit, spoiling and huffing … but … skill … and ambition [are] absent from their ranks.

(11 June 1995, p. 28)

Rarely are these stereotypes mentioned extensively. However, this does not detract from their power or significance. In some instances, a single word can stand in for a more general aspect of national character. Consequently, the use of stereotypes should be seen as a way into the larger discourse of national identity, habitus codes and identity politics at play (Tuck, 2003). However, it is also worth observing that with the influx of foreign coaches, the ongoing professionalisation of the game, the organisation of clubs along provincial lines, and the success of such clubs in European competition, such stereotypes may well be waning. A more professional, scientific and cosmopolitan style of play has come to the fore.

In summary, the evidence suggests that the imaginary national self-image of the Irish, with all its political, symbolic and stereotypical components, is invented, reinvented and reinforced through lived and meaningful habitus codes surrounding and underpinning the sport of rugby union. Rugby provides, for some Irish, the soil from which an imaginary Ireland can grow and become more real. In the context of international rugby, a series of 'us' and 'them' identifica-tions are subsumed by a powerful we-image reflected within and between individuals who are able to embody 'their' Ireland.

Conclusion

The process-sociological framework employed here has shed some valuable light on the triple-bind that enmeshes individuals, nations and global processes. The Eliasian use of 'habitus' is of central importance to the under-standing of the process of identity and the multi-layered, dynamic nature of personal and national identity. It is only by considering the connections between the subjective and the objective, the cultural and the political, the modern and the ancient, the real and the imagined, and the established and the outsiders, that one can start to appreciate what 'the nation' has been, is, and might be.

The notion of identities in competition in a more global world also provides a useful viewpoint for the study of the dominant, emergent and residual layers of habitus, and how these layers are 'locked' into broader processes of social trans-formation. By employing a figurational framework, globalisation is seen as multifarious rather than unilinear. In other words, there is a local–global nexus in operation which allows for 'resistance' from the local in processes of 'glocalisa-tion'. The resulting tensions of identity placed at the level of the nation, through the diminishing of contrasts and increasing of varieties, therefore have the potential to either strengthen, weaken or pluralise national identity. In this regard, the competing layers of national habitus and the employment of personal pronoun pairings (such as we/they) provide an indication of the process of national identity politics writ large.

The development of sport is also a significant part of this process. International sport provides one of the most powerful and popular arenas for the display, and employment, of national habitus codes. With the nation becoming more easily identifiable through a series of 'concrete' national symbols on sport fields, the nation becomes more visible, more objective. Sport provides an environment for the awakening of the nation – a process which transforms imagined communities into real nations. The study of sport as a national dream which reflects the special charisma of nations provides a useful insight not only into the place of sport in regards to the formation and re-formation of national habitus, but also the processual character of identities.

In relating this framework to the context of Irish rugby, it is possible to identify several general themes. First, rugby union does appear to have been significantly connected to the national habitus of Ireland during the post-war period (especially since the 1960s) and creates a highly visible, 'glocal', arena for the testing of 'Irish' and 'British' identity. Second, the players are, in many ways, portrayed as embodied symbols of Irish national pride and patriotism. The slow emergence of a more confident we-identity and assertive group charisma, freed from the legacy of colonial rule, is evident. Third, habitus codes related to styles of play and national stereotypes are used by the media as signifiers to differentiate between nations – some of which still survive in the internalised views of the players themselves. Finally, rugby in the British Isles appears to foster a complex of I/we and us/them relations, which is exemplified in the juxtaposition of the so-called Celtic fringe with the Anglo-Saxon English.

From this, it is also possible to identify some key components of a sport–national identity nexus, which have significance for the study of sport and national identity more generally. First, the sport–national identity nexus has a processual, or historical, dimension. The connection between sport and national identity appears to have been developing (at least in the British context) for a century and a half, but has accelerated notably in recent years with sport and the symbolic rank order of nations becoming more closely intertwined. Second, this acceleration has been partially fuelled by the increasing use of national habitus codes, such as in the discourse of the mass media. Third, it appears that processes of identity politics are intimately bound up in the nexus. For example, politicians and sports officials are becoming more aware of the significance that sport, and identity, have to the health of the nation and the feel-good factor that international sporting successes can bring. Fourth, international players surrounded by national symbols do tend to view themselves as embodiments of their nation (and this union of private and public worlds becomes even more political when players possessing more than one 'nationality' have to select an affiliation).

In summary, the sport–national identity nexus is complex, dynamic and particularly relevant to the study of sport and nations in an increasingly globalised world. The nation-state remains a powerful player in shaping the habitus of people and the conduct of world affairs. Whilst the specific dynamics of this nexus are sometimes temporary, shallow and imagined, they can become, through the actions of people and especially in the context of international sport, very real and long-lasting indeed.

6 'Not the Germans again'

Soccer, identity politics and the media

Joseph Maguire and Michael Burrows

In this chapter we wish to revisit some of the ideas, concepts and evidence contained within the work of Maguire and Poulton (1999), and Maguire, Poulton and Possamai (1999) on association football and national identity. Using an Eliasian perspective (set out more fully in Chapter 5) we focus once again on association football. Specifically, we examine a single match between Germany and England that took place on 1 September 2001, and the ways in which sport intersects with habitus and identity at the level of the nation. The chapter first reviews the findings of the earlier work on the Euro 96 soccer tournament held in England. In so doing, we can compare and contrast the media coverage that surrounded the match in 2001. On this basis, we make the case that the media's representations of identity politics can be understood from the vantage point of national habitus codes.

Anglo-German identity politics, habitus codes and 'national character'

In his introduction to *The Established and the Outsiders* (Elias and Scotson, 1994), Elias makes the connection between issues of identity and national character, and in his work on the Germans (Elias, 1996), these links are most fully substantiated. In this latter study, Elias investigates the deeply embodied aspects of German habitus, personality, social structure, and conduct, and how these features emerged out of the nation's history and pattern of social development. The fortunes of the nation became sedimented, internalised and fused as part of the 'second nature' – the habitus – of its citizens, whose actions remake the national habitus anew. The image of the nation is also constitutive of a person's self image. The emotional bonds of individuals with the nations they form can have, as one of their levels, sleeping memories which tend to crystallise and become organised around common symbols – national sport teams being one example – that powerfully reinforce the notion of I/we relations and form the focal point of a common belief system. Examining these habitus codes allows investigation of why, for example, European integration at the level of political institutions is running ahead of the degree of identification that many of the citizens of European nation-states feel towards the notion of being Europeans. Elias (1991) states that:

This make-up, the social habitus of individuals, forms, as it were, the soil from which grow the personal characteristics through which an individual differs from other members of society. In this way something grows out of the common language which the individual shares with others and which is certainly a component of the social habitus – a more or less individual style, what might be called an unmistakable individual handwriting that grows out of the social script.

(p. 182)

Emotional bonds and I/we images are relatively fixed and tend to go unchallenged. In all nations there are, to blend aspects of Elias's conceptualisation with that of Raymond Williams, 'dominant', 'emergent' and 'residual' habitus codes (Williams, 1977). When examining national characteristics, we are dealing with interconnected ways of knowing that have been termed by Anthony Giddens (1986) practical consciousness and discursive consciousness. The level of practical consciousness is more taken for granted, yet finds expression in, and is influenced by, the two-way traffic conducted with the discursive consciousness of an individual. While the concepts of invented traditions and imagined communities are also fruitful in exploring European identity politics, such concepts seem to us to be dealing only with the level of discursive consciousness, ignoring the level of practical consciousness and overlooking the interplay between the two. Hence, we lay emphasis on an Eliasian position that focuses on issues of habitus. As Elias (1991) notes:

> The deeply rooted nature of the distinctive national characteristics and the consciousness of national we-identity closely bound up with them can serve as a graphic example of the degree to which social habitus of the individual provides a soil in which personal, individual differences can flourish. The individuality of the particular Englishman, Dutchman, Swede or German represents, in a sense, the personal elaboration of a common social, and in this case national, habitus.

(p. 210)

Habitus 'codes', embodied feelings and discursive practices of the individuals who make a nation play a powerful role in both the foundation of cultural relations and the construction and maintenance of national identities. People in complex nation-states have multiple identities that are many-layered – local, regional, national, global. These layers form the flexible lattice work of the habitus of a person. Individuals do not only have an ego-image and an ego-ideal, but also a we-image and a we-ideal. 'The image of this "we" 'forms an integral part of the personality organisation [social habitus] of the individual who ... uses the pronouns "I" and "we" with reference to him- or herself' (Elias, 1996, p. 153). We argue that one of the most potent I/we identities of an individual is that associated with that individual's nation. 'The "traits" of national group identity ... are a layer of the social habitus built very deeply and firmly in the personality structure of the individual' (Elias, 1991, p. 209).

Through discursive practices and practical actions, both of which have an often unacknowledged affective component, our I/we identity is constructed. The familiar, taken-for-granted, daily actions bind us to a particular I/we identity – a process that occurs through childhood and adult life. The deepening and consolidation of an I/we feeling is also a double-bind – a cognition or sentiment which, while it enables us to share things in common with others like us, also acts to separate us from them. The I/we habitus code gives a sense of individual self, but also we-group identity. When confronted with outsiders, such codes tend to harden and become more sharply defined. While the process of national habitus/character formation is framed, constructed and represented by and through discursive practices (such as through the production and consumption of media–sport discourses), these practices themselves are interwoven with activities occurring at the level of practical consciousness. The fantasy shield and imagined group charisma of European nations are based on such practices and actions. Yet, of course, citizens of these nations are confronted with the twin, interlocking processes of Europeanisation and globalisation. Citizens of European countries tend to have a stronger and more emotive I/we identification with their nation rather than with the we-identity notion of themselves as *Europeans*. A question that arises in this regard is whether, as a result of processes of Europeanisation and globalisation, I/we national identities are being strengthened, weakened or pluralised.

Only in the course of the twentieth century has a more complete integration of citizens in European countries occurred. As Elias observes: 'in all nation states the institutions of public education are dedicated to an extreme degree to deepening and consolidating a we-feeling based exclusively on the national tradition' (Elias, 1939/1994, p. 210). Just as it takes several generations for the collective group memories of former greatness and superiority to dissipate, so it may be that today's European citizens are but the first generation voluntarily moving towards European I/we group identification – within a 'United States of Europe'.

On the basis of the arguments outlined above, we examined the role that Euro 96 played in European identity politics and habitus construction more generally (Maguire and Poulton, 1999; Maguire, Poulton and Possamai, 1999). Four main findings were identified. First, while the dominant form of English press coverage of Euro 96 served to divide sections of the British/English from the nations of Europe (especially Germany), this was not a common trait of the German press. The English coverage appeared typical of the response of nations whose former power superiority in relation to other groups has been lost. A fantasy shield entailing an imagined charisma – an illegitimate superiority complex, born of an inferiority complex – manifests itself in a hostile reaction to more powerful contemporary nations, like Germany.

Second, the press coverage in both the English and German newspapers reflected several social currents that were evident in the countries' respective domestic politics of the time. For England, these social currents included: an anti-Europeanism, particularly with regard to the so-called 'Beef War', the prospective single currency, and the perceived interference by Brussels in internal British concerns; a latent anti-German sentiment reflecting long-standing rivalry, brought to the fore due to Germany's current standing and influence in Europe; and the desire of the (then) British Conservative government, and its allies in the right wing press, to foster what was termed a 'feelgood factor'. For Germany, a nation not proud of its immediate past, emphasis was placed on contemporary international relations, with reactionary taunts towards England/Britain regarding the *Rinderwahnsinnskrise* (Mad Cow Crisis).

Third, the identity politics evident in the media discourse underpinning the English coverage of Euro 96 reflected a more deep-seated British, mainly English, concern regarding national decline and rapid social change which was identified by the German press and some of the English broadsheets. As a result, the dominant English media discourse tended towards two interwoven themes: nostalgia and ethnic assertiveness/defensiveness. The sense of nostalgia was particularly evident in the build-up to and in the early part of the tournament. Ethnic assertiveness/defensiveness became more evident as the tournament developed and the English team encountered a series of old European foes, specifically Scotland, Holland, Spain and Germany. It was, and remains, our contention that English media discourse of this kind can be understood as part of an active construction of fantasy group charisma, based on both the invention of traditions and, at a deeper and more enduring level, the habitus codes that underpin the dominant national character of European nations.

Finally, in light of this, the German press coverage was marked by a distinct disinterest in nostalgic or otherwise historical references of their own, and dismay at the English press's evocation of past hostilities between the two nations. The German press preferred to enjoy the present by depicting Germany as a powerful nation on the European/world stage, a position which Britain/England can no longer really claim to have, despite its 'imagined charisma'. While a minority of English supporters still chanted 'two World Wars and one World Cup' across the crowded platforms at Wembley central station within an hour of England's victory over Spain (*Times*, 25 June 1996, p. 56), the reality was that the English had to look back to their World Cup victory of 1966 to claim any form of superiority over Germany, on or off the football field.

It is this fact that characterised the press coverage of Euro 96, with the English press dwelling nostalgically on former lost glories and power relations and a marked ethnic assertiveness/defensiveness. The German press, on the other hand, appeared quite content to let their football team do the talking, seemingly taking satisfaction from the contemporary European political situation. In the build-up to the match between Germany and England on 1 September 2001, similar themes were evident. In the previous year, in the home tie between the two, England had lost to Germany. The result had led to the resignation of the then England manager, Kevin Keegan, and the subsequent appointment of Sven-Goran Eriksson, the first foreign manager of the national team. Qualification for the 2002 World Cup was dependent on the outcome of the game. Yet, deeper issues concerning Anglo-German identity politics were also at stake. The English victory also seems to have prompted some deep-seated aspects of national habitus to find more open expression. It is to this reaction, and how it compares and contrasts with the earlier findings, that we now turn our attention.

Old scores, new games: 'them' versus 'us'

In the same way that military references and the vocabulary of war can help to reinforce the 'we' image at the expense of outsider groups, the celebration of tradition and the nostalgic glorification of past triumphs may also be very influential in shaping one's national identity. The media coverage of the 2001 England–Germany game regularly implied that: 'The forgetting of history is easier said than done' (*Guardian* (*Sport*), 1 September 2001, p. 7). This nostalgic discourse was far more cautious before the result had been decided, as the media appeared to be preparing the English public for another loss at the hands of their arch rivals.

Readers were reminded that 'history is against England ... [having] never won a competitive international in Germany' (*Daily Express*, 1 September 2001, p. 119), and that: 'the Mother country so often casts herself as a victim of fate sketched out by German hands' (*Daily Telegraph* (*Sport*), 1 September 2001, p. 15). However, the press also implied that England's poor results against Germany stemmed from more deep-seated political feelings that existed in the early twentieth century when England was socially and politically a dominant nation, and: 'Germany first gave a political edge to its football when England ... wanted to overtake them in other terms' (*Times*, 1 September 2001, p. 21).

In contrast to reports concerning the post-war revival of Germany, and the decline of the British/English, the press chose to refer to the finest hour of English football, the 1966 World Cup victory over (West) Germany. The manager, Eriksson was viewed as attempting 'to emulate Ramsey and become first to win in Germany in 36 years'. Also, if the current team were to go on to win the World Cup in 2002, it would 'forge another link with England's football past if the side can do what Ramsey's did in Nuremberg in 1965' (*Daily Mail*, 1 September 2001, p. 96). In the light of victory, the English press attempted to arouse more 'sleeping memories' of World Cup success in 1966 that still exist within the national habitus. The media highlighted the fact that at last there was a new hat-trick hero who was worthy of an association with the 1966 match winner: 'Owen's three goals evoked memories of Hurst in victory over Germany' (*Sunday Times*, 2 September, 2001, 24).

The fact that the nation had just witnessed the 'largest margin in the history of Anglo-German rivalry' (*Independent On Sunday* (*Sport*), 2 September 2001, p. 2) seemed to justify the reliving of past encounters with Germany that were rooted in the habitus of the English football fan. Previous triumphs were also relived through separate features within the sports pages, which included photographs to evoke past memories. This use of nostalgic discourse occurred in both tabloid and broadsheet newspapers – the media message was clear: England's 5–1 victory over Germany on 1 September 2001 was 'one of those moments you will always remember ... like VE Day' (*Daily Mail*, 3 September 2001, p. 10).

On the day of the match, visual representation also conveyed notions of us versus them. For example, Ladbrokes (the bookmakers) had produced an advertisement with pictures of England fans on one side of a double page, and German fans on the other, with the two groups clearly segregated. A photograph on the front page of *The Mirror* showed David Beckham, the England captain, draped in the cross of St George, which seeks to generate a feeling of 'togetherness' and shared history. In terms of text, the press coverage, both tabloids and broadsheets, stated their intent to employ patriotic ideas and images from the outset, revealing that: '... one should not discount patriotism as a pertinent potion' (*Daily Express*, 1 September 2001, p. 119).

Readers were also reminded that: 'England versus Germany has become a metaphor for our relative standing in the world' (*Times*, 1 September 2001, p. 21). Broadsheets and tabloids contained patriotic quotations from England's Swedish manager Sven-Goran Eriksson, and he was sighted in a sub-heading as saying: 'Today I am an Englishman' (*Mirror*, 1 September 2001, p. 2). This idea of the foreign manager being on the 'same wavelength' as the whole country was being used to promote feelings of national identity. The tabloids also brought the readers' attention to events that were taking place away from the football itself. This included *The Sun*'s coverage of their makeshift 'Oompah' band that had sought to reek havoc near the German team's hotel. Additionally, the press informed its readership of how a Cleethorpes pub removed all 'Becks' (a German beer, but also the abbreviated name of the England captain) from their shelves, and had large St George flags hanging from their walls (*Daily Mail*, 1 September 2001).

The tabloids also employed a range of personal pronouns when referring to the football match itself. It was made clear that there is a 'particular sweetness in beating them ... and a special bitterness in losing to them' (*Mirror*, 1 September 2001, p. 6). Reference was made to the Second World War film *The Great Escape* – with Sven-Goran Eriksson compared to one of the actors in the film, Richard Attenborough. In being wished 'good luck', Attenborough, and now Eriksson, had replied: 'We will need it' (*Sun*, 1 September 2001, p. 71). The national importance of the game was often highlighted with comments such as the 'fixture has relegated England versus Scotland to a minor domestic dispute'.

Despite this stirring of national sentiments, the broadsheet papers did hint at maintaining some realism amongst all this optimistic reporting in the press coverage. The reader was reminded that: 'Britannia doesn't rule the waves and World Cup Willie doesn't rule football ... something in the English psyche has never fully absorbed either fact' (*Times*, 1 September 2001, p. 28). Many of the issues used by the press on the day of the match were developed in the subsequent post-match coverage. However, emphasis was also placed on a number of new topics that were clearly employed to express feelings of national identity. A range of key themes reflected some deep-seated anxieties that sections of the English have with regard to relations with Germans.

'Sweet revenge': exorcising national habitus memories

The post-match articles and headlines, like those on the day of the game, again demonstrated a range of 'us/them' discourses (Blain, Boyle and O'Donnell, 1993; Elias, 1939/1994). For example: 'Uli Hoeness, Beckenbauer and all other German history men, your team took a hell of a beating' (Observer (Sport), 2 September 2001, p. 2). This by-line deliberately alludes to the Norwegian press coverage of Norway's victory over the English some years previously. Using photographs, head-lines and storylines, the press reminded its readership that the evening of the game was 'a night we'll never forget' (Sun (Sungoals), 3 September 2001, p. 5), and that 'they'd lost only one home World Cup tie ... and their last loss in Munich was 1973' (News Of The World, 2 September 2001, p. 4). The Sun proclaimed: 'We munched em in Munchen' (Sun, 3 September 2001, p. 4). Although the broad-sheet coverage had very few headlines of this nature, personal pronouns were included as part of a more subtle message, which reflected those in the tabloids. For example: 'We tend to be disgracefully rude when we play them, but such behaviour is so transparently the product of our envy of their success ... it's forgivable' (Daily Telegraph, 3 September 2001, p. 19).

Whereas the tabloids utilised headlines to express notions of 'us' versus 'them', the broadsheets tended to focus on the significance of the game for both the German and English teams. The broadsheets re-emphasised the fact that England had 'inflicted their heaviest defeat' on the Germans (Observer (Sport), 2 September 2001, p. 2). The reporting also seemed to revel in the fact that the England team had taken 'sweet revenge for all those penalty shoot-outs by them' (Sunday Telegraph (Sport), 2 September 2001, p. 2) – a reference to the fact that England had lost twice at the semi-final stage of major tournaments to the Germans as a result of the game being decided by penalty shoot-outs. Reviewing the history of these fixtures, a writer in the Sunday Times thus argued: 'they were soon wallowing in the illusion that their habit of being invincible on home soil would be sustained' (Sunday Times (Sport), 2 September 2001, p. 2). In the light of victory, the message to English people was unsurprisingly much more optimistic, and stressed ideas of togetherness: 'We're all in this together, and we can all rejoice together' (Times (Sports Daily), 3 September 2001, p. 4).

As a result of the triumphant result, the Mail on Sunday, (2 September 2001, p. 21) felt able to claim the Swedish manager as 'one of us Dear old Sven. One of us? You'd better believe it'. A Times reporter went on to suggest what the result implies for 'our' future in terms of playing the Germans: '... nothing to fear from the Germans anymore' (Times (Sports Daily), 3 September 2001, p. 2). These examples clearly demonstrate the way nations are segregated through media–sport discourse, and reinforce the earlier findings of Maguire, Poulton and Possami (1999). Though 'Sven' was now proclaimed as 'one of us', questions were also raised as to whether he could grasp that the significance of the victory lay beyond soccer, with one writer in the Daily Express (3 September 2001, p. 44) posing the question whether he could 'understand how much Saturday's result meant to us'.

The war of the words revisited

The research examining Euro 96 had highlighted the use of war vocabulary and military metaphors in English press coverage of the tournament (Maguire, Poulton and Possamai, 1999). Media coverage of the September 2001 England – Germany game again deployed similar war vocabulary and militaristic imagery. This appears to link two supposedly crucial areas of national life together: war and sport. As Beard (1998) suggests: 'In international competition, metaphors of war appear most frequently when the media can equate the sporting contest with the actual wars which have taken place' (p. 35). This statement clearly holds true with England–Germany games, and in both 1996 and 2001 reporting of the match contained numerous examples. This reference to war in a sporting context may well reinforce feelings of national identity, especially when the two opponents have such a history of rivalry.

On match-day the media set the scene for what was to be a historic encounter through statements such as: 'England battle to beat Germany in their own backyard' (*Daily Mail*, 1 September, 2001, p. 7). Advertisements for betting questioned whether England could stage a 'Great Escape'. Within the day's coverage, distinctions can be made in terms of broadsheet and tabloid reporting, where the latter used the vocabulary of war almost exclusively to refer to events leading up to the game, and the broadsheets focused more on the actual match. Readers were reminded of previous battles between the teams through the English footballing veteran Nobby Styles' memories of: 'having a running battle with a German winghalf' (*Daily Express*, 1 September 2001, p. 115). *The Sun* newspaper focused on their own constructed story. As noted previously, dressed as a German 'Oompah' band, *The Sun*'s own models made a surprise visit to the German team hotel in the early hours. The report emphasised that: 'The Sun's Raid' led to the players 'being shaken from their beds by the deafening dawn swoop', and when the paper's PR manager was questioned he simply replied 'I was only following orders' (*Sun*, 1 September 2001, p. 2).

Whereas *The Sun* reported their own actions as a military operation, the broadsheets suggested that the real warfare would occur on the pitch. Coverage implied that viewers were to witness: '90 minutes of international combat – no world will exist outside' (*Daily Telegraph* (*Sport Saturday*), 1 September 2001, p. 3). Reports continued to suggest that a battle was soon to commence as the England leader David Beckham had ' beaten the drum fiercely', and his role was further linked to the role of military general as it entailed 'more about influence in the trenches than being high profile and enthusiastic' (*Independent*, 1 September, 2001, p. 26). *The Guardian* also employed militaristic language when acknowledging the significance of this game in terms of qualifying for the World Cup. Although the importance of the game for the English team was played down, a battle was still to take place: 'Less a question of apocalypse now than the day of judgement being postponed ... if the main parachute fails to open they should still enjoy a reasonably soft landing' (*Guardian* (*Sport*), 1 September 2001, p. 2).

Both tabloid and broadsheet coverage continued to use wartime language to report the victory that had been witnessed by 'England's army of travelling fans' (*Sunday Times*, 2 September 2001, p. 24). It was almost as if a famous battle had been won by 'Eriksson's brilliantly deployed forces' (*Mail On Sunday*, 2 September 2001, p. 108), who inflicted the '5–1 Slaughter of Germany' (*Sunday Times (Sport)*, 2 September 2001, p. 1) and 'put the old enemy mercilessly to the sword' (*Sunday Times (Sport)*, 2 September 2001, p. 3). The match was also referred to as a time of combat, being the 'sporting equivalent of the last days of Saigon' (*Sun*, 3 September 2001, p. 41). Readers were informed of how the England team had 'surrendered to the old enemy back in October' (*Sunday Mirror*, 2 September 2001, p. 77), but now it was the turn of the Germans who 'surrendered three to Michael Owen' (*Sunday Times (Sport)*, 2 September 2001, p. 1).

The war vocabulary and militaristic imagery continued with reference to the German goalkeeper Oliver Kahn, represented as a symbol for the German national game, who 'held hands up in surrender' (*Observer (Sport)*, 2 September 2001, p. 3) to England's hat-trick hero Owen, who was referred to as 'The Spitfire' (*Mirror*, 3 September 2001, p. 51). The five goals conceded by Kahn prompted *The Sun* to headline its report: 'The Shell Shocked Bayern keeper' (3 September 2001, p. 43).

Who mentioned the war?

In stark contrast to the codes used by the tabloids to construct a view of the match as a question of 'us' and 'them', some reports were highly critical of the connections made between war and sport. The *Daily Mail* (3 September 2001, p. 71) noted: 'Eriksson's realism ... contrasted with the jingoism being expressed by all those around him'. In addition, the overall press coverage prompted some lengthy articles that focused specifically on these issues. John Hooper, writing in *The Observer*, suggested that: 'Socially acceptable xenophobia has developed in Britain ... the media [has] worked itself into a frenzy of racist anticipation ... xenophobic insults would not be printed in other countries', and concluded that 'Britain now displays values of Hitler, Mussolini and Franco' (*Observer*, 2 September 2001, p. 16). Other reports were more apologetic, with *The Times* (3 September 2001, p. 39) noting that it is a 'shame that we are so desperate for anything to unite and excite the nation that a football match can be treated as such a historic event'. Reinforcing this critique, one report contrasted the behaviour of the English team captain with the supporters of the national team. The *Mail on Sunday* (2 September 2001, p. 108) observed that David Beckham was 'a symbol of sophistication amidst the dross of xenophobia – he sees no need to swathe himself in the Union flag. He has an innocent empathy with the Stansted battalions, whose patriotism swills about in the 3 litre steins of local lagers'.

Some journalists, from a variety of papers, attempted to make clear that war references had no real bearing on a game of football. In the light of the English victory several reporters sought to establish some distance from the more jingoistic reports. However, in doing so, some press stories played with the rhetoric of war. As the

Daily Mail (3 September 2001, p. 8) noted: 'Oh, none of that ... Don't mention the war'. Other reports claimed that Eriksson 'would never think to mention the war in his warm-up talk' (*Guardian*, 3 September 2001, p. 16). In fact, the broadsheets, again similar to the evidence relating to Euro 96 media coverage, adopted a more subtle approach. While condemning jingoistic tabloid journalism, broadsheet newspapers used more subtle techniques to frame the match in such terms. *The Guardian*, for example, while criticising the use of war language, continued to cite examples from tabloids, including headlines such as: 'We still cannot forget the war ..."Blitzed" (*Sunday Mirror*) and Churchillian "Our Finest Hour" (*Sunday Express*)' (cited in *The Guardian*, 3 September 2001, p. 17).

While the military language of broadsheet coverage was more subtle, it was not absent. Nevertheless, more vivid examples of the use of war rhetoric came from the tabloids. The *Daily Mail* (3 September 2001, p. 76) observed: 'The English have been making an effort to move on from the dark days of war' but followed this up with the phrase that the 'Germans shot us down by penalties'. *The Mirror* (3 September 2001, p. 10) was more explicit: 'We gave your boys a hell of a beating! And we didn't even mention the W**'. Yet, while the reporters were conscious that use of such war metaphors was problematic, they were still able to weave such images into reports. Referring to the play of one English player, a *Sunday Mirror* reporter stated: 'I know we should try to avoid military metaphors ... but ... Operation Stifle Deisler ... was his order' (2 September 2001, p. 77).

From the examples outlined above it is clear that while there were differences between broadsheet and tabloid newspapers, all were engaged in a style of reporting permeated by references to the war and past conflicts between these two nations. Which style was deployed may well be connected to how reporters and editors from specific newspapers felt coverage needed to relate to their readerships tastes, traditions and memories.

What the English victory meant, and revealed

Was this the game that: 'Shook world order' (*Sunday Telegraph (Sport)*, 2 September 2001, p. 3)? Central to all the post-match coverage was the idea that victory was extremely important for 'our' nation as a whole. Football was referred to as 'the game by which most Englishmen measure our national pride' (*Daily Mail*, 3 September 2001, p. 76). The press suggested that the English public should take great pride in witnessing this shared experience, and implied that the match would become incorporated into the national character and even become as significant as events such as the wedding of Prince Charles and Lady Diana Spencer. Broadsheet readers were reminded that they had witnessed not only the 'most astonishing victory ever recorded by the national football team' (*Sunday Times (Sport)*, 2 September 2001, p. 1), but also 'the best result in England's history' (*Times (Sports Daily)*, 3 September 2001, p. 5).

While reports of the game were a major feature of the press coverage, the media also stressed the importance of the result in a broader context. A reporter in *The Times* noted that there has 'always been a political edge to Germany – England games – little doubt of the national significance of Munich encounter' (*Times*, 3 September 2001, p. 4). Great pleasure appeared to be taken in reporting that 'we' had seen 'a win which turned history on its head' (*Independent On Sunday* (*Sport*), 2 September 2001, p. 2), and that the result 'rewrote that chapter of the history book in red, white and blue' (*Sunday Times* (*Sport*), 2 September 2001, p. 3).

The enormity of the result for the history of the nation continued to be stressed over the following days. As one report in the *Daily Mail* observed: 'There are epic moments in our national life which are to be treasured ... this is one for the ages' (*Daily Mail*, 3 September 2001, p. 76). The match 'has already taken its treasured place in the folklore of English football' (*Mail On Sunday*, 2 September 2001, p. 1). Press coverage made continual and nationalistic references to the World Wars. Yet, despite this, the result was seen as so significant that 'it may mean we never have to mention the war again' (*Independent On Sunday*, 2 September 2001, p. 1).

The press coverage made many references to the reaction of national celebrities to the game as well as showing the press reaction in Germany. By quoting non-football figures the coverage was again able to imply that this football match was of wider social and political significance. For example, the British Prime Minister and other members of the British Parliament were cited at length in the broadsheet papers. Tony Blair himself passed on his congratulations for a 'truly incredible performance and a marvellous victory' (*Observer*, 2 September 2001, p. 1). Readers were also informed that the Sports Minister, Richard Caborn, was 'very proud' (*Observer* (*Sport*), 2 September 2001, p. 3) and that the Home Secretary, David Blunkett, admitted: 'For once in my life I am speechless' (*Independent On Sunday*, 2 September 2001, p. 5). The tabloids also used comments from famous sportsmen and showbiz icons, including the former England managers Terry Venables and Bobby Robson (*News Of The World*, Score, 2 September 2001), as well as pop groups such as S-Club 7, glamour model Jordan and soap actor Mike Reid.

Matches between Germany and England were framed in terms of a sense of togetherness, and that the result 'united the country with a potency that every politician would kill for' (*Daily Mail*, 3 September 2001, p. 10). Reporting suggested that all myths of German superiority had been laid to rest and 'the mystique surrounding Teutonic superiority finally evaporated last night' (*Sunday Mirror*, 2 September 2001, p. 76). This theme was accentuated in what may well be the most xenophobic piece of reporting:

> In affectionate remembrance of arrogant, clinical, penalty-scoring, and downright bloody irritating German football, which died at the Olympiastadion, Munich, on 1st September, 2001. Deeply unlamented by a large circle of English football fans, RIP.
>
> (*Mirror*, 3 September 2001, p. 1)

This front-page statement was accompanied by an image of the German goalkeeper Oliver Kahn's gloves on fire. The coverage highlighted how this occasion was a priceless shared experience, with victory the 'nation woke up to a collective feeling of utter euphoria ... the result ... stirred the patriotism of the millions' (*Sunday People*, 2 September 2001, p. 2). The tabloids used images of fans celebrating across the country to demonstrate these joyous scenes, especially in places of national significance such as Trafalgar Square. For sections of the press, the significance of the game for the English was captured by comments in *The Mirror* (3 September 2001, p. 6). 'Being English was a cause for celebration, not embarrassment'.

Readers were also advised to forget 1966 and to 'start dreaming of the future rather than the past' (*Sun*, 3 September 2001, p. 43). Despite the nostalgia and sense of tradition evoked in the coverage, some reports sought to highlight how readers should jettison the past. A reporter in the *Daily Telegraph* (3 September 2001, p. 3) argued: 'All that "35 years of hurt" gulf is just the usual English obsession with nostalgia impeding progress ... It's irritating, pointless and belittling to the modern players'. Indeed, the war rhetoric needed to be abandoned – not least due to the Swedish heritage of the national coach: 'Eriksson could never ... pledge to get back at the Luftwaffe for bombing his Granny' (*Guardian*, 3 September 2001, p. 16).

Conclusion

In the case of both Euro 96 and the 1 September 2001 match, sport plays a central role in European identity politics and habitus construction. The dominant English media coverage served to divide the English from the Germans. For Euro 96 such coverage reflected broader social currents. While more contemporary social currents did not figure in press coverage of the 2001 match, deeper, long-term anxieties of a sporting and cultural kind found expression. Issues of national and sporting decline permeated the coverage. While we did not examine German press coverage extensively, the German reaction which was commented on in the British/English press did not contain a sense of anxiety about Germany's role in European integration or the wider global order. What bearing does this have on discussions about national identity and global processes more broadly?

Elias (1991) identifies globalisation processes as a new stage of worldwide integration, which both decreases the social distances between groups and increases the scope of identification by offering a variety of identities for individuals to invest in. In this more global era, it is tempting to regard the greater interdependencies between nations, and the changing power ratios between them, as reducing the significance of national identity. However, such rationalisation of the nation would fail to appreciate the powerful emotional attachment the nation still holds as an 'inner circle' of identification (De Swaan, 1995, p. 36). Elias (1991) explains this enduring power of the nation in terms of a 'drag effect', whereby the power of the nation to resist global processes, at least in the short term, makes them appear as 'islands of nationalism' in a sea of lengthening and deepening chains of interdependence. In the words of Elias: 'The [national] we-image trails far behind the reality of global interdependence' (1991, p. 227). This is also true in connection with the role of the nation-state in European integration. It also applies with regard to the role that sport plays in each of these areas. What is being raised is the question of how societies – the people who compose societies – remember. One dominant way is through embodied (male) sport identity practices (Connerton, 1989). It becomes important, then, to re-examine the role that such practices play.

Identities are not 'natural', nor are they fixed. Rather, identities are socially constructed and are subject to change over time and across place. People have multiple identities that are formed and transformed in social interaction. That is, people's identities are composed of a set of interwoven features that have both territorial and non-territorial aspects. People's multiple identities are expressed in terms of networks of interdependencies, with aspects of identity intersecting across time and space (Elias, 1978). Multiple identities – of which national identity is a key feature – are constructed by a process of cultural representation. In this interchange, there are dominant, emergent and residual notions of identity. The dominant view of identity tends to invent a specific origin and tradition, recount habitus-based experiences, and emphasise a view of who does and does not belong. These are crucial issues in identity politics (Elias, 1978, p. 128).

Sport is an arena in which processes of personal identity testing and formation are conducted. Different sports represent individuals, communities, regions and nations. A key feature of the sports process is that it is used by different groups – established, emergent and outsider groups – to represent, maintain and/or challenge identities. Sports have performed this role since they became important national practices in the 1880s (Maguire, 1993a). Here, in this chapter, notions of sport and national identity are vividly displayed in what Schwarz has termed 'daily unnoticed practices' (1992, p. 203).

Britain/England provides an ideal typical exemplar of broader globalisation processes at work. At the level of national societies, for example, problems of heterogeneity and diversity have arisen. Internal and external pressures have developed that seek to reconstruct collective identities along pluralistic lines. Closely connected to this is the process by which individuals have become subject to competing ethnic, cultural and religious reference points. The system of international interdependency chains in which Britain is located has also become more fluid, multipolar and dynamic. European, Commonwealth and United Nations networks are undergoing processes of rapid change. The loss of positions of power in sporting politics goes hand in hand with decline in global political terms. In seeking to arrest this decline the British government is seeking to secure world-class events such as the 2012 Olympic Games. Perhaps it is less surprising to observe that in some societies, resistance to globalisation processes has grown more intense. This is especially so where older, more established empires have been overtaken by previous competitors who had been defeated, on and off the field of play. In the cultural identity politics of modern Britain, a 'little Englander' wrestles with a more fluid, pluralistic global identity. As this chapter has shown, in soccer this struggle continues to be played out.

Part IV
Sporting futures

7 'Civilised Games'?

Beijing 2008, power politics and cultural struggles

Joseph Maguire

This chapter seeks to examine these tensions, and to highlight the key groups involved in the cultural struggles that underpinned the awarding of the 2008 Olympic Games to Beijing. In doing so, this chapter draws attention to broader questions concerning global sport and Olympism, globalisation and geopolitical issues, and Sino-Western civilisational struggles (for further discussion of Chinese encounters with other civilisations, see Cho-Yun Hsu, 2001; for globalisation and China see Yeung, 2000; and for a general discussion of civilisational analysis see the Introduction to this collection). The events of what has become known as 9/11 have shaken the interdependencies that pattern the geopolitics of the globe. It is too early to tell what the intended and unintended consequences of such events will be.

Equally, the impact of 9/11 on global sport is yet to be assessed. True, the security arrangements surrounding mega-events, such as the Salt Lake City Olympic Games, and soccer's World Cup, have become ever tighter, but such issues are symptoms of the crisis. Indeed, in a sociological sense, they are relatively less important than the deeper processes at work. These processes concern the emergent global, cultural, economic and political figuration of the twenty-first century. Insights to such issues, as indicated in the Introduction, can be gained from a process-sociological perspective. Take, for example, the comments made by Norbert Elias, writing in the mid 1930s:

> From Western society – as a kind of upper class – Western 'civilized' patterns of conduct are today spreading over wide areas outside the West, whether through the settlement of Occidentals or through the assimilation of the upper strata of other nations, as models of conduct earlier spread within the West itself from this or that upper stratum, from certain courtly or commercial centres ... This spread of the same patterns of conduct from the 'white mother-countries or fatherlands' follows the incorporation of the other areas into the network of political and economic interdependencies, into the sphere of elimination struggles between and within the nations of the West.
>
> (Elias, 1939/1994, p. 462)

As will be argued in the conclusion to this chapter, comments made by de Coubertin, and other Olympic officials, can well be understood in such terms. Consideration must first be given to more current events. While 9/11 may become synonymous with the 'future shock' of the global age and new millennium, the events taking place a few months earlier, around 1 April 2001, may well prove more symptomatic of the changing global order – and its concomitant impact on sport. At least, that is the thesis of this chapter. That is, the spy-plane stand-off between the emergent and current global superpowers, China and the US, with 24 aircrew held for some 11 days, may well mark the incipient stage in a long-term civilisational struggle. Despite frenzied media comment which speculated that the US would seek to make the Chinese 'pay' for the incident, some three months later, Beijing was awarded the 2008 summer Olympic games, and, later in the year, became a member of the World Trade Organisation (WTO).

In seeking to understand Beijing's success it is necessary to examine the complex figuration in which the International Olympic Committee (IOC) decision was embedded. Attention must be paid both to the position of several key groups and to a number of decisive issues. These issues include: the interconnections between geo-and sporting-politics; Sino-Western relations and occidental perceptions of the Chinese; the role and structure of the IOC; the meaning and purpose underpinning the allocation of the Olympic Games; and, the role and influence of political economic concerns. Before consideration is given to these issues, attention must first be given to some key issues involved in studies examining the media and the Olympics.

The Olympics, the media, politics and identities

The Olympics is a global event, not merely of supreme significance in the world of sports, but as a carrier of cultural meanings which are almost uniquely available to vast international audiences (MacAloon, 1999; Bale and Christensen, 2004). Such meanings are re-represented, distributed and circulated by the media-sport complex. Sports in the media in general, and the Olympics in particular, are embedded in local/global processes in three ways: the production of media sport goods, the political economy of sport mediated texts, and the political economic aspect of consumption. These issues have been examined by several researchers (Harvey, Law and Cantelon, 2001; Maguire, 1999; Roche, 2000; Rowe, 1999; Segrave, 2000). What such work indicates is that the study of the Olympic Games must be located within broader local/global processes, with specific reference to media and consumption (Miller et al., 2001; Tomlinson, 1999). That is, a global mega-event, such as the Olympics, must be examined in a way that highlights how it plays out locally, and does so through the lens of the media–sport complex (Jhally, 1989; Puijk, 2000; Rowe, 1999; Toohey and Veal, 1999; Wenner, 1998, Whannel, 1992; Whitson, 1998). In seeking to examine the interdependency between Olympism, consumer culture and advertising, for example, several issues must be considered. Prominent among these include the nature of commodified sport, and the concomitant local/global politics of cultural representation, and identity formation. Issues of class, gender, ethnicity and nationhood are but some of the identity politics that are at stake when expressed through and at such mega-events (Bourdieu, 1999; Bairner, 2001; Blain, Boyle and O'Donnell, 1993; Boyle and Haynes, 2000; Dauncey and Hare, 1999). Such identity politics are contoured and shaped within the context of consumerism, advertising and marketing (Jackson and Andrews, 1999).

The International Olympic Committee (IOC) purport to promote, globally, a message of internationalism, cosmopolitanism, environmentalism and 'fair-play' (Cashman and Hughes, 1998; IOC [online], 2005). To achieve this, IOC officials defend their involvement with commercial interests on pragmatic grounds. Without such commercial support, officials argue, their movement would not achieve its goals of disseminating the ideals of Olympism (Bale and Christensen, 2004; Kidd, 1984). In adopting this strategy in the 1980s, however, this 'message' became embedded in a broader process of commerce (Jhally, 1989). That is, the media/marketing/advertising/corporate nexus is concerned less with the IOC message, and more with building markets, constructing brand awareness and creating local/globalised consumers/identities (Gruneau and Whitson, 2001; Rowe, 1999; Slater, 1998; Wenner, 1998).

In examining the media and media–sport more broadly, consideration of the interweaving of cultural, economic and political dimensions is required. The meanings associated with the Olympics are shaped by general economic dynamics and the wider structures they sustain (VanWynsberghe and Ritchie, 1998). Attention has to be given to the marketing and advertising synergies and the consequences of this consumption process for the control of cultural production and, more specifically, how local/global identity politics are played out in the context of the Olympics (Alt, 1983; Dunn, 1986; Wamsley and Heine, 1996; Wilson, 1997, 1999). The political economy underpinning the Olympics has also played a large part in the global expansion of the games over the past 30 years (Gruneau and Cantelon, 1988; Lenskyl, 2000; Real, 1996). Whilst Olympic officials claim that media globalisation helps to spread aspects of Olympism, the question still remains as to whether using the commercial and media networks of big business compromises the stated ideology of the Olympic Movement. In the case study that follows, which examines the Beijing bid for the 2008 Olympic Games, these issues are writ large. In trying to achieve its aim of internationalism, the IOC is dependent on the media as a means of spreading the Olympic message, and is enmeshed in a wider political economy that funds the growth of the Games (Rowe, 1999). The connection with the media–sport complex is through three mechanisms: sponsorship, advertising and product placement (Shank, 1999; Westerbeek and Smith, 2003).

Of equal importance is the role of corporate branding in Olympic coverage. Naomi Klein urges us to 'think of the brand as the core meaning of the modern corporation' (Klein, 2000, p. 5). Advertising is seen as the means by which the brand meaning is conveyed to the world. An examination of branding then looks at not only advertisements, but at any means by which the brand penetrates society, or the individual's psyche. This may include the placement of logos on bodies (through equipment, uniforms, clothes or tattoos); the use of hoardings in arenas, stadia, and billboards in public spaces; and advertisements on television, the radio, the internet and in the press. These are but a few examples, and marketing firms are constantly finding new ways to penetrate the consumer consciousness. The aim of branding in general, and Olympic branding is no exception, is for the company or product to accumulate symbolic meaning through various associations, which serve to differentiate the brand from competitors who are essentially providing very similar products or services (Leiss, Kline and Jhally, 1997).

Synergies are created between brand identity, the corporation and the media, which eventually serve to impact upon consumer spending habits (Shank, 1999). Corporate branding, and the ideology that goes with it, become naturalised in Olympic coverage, to the extent that a point has been reached where Olympic sport and commercialism are almost synonymous (Bale and Christensen, 2004; Gruneau, 1989; Slater, 1998; Roche, 2000). The interests of TNC and television networks overlap and advertising revenue is the chief means by which media companies, such as NBC, are able to profit from Olympic coverage.

Considered in the light of the evidence outlined, several key points can be made with regard to the connections between the Olympics, the media–sport complex and globalisation. First, the re-emergence of the modern Olympics and its subsequent diffusion worldwide is bound up in the more recent phases of globalisation processes. Second, the re-birth of the modern Olympics in 1896 must be located the third phase of sportisation processes (Maguire, 2004) and the more general 'take-off' phase of globalisation. Third, the diffusion of the Olympic ideology, movement and games during the twentieth century both reflects and has reinforced the broader fourth and fifth sportisation phases. Fourth, Olympism, the Olympic movement and the Games themselves are contoured and shaped by wider global flows of people, finance, media images, ideologies and technologies. Fifth, the Olympic movement in general, and the IOC in particular, can be seen as symptomatic of the emergence during the twentieth century of transnational movements. The IOC is a transnational organisation – its ideology purports to be internationalist and have global appeal and relevance. Sixth, the Olympic movement, Olympism and the Games have, as part of broader sportisation and globalisation processes, reflected Western values, ideologies and corporate activities – and, as such, have led to greater homogeneity (see Chapter 8). Its competitive structure has been standardised globally and accepted universally – the Games, summer and winter, are global media events that cut across cultures and as such can be said to form a 'global idiom'. Yet and seemingly paradoxically, this movement has led to new varieties of meanings and activities associated with the experience of global sport. Seventh, those involved in Olympism and the Olympic movement will have to trace and understand more fully the linkages between sportisation and globalisation if they seek to maintain and cherish those ideals that are worth preserving in the new millennium (see Introduction).

The academy has to consider critically, in an educationally based manner, the promise and potential of Olympism for humankind. In surrendering that role to multinational corporations – who use Olympic themes as part of their marketing strategies – the academy appears to abandon this mission. The task of educators in contributing to the values underpinning aspects of Olympism is made easier when they articulate the wishes and ideals of a democratic elected and transparent decision-making movement. Let me now turn to a specific case study that highlights some of the general issues that have been outlined.

US media and political reaction to the Beijing bid for the 2008 Olympic Games

The decision to award the 2008 Olympic games was made by the IOC in Moscow, in July 2001. Of the 119 IOC members, 105 were eligible to vote – 14 members were excluded because they were from the candidate countries. The decision was taken under the revised bidding procedure, where only members of a technical committee visited the prospective host cities. In the wake of the Salt Lake City scandal, it was this committee which ruled on the technical merits of each bid – yet no recommendation would be offered. Despite the IOC having launched its Campaign for Humanity programme, claiming that Olympism has a positive role to play in furthering international understanding and that the award of the games to a specific city should also reflect the goal of 'universality', issues of human rights were *not* part of the brief of the technical committee. The committee was concerned with whether bid cities could organise and administer a 'viable' games. This brief was, in fact, compatible with how IOC delegates viewed the Olympic movement. At the Moscow meeting IOC delegates, such as the soon to-be-elected President, Jacques Rogge, noted that the Olympics are not about politics, yet, at the same time, also felt able to claim that the award of the games to any one city would 'help change'.

In the build-up to the Moscow meeting several elements stood out. The US spyplane incident had not only threatened Sino-American relations and raised a series of geopolitical issues; there had, as noted, also been speculation that the Americans would seek revenge for the prolonged stalemate by blocking China's entry into the WTO and/or Beijing's bid for the 2008 games (see Harding, 2001; Li, 2000 for further discussion of US–China relations; Brownell, 2004; Mangan and Hong, 2003; and Wasserstrom, 2002 for further discussion of China, Asia and the Olympics). In the event, the Bush administration chose not to do so. US national security adviser Condoleezza Rice called the selection of host city 'an IOC decision' (*Washington Post*, 14 July 2001). Highlighting this issue, a report in the the *Houston Chronicle* (13 July 2001) observed:

> The Bush administration backed away from opposing China's 2008 Olympic bid in hopes that the ensuing international spotlight would force Beijing to curb human rights abuses and halt threats to Taiwan, officials said … The Bush foreign policy team, after much internal debate, decided to stay on the sidelines rather than opposing Beijing's bid for the Games, officials said. 'This came up back during the EP-3 incident, and it has always been seen as a decision for the International Olympic Committee to make,' said an administration official.

At first sight, then, the decision by the Bush administration not to actively intervene appeared puzzling. Clearly, the right-wing US administration were suspicious of the Chinese – President Bush himself having declared that China was a 'strategic competitor' (*USA Today*, 16 July 2001). The spy-plane incident had not helped to dispel these sentiments. Furthermore, there had been moves in the US Congress, and in the European Parliament, for there to be votes taken against the award of the games to China. Both Republicans and Democrats in Congress urged the administration to oppose China's bid. Tom Lantos, ranking Democrat on the House International Relations Committee, was reputed to have observed, after a failed attempt to get Congress to vote against Beijing's bid:

> We only need to look at the 1936 Olympics in Berlin to see how authoritarian governments use the Games to strengthen their hand. If Beijing receives the Olympics this Friday, they will put on a dazzling show designed to fool other countries into believing China is a model world citizen, just as the Nazis did in 1936.

> (*Houston Chronicle*, 13 July 2001)

While such moves proved unsuccessful in the US Congress, the European Parliament did vote against giving the games to Beijing. The Bush administration was also under pressure from groups across the political spectrum. Amnesty International were vocal in their criticism and used the media to highlight human rights abuses. Such criticism also found expression in statements issued by the Heritage Institute, a right-wing, conservative think tank located in Washington, DC, and known for their support of the Bush Presidency. Julian Weiss, one of the Heritage Institute's analysts, observed that if China won the games 'the Olympics will be used very effectively for the nationalistic, xenophobic campaign already under way by the government' (*Houston Chronicle*, 13 July 2001). Views of this kind were also supported by another US pressure group, the Family Research Council (FRC). Bob Maginnis, FRC's Vice-President of policy observed that:

> the spirit of the Olympic games is that of freedom, goodwill, co-operation and high ideals among the nations of the world ... Allowing Beijing to host the games sends the message there is no price for a very serious record of human rights abuses.

> (PR Newswire, 13 July 2001)

It may well be that the Bush administration adopted a pragmatic or geopolitical realist view. Officials may have felt that they had insufficient clout to influence the IOC decision. In addition, US strategic interests in Taiwan may well have outweighed any concerns or criticisms of China's human rights record. Furthermore, US big business had already made it clear to the government that a Beijing Olympics would prove a very attractive proposition. US companies like General Motors and Xerox had been involved in underwriting Beijing's bid and, as a report in the *Atlanta Journal and Constitution* (14 July 2001) concluded:

Let the marketing games begin! With Beijing now cemented as the site for the 2008 Olympics, huge corporate sponsors like Coke and McDonald's can prepare to reach deeper into China's vast market. For Coca-Cola, it offers a chance to boost its image and, perhaps, its sales. Coke's per capita consumption is eight servings per year in China, the lowest total in any major region of the world that Coke serves … 'There's a tremendous amount of room for growth,' said Coke spokesman Rob Baskin. 'The Olympics provide a nice marketing platform for us.'

These economic and political elements, combined with a realistic assessment of the likely outcome of the vote, may well have persuaded the Bush team to remain neutral. Input from the United States Olympic Committee (USOC) may well have also proved influential. Several American cities were in the process of seeking the nomination of the USOC to bid for the 2012 games. Toronto's loss would prove advantageous to aspiring rival American cities. Indeed, after the vote was announced, such sentiments were expressed by leading USOC officials. Here, then, politics and sport and sporting politics interweave.

The criticisms that had been levelled at the Beijing bid prior to the IOC meeting were matched by demonstrations in Moscow organised by Amnesty International and supporters of the deposed Tibetan leader, the Dalai Lama. These demonstrations, occurring during the congress deliberations, were broken up by Russian police. There were five cities bidding to host the games: Beijing, Toronto, Paris, Istanbul and Osaka. The IOC technical committee had described the first three cities' bids as excellent, but had found flaws with Istanbul and Osaka. During the presentation the Chinese delegation fielded at least twice as many questions as their rivals.

With the revised IOC structure in place, the voting congress included, for the first time, 15 athletes, including the Norwegian speed-skater and Olympic champion, Johan Olav Koss. Yet, the *Atlanta Journal* (14 July 2001) reported 'IOC delegates asked about pollution in the Chinese capital, traffic and infrastructure concerns – 60% of the Olympic event sites remain to be built [but] no IOC delegate asked about China's human rights record'. In the first round of votes Osaka was eliminated. In the second round, Beijing with 55 votes exceeded the 53 votes needed to win the nomination – Toronto received 22, Paris 18 and Istanbul 9.

Several themes emerge in the reaction of the six main stakeholders involved with the IOC decision. Chinese official delight with the result was matched by scenes of euphoria in Beijing. Having hired a top Western public relations firm, Chinese officials, such as Beijing's mayor, Liu Qi, were astute enough to stay 'on message'. Commenting on the vote, he observed that the games will:

Help promote economic and social progress, and it will also benefit the further development of our human rights course. It will promote an exchange of the great Chinese culture with other cultures. It will mark a major step forward in the spread of Olympic ideals

(*Denver Post*, 15 July 2001)

Sentiments of this kind had also been used during the Beijing bid presentation. Zhen Liang, a member of the IOC executive board, had argued before the assembled council:

> The Olympic values are universal, and the Olympic flame lights the way of progress for all humanity. I, as well as my countrymen [sic], dream of having the eternal beauty of the Olympics come to our homeland. The message you give today may signal the beginning of a new era of global understanding.
>
> (*Denver Post*, 15 July 2001)

Chinese officials not only showed a sophisticated grasp of Olympic ideology, but also sought to take the sting out of Western criticisms of the IOC decision. At his embassy party to celebrate the victory, the Chinese Minister of Sport proclaimed that: 'I can assure you China is going in the right direction with human rights. There will be improvements' (*Wall Street Journal*, 16 July 2001). While observations of this kind could thus be interpreted as part of the ongoing public relations campaign – with the Western media noting that some sport stadia had been used during the past year for public executions – Chinese reactions also highlighted the significance of the result for their country's standing in the new global order.

Focusing on slogans that had covered Beijing such as: 'The Giant is Rising!', the *Boston Globe* (14 July 2001) gave prominence to the views that echoed the official position. One Beijing worker was reported to have argued 'Now China can stand up in the world'. The *Washington Post* (14 July 2001) reported similar claims. Citing another worker, the newspaper noted 'this means people around the world will stop bullying China for a while'.

The IOC's attempts to justify the decision highlighted the contradictions that lie at the core of the Olympic movement, its stated ideology and the rationale of allocating the games to a specific city and, more fundamentally, spreading Olympism across the globe. Francois Carrard, Executive Director of the IOC, claimed in the *New York Times* (14 July 2001):

> We are totally aware at the I.O.C. that there is an issue on the table and that issue is human rights. It is not for the I.O.C. to interfere, but this is a bet that in the coming seven years up to the 2008 Olympic Games, the interaction, the progress and the development in many areas can be such that the situation in China can be improved.

Carrard was not alone in maintaining the long-standing IOC view that the Olympics was not about politics. After his election as IOC President, Jacques Rogge argued:

> It is not the role of the co-ordination commission to do whatever monitoring. The role of the co-ordination commission is to take care of sport and to prepare the best possible Olympic Games with the organizing committee ... The IOC is not a political body. It is a sports organization, so we will not get

involved in politics. The IOC is of course in favor of the best possible situation of human rights in all countries in the world ... Having influence on human rights is the task of political organizations and human-rights organizations. It is not the task of the International Olympic Committee to get involved in monitoring or lobbying or influencing.

(*Wall Street Journal*, 28 August 2001)

Observations of this kind demonstrate the difficulties that officials of the Olympic movement face in making the case for universalism yet denying that they should consider the issue of human rights in awarding the games to specific cities and nation-states. While purporting to be apolitical, yet aspiring to promote Olympic ideals, IOC officials also claim that the movement builds international goodwill. This contradiction was further demonstrated in comments made by two of Rogge's rivals for the IOC presidency. Richard Pound, IOC member from Canada, argued that the new president would 'have to insist that these commitments [to human rights] are honoured' (*Wall Street Journal*, 28 July 2001) and that the hosting of the games 'can be seen as presenting the chance to be an agent for change' (*Houston Chronicle*, 15 July 2001). Other senior IOC officials were more concerned with how the decision affected their movement. Kevan Gosper, IOC representative from Australia, focused on the issue of Olympism, and thought that the decision to award the games to Beijing 'was very, very good for the Olympic movement' (*Denver Post*, 15 July 2001).

Reactions of this kind – from the IOC and the winning city – are perhaps not surprising. Nevertheless, they stand out in sharp contrast to the other key groups involved in the cultural politics surrounding Beijing's award of the games. Here, I want to focus on the transnational human rights groups, the American political elite, and, selected American media outlets. Significantly, criticism of the specific decision, and the IOC and Olympism more broadly, was common *across* the political spectrum.

Transnational groups such as Amnesty International and Human Rights Watch had already been linking the debate about the award of the games with questions of human rights. Though unsuccessful in their attempt to foil Beijing's bid, these groups swiftly used the media to ensure that the Chinese would be held accountable. Sydney Jones, Asia director of Human Rights Watch commented: 'If abuses take place as preparations for the Games proceed, it won't be just the Chinese authorities who will look bad. The IOC and the corporate sponsors will be complicit' (*USA Today*, 16 July 2001). In a similar vein, Amnesty International observed: 'For every day of the next seven years the Chinese authorities will have to demonstrate that they deserve [the Games]' (*Houston Chronicle*, 14 July 2001) and the International Committee for lawyers for Tibet recorded that they were 'appalled' at the decision (*San Francisco Chronicle*, 14 July 2001).

Criticisms of this kind also found expression among hardline Republicans and Liberal Democrats. Tom Lantos had, as noted, proposed a congressional measure in March 2001 calling on the IOC to not award the Olympics to Beijing. Lantos was forthright in his criticism, arguing that: 'This decision will allow the Chinese police state to bask in the reflected glory of the Olympic Games despite having one of the most abominable human rights records in the world' (*Washington Post*, 14 July 2001). He was not alone in these criticisms. Right-wing hawks, such as Jessie Helms, castigated the IOC for rewarding a government that 'arbitrarily imprisons, tortures, murders, and harvests the organs of its own people' (*Wall Street Journal*, 16 July 2001). A more wide-ranging critique was offered by a Democrat representative from San Francisco, a city with a large Chinese population. Nancy Pelosi linked her criticism of the IOC with 'corporate business'. She observed that: 'It is incumbent on the IOC and the Games corporate sponsors to demand that the Chinese government respect these basic freedoms at the time of the Olympics and the years leading up to 2008' (*San Francisco Chronicle*, 14 July 2001).

Despite criticisms of this nature, the Bush administration maintained its politically neutral stance. Contrary to the evidence outlined, Ari Fleischer, spokesman for the White House, tried to maintain the line that sport and politics are separate issues, yet inadvertently confirmed the linkage. Fleischer noted that: 'The President believes that the Olympics are a sporting event, not a political event. But having said that, this now is an opportunity for China to showcase itself as a modern nation' (*Houston Chronicle*, 14 July 2001).

In addition to current politicians, the media sought out the views of the elder statesmen of America. Henry Kissinger, formerly secretary of state in the Nixon Presidency, and currently an auxiliary member of the IOC, struck a more supportive tone when he observed:

> I think this is a very important step in the evolution of China's relation with the world. I think it will have a major impact in China, and on the whole, a positive impact, in the sense of giving them a high incentive for moderate conduct both internationally and domestically in the years ahead.
>
> (*New York Times*, 14 July 2001)

In contrast to this assessment, Zbigniew Brzezinski, formerly national security adviser in the Carter administration, posed a more long-term evaluation. In an article entitled 'Can Communism Compete with the Olympics?', Brzezinski commented: 'The Olympics in Beijing may be a triumph for China, but by intensifying the pressures for change the games are quite unlikely to be a triumph for China's waning Communism. In fact, the Games may accelerate its fading' (*New York Times*, 14 July 2001). Perhaps echoing the ambivalent nature of Beijing's success, current secretary of state Colin Powell observed that the 2008 games would put Beijing under 'seven years of supervision' and noted, somewhat dryly: 'I hope they know what they got' (*USA Today*, 17 July 2001).

It is clear, then, that such observations highlight how deeply political the decision to award the games to Beijing actually was. Most US political criticism was levelled at the Chinese and the actual decision to award the games to Beijing. In examining editorial commentary in US newspapers, however, a more fundamental critique of the IOC was evident. Take, for example, this leading article in the *Atlanta Journal and Constitution* (14 July 2001):

> The Olympics do not change the world. The Olympics merely reflect it. The Olympics are a collision of political force and venal interest, pretty much like everyday life in every corner of the globe. The modern Olympics began as a noble concept and have become an engine of international commerce overseen by the former deputy of a Fascist dictator. Tons of nobility in that ... His excellency Samaranch wanted the 2008 Games in Beijing, and that's where they'll be ... The Olympics are a noble concept overwhelmed by reality. Prospective hosts roll out the bribes. IOC members hold out both hands. Nations hit one another over the head with the splendor of their athletes and the glory of their nationhood. Athletes drug themselves in the effort to snatch glory. Terrorists intrude on the quadrennial spectacle of sport just to prove that terror observes no moratorium.

Similar views were expressed in the *Washington Post* where a report linked Beijing's success to the political economy that underpins the Olympic movement. This is what the reporter had to say:

> The awarding of the Olympics to Beijing by the IOC has an unintended consequence: It begs an inquiry into the very meaning and existence of the Games. The Olympics have long been a matter of politics and commerce in skimpy garb. World peace is only partly what the IOC, which the bribery scandals of the last few years have revealed as a profiteering, junketeering cartel, actually had in mind by awarding the Games to Beijing. What the IOC had in mind, actually, was that China is the location of one-fifth of the world's population and an enormous new cash register.

The report went on to raise the whole question of the meaning and future of the games and argued:

> The so-called Olympic movement has been fraying at the edges for a long time – it was created by a Euro-colonial aristocracy in decay, trying to hang on to romantic values of amateurism, and it has now been hyped into a combination festival of world peace and advertising extravaganza. The editors of the New Republic go so far as to label the Olympics a 'moral farce', and to call for their abolishment because they do not distinguish between democracies and dictatorships and 'reward the latter'.
>
> (*Washington Post*, 14 July 2001)

An ongoing theme, then, in press reporting concerned the meaning of the games, and the extent to which issues of political economy had undermined the movement, or more radically, whether such processes were indicative of an inherent contradiction within the practice of the concept of Olympism. In an article entitled 'Corporations Ignore Beijing's Tarnish in the Hunt for Gold', the *St. Louis Post* (19 July 2001) emphasised how corporate interests undermined IOC rhetoric regarding the Games as building peace and international goodwill:

> Every now and then, there is a beautiful scene, a stirring triumph or a wonderful story to give the Olympics a warm glow. These moments are genuine, if rare, and they make us tingle. Sponsors are willing to pay a large fortune to be associated with these feel-good dramas. And it's all about marketing now. Buying, selling and brand recognition. In that sense the athletes are props, used to create the commercial appeal. If they are clean and free of banned performance-enhancing drugs, that's even better. The 2008 Summer Olympics will be held in Beijing for a predominant reason: There are 1.26 billion potential customers in China. The Chinese government supervises an economy of $1.1 trillion, the second-largest in the world.

Several features stand out in the US media reaction to the awarding of the 2008 Games to Beijing:

1   An overwhelmingly negative reaction can be observed.
2   Editorials consistently argued that the Games should not be awarded to Beijing.
3   Columnists observed that, at best, the award should be used to cast a critical light on the communist regime over the ensuing seven years.
4   Reporters were equally critical of the IOC – seeing the decision as reflecting the interests of global capitalism, and highlighting the need for further reform.
5   Commentators were also keen to highlight how the decision both legitimised the Chinese government and signalled China's arrival on the global stage.
6   Journalists also noted that while the 2008 Beijing Games would consolidate the IOC goal of 'universality', the award also highlighted the contradictions that lie at the heart of Olympism and the still opaque criteria by which the games were awarded.

US media reporting tended, then, to emphasise several themes regarding the Beijing Games: one, that no beneficial effect in terms of human relations would occur; two, that the communist party would be internally 'validated'; three, that China would be legitimised as a global player on the geopolitical world stage; four, that corporate capitalism had further co-opted Olympic values; and five, that the whole purpose of the Olympic movement was thus called into question. What is also clear is that this intense media and political debate will not subside. An editorial in the *Atlanta Constitution* (16 July 2001) signalled how this debate might be sustained, and, indeed, gather momentum as we approach 2008:

Now that Beijing has been handed the honor of hosting the Games, the International Olympic Committee ought to make clear that its government has special obligations. So should the corporate sponsors who take advantage of the Games' popularity to advertise their products – Xerox, Coca-Cola and McDonald's among them. At every step of the way, private executives and public officials ought to be pressing the Chinese government not only to give visitors basic freedoms but also to extend those same freedoms to Chinese citizens. The relationship between the West and China must be a delicate balance of diplomacy, engagement and criticism of its repression. The awarding of the Games to Beijing was a major step forward in diplomacy and engagement. Now it is time to step up U.S. criticism of China's repression.

Conclusion

Clearly, the ongoing debate surrounding the Beijing Olympic Games is worthy of further sociological enquiry. What is evident, even at this stage, is that the awarding of the 2008 Olympic Games to Beijing provides a powerful case study of the interconnections between Olympism, global sport and geopolitics more generally. Let me try to place this in some historical context. Writing in the *Revue Olympique* in May 1913, Pierre de Coubertin speculated on the development of an Olympiad in the Far East. Arguing that he was witnessing the 'beginnings of exotic athleticism', he continued:

> For us, who are merely chroniclers of the event, there is nothing in this business that can disturb or surprise us. We have always believed that athletics would soon reach all parts of the Far East. We are convinced that sports will play a capital, decisive role there. We would be willing to bet that in twenty years, athletic associations will abound in the region. The 'yellow men' seem to us to be admirably prepared to benefit from the athletic crusade that is taking shape. They are ready individually and collectively. They are ready individually because endurance, tenacity, patience, racial flexibility, the habit of self-mastery, of keeping silent, and of hiding pain and effort have shaped their bodies most effectively. They are ready collectively, because their young imperialism, which has not yet had its fill of domination, will impel them to taste the flesh joys of athletic victories, as well as the honor this brings to their national flags.
>
> (Cited in de Coubertin, 2000, pp. 696–697)

It was not until 1964 that Japan became the first Asian country to host the summer Olympic Games. However, Tokyo was scheduled to host the Olympics as early as 1940. In addition, South Korea held the Games in 1988. Each had significance in terms of East–West relations. Yet, it may well be that the Beijing Games may signal something even more significant – namely what Johann Huizinga, in a different context, called the 'waning of the west'. New varieties of power balances may emerge in which the West is no longer dominant. On the other hand, irrespective of how successful the Games may prove, both on and off the field of play, the Chinese will be playing on Western terms – be they sporting rules or human rights. The contrasts between nations are thus reduced by such athletic contests and the global marketing of brands. Pierre de Coubertin was seemingly well aware of the cultural struggles that were at stake when he wrote, in 1931, on this issue of athletic colonisation:

> If one wishes to extend to natives in colonized countries what we will boldly call the benefits of 'athletic civilization', they must be made to enter into the broad athletic system with codified regulations and comparative results, which is the necessary basis of that civilization. More than one colonizing country balks at this decisive step. Yet we are going to have to reach a decision, or the natives will end up organizing on their own. After all, perhaps they would not be any the worse off that way, but perhaps so for those who direct them.
>
> (Cited in de Coubertin, 2000, p. 704)

The 2008 Beijing Olympics may then be interpreted in two possible ways: as symptomatic of the relative rise of the East, and the concomitant waning of the West; or the triumph of global Western capitalism and its civilisational tradition. Perhaps it is a blend of both. While it is also too early to reach a conclusion with regard to the Beijing Olympics, it is clear from the evidence so far accumulated that a range of geopolitical and civilisational struggles are already at work.

8 The sports–industrial complex

Sports sciences, social development and images of humankind

Joseph Maguire

Using sport to search for the hero inside of us appears to be part of the quest for exciting significance (Maguire *et al.* 2002). In this chapter, however, I seek to highlight two questions posed by Hoberman (1988, p. 325): 'Why has the world chosen as its predominant physical culture competitive sport rather than expressional dance?'; and 'What makes the modern body an efficiently performing body rather than a different sort of body?' An answer to the first question can be gained from tracing the emergence and diffusion of global sport (Maguire, 1999) and, in this connection, several key processes highlight how this 'choice' of competitive sport was highly structured (Maguire *et al.* 2002). Unless this choice is challenged, body cultures will remain locked in the iron cage of modern achievement sport. As to the second question, an examination of what I term the sports–industrial complex reveals the emergence and implications of the efficient body as the predominant corporeal form. Whatever merit this sportive culture has, it has come at the cost of a loss of other body cultures and a marginalisation of alternative views of physical education and sports science (Crum, 1999).

This chapter challenges aspects of the sports–industrial complex and, in so doing, provides an opportunity to consider 'human development' as an alternative way of viewing this subject area. The main line of argument being proposed is that the pursuit of performance efficiency in achievement sport is damaging in specific anthropological, natural scientific, and sociological respects to individuals, sport, sports sciences, and to humanity as a whole (Heinilä, 1984/1998; Hoberman, 1988, 1992; Ingham, 1997; Ingham and Lawson, 1999; Ingham, Chase and Butt, 2002; Sage, 1993). While it is important to describe what might be called this current malaise, it is also important to plot an alternative route, based on a map that emphasises human development. For reasons to do with fundamental science, involved advocacy and committed service, and in a period of intensified globalisation, it is necessary to reconfigure the nature and scope of sports science. However, just as the military–industrial complex dominates aspects of broader global processes, advocates of the sports–industrial complex may well seek to thwart such alternative possibilities. As a result, the role of academics will be confined to the production of world and Olympic medals – sports scientists will be the technicians, and athletes the cogs, in the machine (Brohm, 1978; Heinilä, 1984/1998; Hoberman, 1992). If we cannot think beyond the present state of play, then the totalising process in international sport to which Heinilä directed our attention will have enveloped us. This chapter, then, is an intervention, an attempt to provide an alternative view of sports science and future sport worlds (Maguire *et al.* 2002).

The global state of play – performance efficiency and the quest for success

As sports science research emerged out of the shadow of physical education, in the guise of exercise physiology, biomechanics and sport psychology, it was increasingly funded and developed by the state and sport organisations. Being tied so closely to these agencies, sports science research has tended to reflect the demands of competitive sport – the achievement of records, and 'winning' outcomes (see also Voy, 1991). This should not surprise us. As Alvin Gouldner noted in his discussion of the connections between ideology and technology:

> The rational-scientific elements of the bureaucratic organisation remain encased within and limited by nonrational, nonscientific political and economic interests. Scientific and technological expertise thus rationalize and legitimate only the means used to achieve the organisational goals given, but *not the goals* [original italics] themselves ... Even within the most modern bureaucratized state apparatus, science and technology thus operate within the limits set by ideology and interest.
>
> (1976, p. 241)

That the sports science – industrial complex operates in this fashion is only too evident. Tracing sportisation processes over time, it can be observed from one society to the next that in the development of sports science, research into human well-being, the quality of the sport experience and aesthetic values have been squeezed out. Other features of this subculture are closely connected to this achievement striving, rationalisation and scientisation. Such features are themselves embedded in wider processes (Elias, 1995). Over time, sportisation processes have been marked by a high degree of specialisation. Sports performers have come increasingly to participate in only one sport and, within that sport, they specialise according to task or positional requirements. The demands of elite-level achievement sport have become so great that professionalisation processes have also been a recurring feature, as one sport after another, in different societies, in different time periods, moves in the direction described (Ingham & Lawson, 1999; Maguire, 1999).

Different disciplines have become established features of, or outsiders in, the development of sports science. Biomechanics, exercise physiology and sport psychology remain part of the established group within this sub-discipline. The sociology of sport has been at the margins since the development of sports science or kinesiology. In one sense, this was deliberate – on the part of sociologists, but also on that of the natural scientists. In the shift from physical education, the quest for respectability lay in adhering to a specific view of science, 'Popperian' rigour and statistical accuracy. The wearing of a lab-coat is part of the cloak of respectability. In this way, sports medicine advocates and sports scientists would be more likely to be accepted by more established scientists in the academy, or so they hoped (Elias, 1971, 1974). This is a process not uncommon in the academy more generally whereby scientific establishments wax, and sometimes wane, in power and influence (Elias, 1982, 1987b). The philosophy of sport and the history of physical education are prime examples of areas that have been actively marginalised in the development of this subject area.

What counts in sports science also relates to what matters in terms of the 'sports ethic' – this not only reinforces the marginalisation of the social sciences, but also ensures that sports science does not fulfil its potential as an academic subject. This issue will be returned to in outlining an alternative agenda for the subject area (see also Ingham, Chase and Butt, 2002). The sports ethic is not an abstract set of principles dreamt up by armchair philosophers. The sports ethic reflects the actual practice of sport. Also, the practices of sports science teaching and research are embedded in these assumptions. Four key features of the sports ethic can be identified. These include: a willingness to make sacrifices; a striving for distinction; an acceptance of risk and the possibility/probability of participating while enduring pain; and a tacit acceptance that there is no limit to the pursuit of the ultimate performance (Coakley, 2003). The practice of this sports ethic is learnt early on and becomes normalised and taken for granted – it is part of the habitus of the performer and the agenda of the researcher.

Sociologists have documented the logical consequences of this sports ethic – cheating, drug abuse, disorderly eating and psycho-doping (Coakley, 2003). The debate on drugs and sport indicates that the binary dichotomies between what counts as natural and synthetic, diet supplementation and drug-taking, and restorative and enhancing treatments, are difficult to maintain (Waddington, 2000). Academics, and more recently some sports officials, have realised that the next frontier in achievement sport is genetic engineering. The World Anti-Doping Agency (WADA) now pronounces not only on drugs, but also on gene transfer. News that Australian scientists had 'discovered' a gene variant linked to athletic performance prompted the then Chairman of UK Sport, Sir Rodney Walker, to observe:

Whilst it is *inevitable* [italics added] that science will eventually identify and isolate genes that can enhance performance levels, whether we should actually begin to screen young people for talent at an early stage is an entirely different matter … To this end, although this research has identified genes that would seem to affect two elements that go into creating the ultimate sportsman or woman, screening would only ever give an indication, albeit a potentially valuable one, as to their athletic promise.

(www.uksport.gov.uk, 8 September 2003)

While rightly reacting with caution, what is striking is Walker's acceptance that biomedical factors on their own are what account for sports performance. Although he also acknowledges the role of psychological factors, the social roots of performance are overlooked. Such sentiments are not uncommon. Take, for example, the recent observations made in *Sport Supplement*, an internet publication by the United States Sports Academy:

> One can see that physical training for sport-performance today, has become very scientific. Coaches and athletes must have a thorough understanding of human movement, the biomechanics and the physiology involved and how these scientific concepts and factors apply specifically to sport-performance.
> (www.thesportjournal.org/sport-supplement, 8 October 2003)

The same set of social and scientific issues that arise in the context of drug use also emerge in considering gene transfer technology and sport performance. And what of eugenics and the production of the cyborg? British scientists are now playing with such an existence, with one Oxford scientist in 2002 even claiming to be a cyborg (*Guardian*, 22 March 2002). Implicit within the logic of the sports ethic, and in the Olympic motto of 'Faster, Higher, Stronger', is the idea that human beings *must* quest beyond their present state of imperfection. As Norway's Olympic gold medal speed skater Johann Olav Koss recently remarked: 'This is not only an issue for sport, it's a broad ethical issue for human beings'. Viewed in the light of Max Weber's concepts of rationalisation and vocations, athletes are compelled to strive for perfection: it is their *duty* (Weber, 1949). And, to succeed, athletes, their coaches and their sports science support teams must adhere to the performance efficiency model. This form of sporting body has also become a key figure in global conceptions of humankind (Maguire, 1999).

Such features of global sport are reinforced by and reflected in the assumptions and practices of the sports–industrial complex. This complex, or figuration, has several dimensions – structural, institutional, ideological and cultural. It is composed of several key groups, including state agencies, transnational corporations, non-governmental agencies and sport associations. The institutional framework of this complex involves at least four main elements: sports medicine, sports science, sports science support programmes and regional/national centres of excellence. The emergence of this complex – initially in those Western/developed nations less restricted by the legacy of a play and player-orientated amateur attitude to sporting success – should not surprise us. Having jettisoned this amateur tradition, the British have been keen to catch up. Under the Conservatives, but more especially New Labour, UK governments have embraced a 'modernisation' agenda – adopting a professional approach to talent identification, production and performance – with advocates of coaching science, sports science and sports medicine recruited to help deliver 'success'.

Developments of this kind – which are not dissimilar in form and sentiment to practices in the former German Democratic Republic – were predicted and encapsulated by Heinilä in what he termed his eighth, ninth and tenth theses on totalising sport (1984/1998). Thesis eight, the 'iron-law of totalisation', concludes that 'as a consequence of continuous upgrading of demands in international sport, competition totalises into a competition between "systems"' (Heinilä, 1984/1998, p. 128). States increasingly mobilise and utilise all relevant national resources in order to guarantee success in international competition. While this totalisation process varies considerably with regard to the strength and comprehensiveness of the system in different countries, thesis nine notes that the overall process aims at 'covering all kinds of resources which affect the productive capacity of the system' (Heinilä, 1984/1998, p. 129). Thus, as Heinilä in thesis ten observes: 'The more total the utilisation of relevant resources, the greater the probability of international success' (Heinilä, 1984/1998, p. 129). Heinilä recently returned to this theme when he observed in an interview in 2004, on the eve of the Olympic Games, 'With totalization, sport has lost its sine qua non – fair competition on equal terms' (Wuolio, 2004: p. 38).

The UK's approach to sports science and sports medicine provides a vivid example of how the logic underpinning the sports–industrial complex operates in practice. Given the observations made so far, consider the mission statement of state-funded UK Sport:

> UK Sport is the agency charged by the Government with providing support to high-performance sport at the UK level, with the aim of achieving sporting excellence on the world stage. The work of UK Sport is all about building a framework for success – developing and supporting a system capable of producing a constant flow of world class performers in a fair and ethical way. UK Sport takes the lead … in aspects requiring UK-wide strategic planning and administration, co-ordination or representation. Our focus is on performance, and providing a winning environment.
>
> (UK Sport, 2001, p. 3)

While the document makes clear that UK Sport seeks to pursue its mission in a 'fair and ethical way', this primarily relates to issues of anti-doping, and only limited attention is given to sporting conduct, equity and corporate governance. The logic at work is to 'ensure the most effective use of funding available from the Lottery' (UK Sport, Annual Report 2001, p. 14). As a result, UK Sport prioritises both between and within sports, and draws on and further funds the knowledge base of sports science and sports medicine. Their concern is with the 'co-ordination of the many strands of sports science and research to make sure that sports are receiving the most appropriate services' (UK Sport, 2001, p. 14). The system is thus aimed at producing 'effective systems and strategies … to help sports monitor and evaluate sports science and sports medicine' (UK Sport, 2001, p. 10).

UK Sport is explicit as to the logic that was at work in the funding of sports science support and sport associations prior to the Sydney Olympic Games:

Prioritisation criteria focused on: medal potential; evidence of a performance system that should continue to produce a high number of talented
athletes; track record; and the significance of the sport in the eyes of the
public. In terms of decision-making most attention was given to the criteria
relating to: medal potential (which hinges on whether the performance gap
to the podium is bridgeable); the number of World Class athletes; and the
number of medals targeted. Track record merely provided some confidence
in the level of risk in the investment.

(UK Sport, 2001, p. 7)

International sporting success in the late twentieth century thus involves a contest between systems located within a global figuration (Maguire, 1999). As can
be seen, sporting success is believed to depend on several elements: the availability and identification of human resources; methods of coaching and training; the
efficiency of particular sports organisations and the depth of knowledge of sports
medicine and sports sciences (Heinilä, 1984/1998). These national sports system
mechanisms are a necessary but not fully sufficient explanation of international
sport success. In addition to these elements, the development of a sport within a
particular society also depends on the status of that society in the international
rank order of specific sports. Less developed nations tend to under-utilise their talent and performers and/or lose them to more powerful nations in the global sports
figuration. Global sports figurations can thus lead to the under – or dependent –
development of a nation's talent. Kenyan athletics is a case in point (Bale and
Sang, 1996). In addition to the elements already identified, these global sports figurations are shaped and contoured by a range of global flows, particularly of
people, technology, capital, mediated images and ideologies (Maguire *et al.*, 2002).

Following the logic outlined above and keen to highlight the 'success' of state
investment in elite sport, UK Sport have also produced what they term a 'World
Sporting Index'. According to UK Sport this 'works by calculating performances by
the world's best athletes and teams in over 60 sports, over a four-year cycle' and thus
'can produce a basic guide to the world's best sporting nations' (UK Sport, 2001, p.
29). Of the top ten, all are industrial nations; all G8 countries are represented; eight
are Western and two are former state socialist/communist societies – here, sport and
military–industrial complexes interweave. Yet, officials of UK Sport do not appear
complacent. The 2001 report concludes with the words: 'Competition from developing countries is increasing and it will now be tough to stay one or two steps ahead'
(UK Sport, 2001, p. 11). Through further investment in the performance efficiency
model, UK officials hope to maintain or increase their sporting lead. Not surpris-
ingly, then, in the UK Sport Annual Review 2002/2003 *Countdown to Athens*
(2003), its Chief Executive, Richard Callicott, declared that: 'Our Lottery-funded
World Class Performance Programme continues to be unashamedly about the pursuit of success – targeting sports and individuals most likely to deliver medals at
major events' (UK Sport, 2003, p. 10). Its stated overall aim is even more stark: 'UK
Sport is committed to a goal: putting the UK among the world's top five sporting
nations by 2012' (UK Sport, 2003, p. 10).

But UK Sport is not alone in adopting the strategies that have been modelled on the practices of the Australian Institute for Sport. Involvement in international sport involves a 'double-bind' in which such practices *have* to be adopted – it is inherent in the logic of competing. Recently, UK Sport also signed 'co-operation agreements with two Olympic superpowers', China and Cuba – Sir Rodney Walker viewing the former as 'a superb example of a country that firmly believes in sport as a tool to enhance society' (UK Sport, 2003, p. 27). There is much irony in these agreements – given that China could be a source of alternative body cultures and that both it and Cuba represent an echo of the state socialist sport systems much derided by the West in the recent past (Brownell, 2004; Maguire, 2002).

Such strategies between so-called 'Olympic superpowers' reinforce the structure of the global sports–industrial complex. Its mechanisms of production, experience and consumption involve several elements: the identification and development of talent; its production on a global stage, in a single or multi-sport event; and its consumption by direct spectators or, through the media complex, by a global mass audience. The logic of elite sport is such that there has now developed a trade in elite athletes involving developed nations or those developing such as Qatar which seek to project a modern image on a global stage. IOC President Jacques Rogge recently commented on this: 'We should avoid this transfer market in athletes. We don't like athletes being lured by large incentives by other countries and giving them a passport when they arrive at the airport' (*Economist*, 14 August 2004, p. 31).

Despite such words, such strategies are built in to the competitive structures of global sport. Traced over time, there is a tendency towards the emergence of a global achievement sport monoculture in which administrators, coaches, sports scientists and teachers promote achievement sport values and ideologies, and competitions and tournaments are structured along highly commodified and rationalised lines. As a consequence of both their actual involvement in elite sport circles, and their quest for status, funding and academic/professional advancement, natural scientists appear unwilling or unable to exercise the degree of detachment which would enable them to understand the wider and longer-term consequences which follow from what they do.

With its over-emphasis on identifying the qualities necessary for winning, sports science is headed towards a technologised view of human beings (Ingham and Lawson, 1999). The dangers of this path were highlighted by Hoberman over a decade ago:

> Sport science does not physically hybridize humans and machines ... instead, sport science treats the human organism as though it were a machine, or as though it ought to be a machine. This technologized human organism comprises both mind and body, for which there are distinct sets of strategies. The implicit demand of these strategies ... is a streamlined and decomplexified image of the human being.
>
> (1988, p. 325)

Operating within this context, it is little surprise that sports scientists should gear their research and teaching towards a performance efficiency model. Exercise physiologists examine the most advantageous biological conditions necessary to train and compete effectively. Biomechanists trace the most rational way specific forces and angles can be utilised for the demands of competitive tasks. Sport psychologists – whether motor learning or cognitive based advocates – plot the optimal mental conditions and conditioning required to reach the performer's peak. As noted earlier, exponents of these disciplines have been joined by geneticists who seek to divide the human population into specific categories, and/or contribute to the early stages of the gene transfer revolution that is unfolding. And, as sports science has grown in depth and range, we now see match analysts, and nutrition and related sports medicine specialists plying their trades, and thereby reinforcing the performance efficiency model.

The rationale and funding underpinning such research ensures that attention is directed at identifying factors that: maximise the development of talent; generate efficient training regimes; contribute to rational performance systems; identify effective recuperation programmes; and highlight strategies that enable performers to cope with pain and injury experiences. Not only are these themes found in sports science journals and at conferences, such as the Pre-Olympic Scientific Congress and the conferences of the European College of Sport Science, but they also find expression in the postgraduate studentships available to a new generation of scholars.

Clearly, the global mono-culture of achievement sport is connected to the quest for success and, as is indicated by UK Sport's 'World Sporting Index', involves the international jockeying for sporting status. Yet another driving force is the dominant culture of science itself, which tends towards a positivist view of the world in which x produces y – a view of the world well suited to a sports science intent both on producing athletes via a rational process and generating their own professional, scientific legitimacy. Yet, science is not monolithic; new conceptions of scientific practice have emerged in the philosophy of science, and social science offers its own, alternative contribution (Maguire, 1991a).

Within sports science, some research does focus less on performance and more on health (Biddle, Fox and Boutcher, 2000; Hardman and Stensel, 2003). This is a welcome development and may signal the ongoing emancipation of this subject area. Indeed, it can be argued that there is nothing less than a cultural struggle at work within the 'natural sport sciences' as to whether further development of the area will take the path of health or performance studies. It should not be overlooked that there are colleagues in the natural sciences who have made this shift. It is also in their interests to challenge the impact of advocates of the sports–industrial complex. Furthermore, there are natural scientists who are concerned with the direction that colleagues within sports science have taken (Ingham and Lawson, 1999). As Alan Ingham has reminded me, some sport psychology colleagues in North America share this humanistic critique of the status quo. However, my aim here has been to highlight how performance efficiency themes have come to dominate the agenda of teaching, research and thus the commodification of the academy – such trends reflect and reinforce the values of the sports ethic, the priorities of funding agencies such as UK Sport, and the concerns of the sports–industrial complex more generally.

This emphasis on performance efficiency within achievement sport also tells us something about what it is to be a 'human'. With its emphasis on rational and efficient performance, specialisation, scientisation, competition and professionalisation, achievement sport reinforces the myth of the 'super*man*'. The existing tendency is to treat individual elite athletes as machines or as though they ought to be machines. Highly rationalised and technologised physical and mental training methods, and scientifically evaluated and scheduled fitness regimes, are designed to produce optimum performance. The ideology and findings of sports science, concerned with identifying the conditions necessary to produce the ultimate performance, sustain the superman myth.

Reconfiguring sports science: fundamental science, involved advocacy and committed service

In order to operationalise the performance efficiency model, a particular style of academic practice is required. The intellectual becomes a technocrat. This technocratic intellectual thinks and speaks in performance terms, and reflects the concerns of the sports–industrial complex. This type of logic was vividly captured in C. Wright-Mills' work *The Power Elite* (1959). Writing about the hierarchies of state, corporation and army (the military–industrial complex), Wright-Mills observed:

> The typical institutional unit has become enlarged, has become administrative, and, in the power of its decisions, has become centralised. Behind these developments there is a fabulous technology, for as institutions, they have incorporated this technology and guide it, even as it shapes and paces their developments.
>
> (Wright-Mills, 1959, p. 7)

We can clearly hear echoes of such themes in the development of sports science, sports science support programmes, and the establishment of centres of excellence. Sports science practice is guided and shaped by a technological discourse which focuses attention on talent identification, optimal training regimes, masking agents, goal-setting and attention styles. Yet, not all sports scientists embrace this focus; the humanistic intellectual still survives, barely, in the study of physical culture. The humanist tradition was once an integral part of physical education (PE) and found expression in areas such as history, philosophy and pedagogy; at its best, it was concerned with themes and issues such as morality, equity, participation, learning, co-operation and the intrinsic properties of play and games. Like folk body cultures, however, humanists, at least in the context of Sport and Exercise Science Departments, are in danger of becoming a residual form.

A reconfiguration of sports science would not only liberate the natural scientist from this technocratic model, but would also promote the mission of the humanistic intellectual in sports science, or whatever name this subject area is assigned. Despite the inevitable resistance of the 'power elite', this reconfiguration can, and must, be undertaken. Three areas in particular require new ways of thinking and doing sports science: 'fundamental science', 'involved advocacy' and 'committed service'. Each of these areas needs to be understood as part of an integrated whole – each mutually reinforcing and reflecting the strengths and emphases of the others. Such an approach would counter the continuing drift towards a restrictive 'scientisation of physical education discourses' (Whitson and Macintosh, 1990) and the consolidation of 'technocratic physical education' (McKay *et al.*, 1993). The alternative proposed here is underpinned by a belief that science is not irretrievably flawed – it still has the potential to be a mode of enlightenment and emancipation – but that left in the hands of the power elite of the sports–industrial complex, this potential will be diminished. Moves away from this model have been taken and some of the thoughts expressed here have found echoes in the position statements of associations such as the International Council for Sports Science and Physical Education (ICSSPE, 2003). Yet the evidence from the everyday practice in our universities, and elsewhere, indicates that the case still needs to be made.

Fundamental science

As I noted earlier, the practice of sports science, in terms of teaching, research and knowledge dissemination, is closely linked to, and dominated by, the sports–industrial complex – many sports scientists are too involved and unable to exercise a sufficient degree of detachment to recognise this and grasp the consequences (Elias, 1987b). The language of the sports ethic permeates the mode of communication of its practitioners. It is not only social scientists who regard this as troublesome. Plagued by the short-term nature of applied projects, some natural scientists also want to get on with 'fundamental' research. This is a matter of both intellectual freedom and the production of more emancipatory knowledge – knowledge that would contribute to a reorientation of the human sciences and which could potentially benefit humanity as a whole. The study of health, exercise and obesity is a case in point.

That is, sports science's scientific model limits the scope and potential of the sports sciences themselves. In order for *scientists of sport* to experience intellectual freedom, and produce emancipatory knowledge, the nature and craft of their scientific enquiry demand critical reflection. Scientists of sport need to recognise that sportspeople are whole selves, not fragmented entities – and that they must be studied as such. This critique of sports science practice and its fragmented view of the athlete also offers an alternative vision of the athlete and the subject area. Rather than sports scientists tackling problems of human performance, scientists of sport could select and focus on issues of human development.

A bolder and more imaginative view of the sports sciences would centre on its potential to tell us something about human beings generally, not solely relating to their performance in elite sport events. A multidisciplinary or interdisciplinary synthesis – involving the natural and the social sciences – would focus the sports sciences on a human-development research agenda and contribute to a reorientation of the human sciences. A more adequate and, in that sense, 'scientific' picture of human beings than is currently available may be produced if we are studied 'in the round' as whole selves, not as isolated physiological or psychological units. That is, through a multidisciplinary synthesis it might be possible to glimpse a fuller potential for the sports sciences. The subject area could also provide a model for a reintegration of disciplines along the lines of *human sciences* (Elias, 1987a; Maguire, 1992, 2003).

In a sense, this is a question of returning to aspects of what we used to know and do. In fifteenth- and sixteenth-century Europe, the growth in knowledge concerning the human form stemmed from an integrated effort by artists and anatomists. Both Renaissance and Enlightenment artists acquired an understanding of the body as a functional system of motion and emotion. This included not only muscular and skeletal mechanisms, but also aspects of the human constitution believed to be responsible for the outer signs of character and emotional expression. It was the broad quest for fundamental knowledge that made possible the intimate union of visions for artists and anatomists (Kemp and Wallace, 2000). Lectures – which in the present day reinforce the separation of the disciplines (in theatres and laboratories that perpetuate this divide) – once drew crowds from across the academy and beyond.

Until recently, PE/Movement Studies undergraduates had to draw the human muscular and skeletal mechanisms, while at the same time learning about the philosophical and historical roots of body cultures. Specialisation came later. Now, we are confronted with departments where there is little or no discussion of philosophy, history or the social sciences. The non-natural science knowledge available to students is increasingly being confined to Sports Management modules that offer an uncritical view of policy and practice. Yet, our history – distant and recent – provides us with examples of how to study *whole* people, people 'in the round' (Maguire, 1992).

Certain consequences would follow from a sports science that studies people 'in the round' and follows a human-development research agenda. First, some existing areas of research would receive less priority – match analysis, for example, may well become the responsibility of clubs and sports. Second, other research areas currently considered crucial would be refocused – the issue of drugs and sport is a case in point. Instead of a biomedical approach, study of the sociogenesis of the recourse to drugs is required. Third, research areas that are, at present, neglected by scientists of sport would receive greater prominence. For example, one task facing human-development orientated sports sciences would be to find out more about the way in which the uniquely large, unlearned human potential for learning is activated and patterned by the learning process itself. In doing so major strides would be taken in understanding how skills and physical dispositions become part of a person's and a culture's movement vocabulary – what various social scientists have termed 'habitus'. This is also what Elias (1987a) was referring to in the phrase 'the hinge' when he sought to highlight how emotions swing on the hinge of learned and unlearned dimensions of a human's makeup. The focus would not only shift toward human development issues, however.

The research agenda could thus broaden from its narrow attention to performance efficiency concerns. Before such agenda setting can occur, however, academics would have to engage in a debate about the possibility of a multidisciplinary synthesis. A synthesis of this kind is, by definition, beyond the scope of any one person or discipline. The task of studying people 'in the round' requires a collective scientific effort. Possible research areas include the emotions and well-being, class, habitus and schema theory, gender and health, violence and on-field conduct, drugs and sport, exercise and lifestyle, alienation, ageing, and child development. All examples indicate the possibilities that would open up with a reorientated sports science programme (Maguire, 1991a).

Sports sciences equipped with a multidisciplinary perspective on studying people 'in the round' would then be better placed to explore aspects of human development more generally. In this way, scientists of sport would not only be contributing to their parent disciplines, they would also be assisting in the process of a reorientation of the academy along the lines of the human sciences (Krüger, 2003; Maguire, 2003). Such a move would be bold: to address fundamental questions of learning rather than specific problems is to go against existing vested interests, funding sources, and the status insecurity evident in the sports science community. But only in this way will a more adequate and, in that sense, more scientific picture of human beings in sport worlds be produced. It is in the process of doing such fundamental research that part of the emancipatory potential of sports science lies. To do that, sports scientists must seek to exercise a higher degree of detachment from the sports world in which they are involved than they have done hitherto (Maguire and Young, 2002).

Involved advocacy

As presently configured, sports science *takes* rather than *makes* the problems it examines. This taking stems from being too closely tied to the here and now, and from seeking to provide solutions to short-term performance-based problems. It is necessary to resist the 'applied knowledge' perspectives of sports management, sports policy, and the sports–industrial complex more broadly which focus attention on short-term 'social problems' and specific 'interest groups' in an often unreflective and atheoretical manner. 'Short-termism' and pandering to vested interests lead potentially to the critical and sceptical character of sports science to be lost. Teaching is no longer a 'subversive' activity (Postman and Weingartner, 1969). Questions of power become neglected. Not challenging the trend towards short-termism in departments, universities and associations will involve its own specific danger, namely that of a further acceleration in the decline of those aspects of physical education promoted by the humanities and social sciences. Sports scientists risk both being seen as technicians involved in the production of high performance and becoming the mouthpiece of the sports industry and the status quo. The generation of fundamental knowledge that would potentially be of benefit to humanity would be thus neglected, and the grounds on which scientists can research the sporting status quo would be reduced to their contributions to performance efficiency.

These issues do not only affect the allocation of research funds and academic posts. Newcomers to the sub-discipline – be they students, academics, politicians or other stakeholders – quickly grasp whose knowledge counts, and how such knowledge is to be used. As Ingham and Lawson (1999, p. 18) remark, students 'learn that technical, market-driven science and professionalism [TMSP] … is more advanced and esteemed than social-trustee, civic science and professionalism'. McKay (1991, pp. 138–139) is equally critical of 'technocratic educators'. In this regard, insights from the sociology of education are instructive – control of knowledge production is power. What requires analysis in sports science, as Michael Young remarked with regard to the academy more broadly, is 'the dialectical relationship between access to power and the opportunity to legitimise certain dominant categories, and the processes by which the availability of such categories to some groups enables them to assert power and control over others' (1971, p. 8). Here, then, there are questions regarding the scale and sources of funding for teaching and research, curriculum design and development, and the status and esteem given to different forms of knowledge and modes of communication within sports science. Reviewing Western sports science, and indeed practice across the globe, it is clear that technical, market-driven science professionalism holds sway. Natural scientists command attention, attract the funds, claim the key academic positions and set the teaching and research agenda. Yet they, too, are imprisoned in the disciplinary practices of the sports–industrial complex. The funding they seek and achieve acts as a 'double-bind', tying them to the sports–industrial complex. They, too, are unable to free themselves from vicarious involvement in elite achievement sport.

There is, however, an alternative. For Ingham and Lawson (1999), the social-trustee, civic science and professionalism approach requires that sports scientists and professionals should 'integrate their formal roles with that of their own citizenship' (p. 19). We have to become sensitive to the production, dissemination, curriculum development and application of the knowledge we provide. The same issues apply whether we are providing knowledge for students, athletes, coaches, administrators, the media, governmental agencies or transnational corporations (TNCs). A series of questions have to be addressed by sports science practitioners, including: How wasteful is the present system? Who are the winners and the losers in global sport – both on and off the field of play, at different levels of sport and in different modes of movement culture? What are the costs, as well as the benefits to the system being constructed – for the individual, the community and the society as a whole?

Answers to these questions lie, as I noted at the outset, in an analysis of the specific position that sports science occupies in the academy and the sports–industrial complex. The shift to a human development model would not only provide emancipatory knowledge for sport communities and societies as a whole, it would also release the sports science community from the tentacles of achievement sport. Thus, 'involved advocacy' of a human development model – with its emphasis on justice, citizenship and equity – is required. Social-trustee, civic science professionals must act 'as stewards of the just society' and act to 'protect and support free spheres of action and public social spaces' (Ingham and Lawson 1999, p. 19). These observations need to be extended and linked to a consideration of environmental concerns, green issues and the development of notions of sustainable sport. In so doing, sports scientists would be engaging in forms of 'committed service' similar to what some physical educationists used traditionally to be involved in.

If this is accepted as the way forward, how best then to nurture such sentiments and practices? How can we build coalitions of advocates for such an approach within sports science? Perhaps in countries in Scandinavia, where social-democratic values still permeate the academy to a greater extent, civic-orientated scientists have a greater chance to survive. Indeed, perhaps it is also no coincidence that the Finnish Minister of Culture, Tanja Karpela, recently broadened out the purpose of sports science, away from elite sport. Karpela concluded:

> The importance of information in sport science and physical education is growing as we answer … society's great challenges … Those challenges include the functional capabilities of elderly people, the working abilities of people of working age, and the health of children and young people … We have to have a deeper grasp of ways to promote exercising throughout a person's entire life.
>
> (Cited in Pyykkönen, 2003, p. 23)

Thus, civic-orientated scientists can act as a candle in the gathering gloom to which Carl Sagan (1997) referred. Citing the words of Ann Druyan, Sagan noted that 'science is forever whispering in our ears "Remember, you're very new at this. You might be mistaken. You've been wrong before"' (p. 37). It would appear, though, that the sports science technocrats are not listening to such advice. To open their – and our – ears, and research agendas, sports science must involve a commitment to a different mission. Perhaps we will have to go back to the roots of the sub-discipline and rekindle what was best in the teaching of physical education?

Committed service

Following Max Weber, if we view involvement in this subject area as a vocation, then it is our *duty* to intervene in sport worlds. We are stewards, today, of tomorrow's sport worlds. As teachers and researchers, we have a part to play in shaping a more democratic, emancipatory sporting future and thus a form of service will be involved. In this regard, we have some things to learn from our feminist colleagues (Hall, 1996; Scraton and Flintoff, 2002). We must ask awkward questions of ourselves, of sports cultures and of the science used in our work. In doing so, we must address questions such as the following: Is there a chance to maintain and cherish a diverse range of body cultures? Can we develop some notion of sustainable sport, and, in so doing, reconfigure sports science? If the structured processes of global sportisation outlined earlier are any indication of future trends, there does not seem that much room for optimism.

Nevertheless, a failure to pose such questions to ourselves and to face the challenges involved will have severe consequences. We need only consider the environmental impact of the global sports–industrial complex to appreciate the urgent need for reconsidering our culture's unquestioning pursuit of 'progress' and the ultimate performance. In environmental terms, the planet faces the loss or diminution of habitat diversity. Species face extinction – due to environmental degradation, climate change or the introduction of new species (Page and Dowling, 2002). What was once dominant becomes residual. In order to combat these processes, the green movement has highlighted the need for new ethics, the celebration of diversity and sustainability, and a challenge to the activities of TNCs.

In similar fashion, TNCs are linked to a sporting goods industry and media–sport complex that pollute the environment, exploit indigenous workers and market homogeneity (Sage, 1999). Across the planet, ways of life, folk cultures and body movement traditions are threatened with degradation, depletion and extinction. The tentacles of modern achievement sport, either through the 'Prolympic' movement, or school-based sport education programmes, ensure that it is elite sport that counts. As for the environment, what is needed is the preservation and promotion of a diverse range of body habituses, and the development of a sustainable sports process. Notions of 'green' sport, though still in their infancy, need to be based on three key tenets. First, there is a need to respect the diversity and richness of local cultures. Second, it must be recognised how different body (sport) traditions have potential meaning and significance not just to local communities, but to humankind as a whole. Third, there must emerge an acceptance that the practice of sport should be based on principles of environmental sustainability. Here, then, questions of habitat and habitus, diversity and sustainability, interweave. A green sport ethics is needed and needs to be taught to our students so that we may confront the version of global sport provided by both conventional sports science and the sports–industrial complex. In this regard, we should develop both a sense of stewardship of the planet (and thus the sporting environment), and an awareness of the rich cultural heritage that still exists in the habitus traditions of different civilisations.

We are currently situated in the most recent phase of sportisation/globalisation. It is one lasting from the mid-1960s to the present day and it contains elements that simultaneously reinforce both the diminishing contrasts between body cultures and the increasing varieties of them. The latter include martial arts, extreme sports and the revival of folk traditions. Several processes are at work in this connection. There is both a consolidation of globally mediated, commodified and technologised sport and, simultaneously, recurrent challenges to modern achievement-sport forms. Commodified sport products are embedded in a complex political economy that reflects the interests of the West in general and TNCs in particular. The fan is a consumer, the athlete a worker, the club a brand and the sport a commodity. Yet that this remains contested terrain is evident in several ways. The West is being challenged on and off the field of play. TNCs are increasingly subject to the glare of publicity from activists and environmental groups and the boycotts that these organise. New varieties of body cultures, as noted, continue to emerge as counter-hegemonic practices – here we witness resistance, reinvention, adaptation and indigenisation. In addition, folk traditions have, like endangered species, an ability to adapt, survive and be renewed (Maguire *et al.*, 2002).

In such a situation, those involved in physical education/sports science programmes must decide whose body culture counts. Modern achievement sport can continue to be promoted in our universities and schools as the dominant, exclusive form of body culture. Sports education replaces physical education, coaches replace teachers, (as teachers once replaced coaches) and talent identification schemes channel young people's early experiences of movement along narrow, prescribed lines. Alternatively, sports science degree programmes underpinned by a model of human development can be formulated. A 'desportisation' of the curriculum can be engineered (Crum, 1999). Diversity can be promoted and the richness of different habitus/body cultures recognised. Through the development of sustainable sport and the teaching of environmental ethics, a sense of stewardship of both habitat and habitus could be encouraged. These changes would be one part of the attempt to move global sport in the direction of being more democratic, with its decision-making more transparent and its decision-makers more accountable. Natural and social scientists of sport can, if they choose, serve a humanistic role in that regard.

Conclusion: human development and new sport worlds

The sports–industrial complex that we experience in our daily lives was made in the past. People in our societies, and across different cultures and societies, contributed to the making of today's sports and sports sciences (Maguire *et al.*, 2002). In sum, there is both a temporal and a spatial dimension to such sport worlds. Just as the shape of the sporting present was made in the past, so a sporting future can be shaped in the present. Future sport worlds can be similar to today, or they can be made anew. Such worlds can enhance the positive aspects of contemporary sport worlds, or they can reinforce, or make worse, what we already experience as negative features. *The choice is ours.* Power resources are unevenly distributed within and between societies. Class, gender, 'race'/ethnicity and 'disability' are but some of the fault lines along which the sports–industrial complex is splintered. Yet, the present state of play can be challenged.

The struggle to change what counts as possible, permissible and pleasurable in sport worlds will begin with consciousness raising and knowledge accumulation. In our teaching and research, we should seek to provide insights into the issues and challenges – and the opportunities – that confront us right now. We can take up the challenge of reconfiguring sports science, just as we can take up the challenge to 'make a difference' – either in our direct participation in sport worlds, or as coaches, consumers, teachers and parents. There will be many obstacles to this struggle for change. The idea that the performance efficiency model in sports science is the 'natural' state of play and here to stay is one such obstacle. If this model really is as destructive as I have suggested, perhaps its advocates will be its own gravediggers? This critique will no doubt strike some as naïve, romantic, unpatriotic or 'sick' – such a reaction would be, to an extent, defensively self-serving (Gouldner, 1976). Whatever the status of this critique, and the alternative proposed, it is perhaps worthwhile to reinforce the logic underpinning it. As Gouldner remarked with regard to technology and ideology more generally:

> ... the romantic critique ... conceives the technocratic society to be the really 'sick' society. It condemns the technocratic society as one in which the goals of life go unexamined; in which men compulsively fasten on the instruments of action; as a society run by grey men without spirit, where freedom, spontaneity, imagination, will, and creativity are crippled; where individuality and personality are buried under the growth of formalization and routinization: 'sick'.
>
> (1976, p. 264)

In contrast to this logic, and as my colleague Alan Bairner has pointed out, perhaps the ideas proposed by Habermas (1972) on democracy can serve as a counterweight to the deadening effects of technocracy. Yet, the quest for exciting significance in such societies tends to be channelled along increasingly narrow body culture lines – the play element is diminished and the human development potential of the subject area of sport is lost (Maguire et al., 2002). In contrast, if, through education, including physical education and sports science degrees, more people were to demand that the sporting power elite should be held accountable, their decisions made transparent and their positions more democratically based, then we would have made some progress towards a better future. Working together towards shaping future sport worlds that are better – better for individuals, for communities and the environment – should inform our academic activities. To promote sport worlds that balance our local needs with growing global interdependence: that is the challenge that faces us both as individual researchers and teachers, and as a community of scientists. The series of readings contained in this book have involved an attempt to show how sport worlds are highly contested, how local/global struggles permeate such worlds, and how people, despite the inequalities in power resources that exist, can make a difference in shaping their own lives and those of others. Further study of how a 'runaway' global sport world can be better regulated, and perhaps transformed, will involve investigation of issues to do with governance and policy, but also with developing alternative futures (McGrew, 2000; Martinelli, 2003). I hope others will take up this challenge.

References

Albrow, M. (1996). *The Global Age*. Stanford: Stanford University.

Albrow, M. (1997). 'Travelling Beyond Local Cultures: Socioscapes in a Global City'. In J. Eade (ed.), *Living the Global City* (pp. 37–55). London: Routledge.

Alt, J. (1983). 'Sport and Cultural Reification: From Ritual to Mass Consumption'. *Theory, Culture & Society*, 3, 93–107.

Anderson, B. (1983). *Imagined Communities: Reflections on the Origin and Spread of Nationalism*. London: Verso.

Andrews, D. (1997). 'The (Trans)national Basketball Association: American Commodity–Sign Culture and Global–Local Conjuncturalism'. In A. Cvetkovich & D. Kellner (eds), *Articulating the Global and the Local* (pp. 72–101). Boulder: Westview.

Andrews, D. (1999). 'Whither the NBA, Whither America?' *Peace Review*. 11(4), 505–516.

Andrews, D., Carrington. B., Jackson. S. & Mazur, J. (1996). 'Jordanscapes: a Preliminary Analysis of the Global Popular'. *Sociology of Sport Journal*, 13, 428–457.

Appadurai, A. (1990). 'Disjuncture and Difference in the Global Cultural Economy'. *Theory, Culture & Society* 7, 295–310.

Arnason, J. P. (2001). 'Civilizational Patterns and Civilizing Processes'. *International Sociology*, 16(3), 387–405.

Arundel, J. & Roche, M. (1998). 'Media Sport and Local Identity: British Rugby League and Sky TV'. In M. Roche (ed.), *Sport, Popular Culture and Identity* (pp. 57–91). Aachen: Meyer and Meyer.

Bairner, A. (1999). 'Civic and Ethnic Nationalism in the Celtic Version of Irish Sport'. In G. Jarvie (ed.), *Sport in the Making of Celtic Cultures* (pp. 1–11). London: Leicester University Press.

Bairner, A. (2001). *Sport, Nationalism, and Globalisation: European and North American Perspectives*. Albany: State University of New York Press.

Bairner, A. (2003). 'Political Unionism and Sporting Nationalism: an Examination of the Relationship between Sport and National Identity within the Ulster Unionism Tradition'. *Identities: Global Studies in Culture and Power*. 10, 517–535.

Bale, J. (1982). *Sports Place*. London: Hurst.

Bale, J. (1992). *Sport, Space and the City*. Routledge: London.

Bale, J. (1994). *Landscapes of Modern Sport*. Leicester: Leicester University Press.

Bale, J. & Christensen, M. K. (2004). *Post-Olympism?: Questioning Sport in the Twenty-First Century*. London: Routledge.

Bale, J. & Maguire, J. (eds) (1994). *The Global Sports Arena: Athletic Talent Migration in an Interdependent World*. London: Cass.

Bale, J. & Sang, J. (1996). *Kenyan Running: Movement Culture, Geography and Global Change*. London: Cass.

Barnett, G. (1990). *Games and Sets: The Changing Face of Sport on Television*. London: British Film Institute.

Beard, A. (1998). *The Language of Sport*. London: Routledge.

Beck, U. (2000). *What is Globalisation?* Cambridge: Polity Press.

Beckles, H. & Stoddart, B. (eds) (1995). *Liberation Cricket: West Indies Cricket Culture*. Manchester: Manchester University Press.

Bellamy, R. V. (1993). 'The Evolving Television Sports Marketplace'. In L. Wenner (ed.), *MediaSport* (pp. 73–88). New York: Routledge.

Bellamy, R. (1999). 'Issues in the Internationalization of the US Sports Media: the Emerging European Marketplace'. *Journal of Sport and Social Issues*, 17(3), 168–180.

Beynon, J. & Dunkerely, D. (eds) (2000). *Globalization: The Reader*. London: The Athlone Press.

Biddle, S., Fox, K. & Boutcher, S. (eds) (2000). *Physical Activity and Psychological Well-being*. London: Routledge.

Billig, M. (1995). *Banal Nationalism*. London: Sage.

Blain, N., Boyle, R. & O'Donnell, H. (1993). *Sport and National Identity in the European Media*. London: Leicester University Press.

Bloom, W. (1990). *Personal Identity, National Identity and International Relations*. Cambridge: Cambridge University Press.

Bourdieu, P. (1984). *Distinction. A Social Critique of the Judgement of Taste*. London: Routledge.

Bourdieu, P. (1999). 'The State, Economics and Sport'. In H. Dauncey & G. Hare (eds), *France and the 1998 World Cup* (pp. 15–21). London: Cass.

Boycott, G. (1990). *Boycott on Cricket*. London: Partridge.

Boyle, R., & Haynes, R. (2000). *Power Play: Sport, the Media and Popular Culture*. London: Longman.

Brettell, C. & Hollifield, J. (eds) (2000). *Migration Theory*. London: Routledge.

Briggs, R., McCarthy, H. & Zorbas, A. (2004). *16 Days: The Role of the Olympic Truce in the Toolkit for Peace*. London: Demos.

Brohm, J. M. (1978). *Sport: A Prison of Measured Time*. London: Ink Books.

Brown, A. (ed.) (1998). *Fanatics! Power, Identity and Fandom in Football*. London: Routledge.

Brownell, S. (2004). 'China and Olympism'. In J. Bale & M. Christensen (eds), *Post-Olympism? Questioning Sport in the Twenty-First Century* (pp. 51–64). Oxford: Berg.

Calhoun, C. (1995). *Critical Social Theory: Culture, History and the Challenge of Difference*. Oxford: Blackwell.

Campbell, N. (1997). 'The NBA way: Globalization. The World Takes Notice'. *The Globe and Mail* (Toronto), 12 June.

Carrington, B. (1998). '"Football's coming home" but whose home? And do we want it?: Nation, Football and the Politics of Exclusion'. In A. Brown (ed.), *Fanatics! Power, Identity & Fandom in Football* (pp. 101–123). London: Routledge.

Carrington, B. & McDonald, I. (2001). 'Introduction: "Race", Sport and British Society'. In B. Carrington & I. McDonald (eds), *'Race', Sport and British Society* (pp. 1–26). London: Routledge.

Cashman, R. (1988). 'Cricket and Colonialism: Colonial Hegemony and Indigenous Subversion.' In J. A. Mangan (ed.), *Pleasure, Profit and Proselytism: British Culture and Sport at Home and Abroad 1700–1914* (pp. 258–272). London: Frank Cass.

Cashman, R. & Hughes, A. (eds) (1998). *The Green Games: A Golden Opportunity.* Sydney: Center for Olympic Studies.

Castles, S. & Miller, M. (2003). *The Age of Migration* (3rd edition). Basingstoke: Palgrave.

Chiba, N. (2001). *Boundaries of Japanese Baseball Players.* Tokyo: Soubun Kikaku Publishers.

Clayton, I., Daley, I. & Lewis, B. (1995). *Merging on the Ridiculous.* Yorkshire. Yorkshire Arts Circus.

Coakley, J. (1994). *Sport in Society* (5th edition). St Louis: Mosby.

Coakley, J. (2001). *Sport in Society* (7th edition). New York: Irwin McGraw-Hill.

Coakley, J. (2003). *Sport in Society* (8th edition). Boston: McGraw-Hill.

Collins, R. (2001). 'Civilizations as Zones of Prestige and Social Contact'. *International Sociology,* 16(3), 421–437.

Conn, D. (1999). 'The New Commercialism'. In S. Hamil, J. Mitchie. & C. Oughton (eds), *The Business of Football: A Game of Two Halves?* (pp. 40–55). London: Mainstream Publishing.

Connerton, P. (1989). *How Societies Remember.* Cambridge: Cambridge University Press.

Copetas, C. (1997). 'Tackling Problems: U.S. Football Finds it Difficult to Score Points with Europeans'. *Wall Street Journal Europe,* 11 February. Retrieved 24 April 2004, from www.global.factiva.cpm/em/arch/print_results.asp.

Coughlan, B. (1983). *The Irish Lions 1896–1983.* Dublin: Ward River Press.

Crace, J. (1993). *Wasim and Waqar – Imran's Inheritors.* London: Boxtree Ltd.

Crick, B. (ed.) (1991). *National Identities: The Constitution of the United Kingdom.* Oxford: Blackwell.

Cronin, M. (1997). 'Which Nation? Which Flag? Boxing and National Identities in Ireland'. *International Review for the Sociology of Sport,* 32(2), 131–46.

Cronin, M. (1999). *Sport and Nationalism in Ireland: Gaelic Games, Soccer and Irish Identity Since 1884.* Dublin: Four Courts Press.

Crum, B. (1999). 'Changes in Modern Societies: Consequences for Physical Education and School Sport'. Paper presented at the 4th Joint International Session for Educationalists and Staff of Higher Institutes of Physical Education in Olympia, Greece, July.

Dauncey, H. & Hare, G. (eds) (1999). *France and the 1998 World Cup.* London: Cass.

De Biasi, R. (1992). 'Comparing English and Italian football'. Paper presented at the Soccer, Culture and Identity Conference in Aberdeen, Scotland, April.

De Coubertin, P. (2000). *Olympism: Selected Writings.* Lausanne: International Olympic Committee.

De Swaan, A. (1995). 'Widening Circles of Identification: Emotional Concerns in Sociogenetic Perspective'. *Theory, Culture & Society,* 12, 25–39.

Dezalay, Y. (1990). 'The Big Bang and the Law: the Internationalization and Restructuration of the Legal System.' *Theory, Culture & Society,* 7, 279–298.

Diffley, S. (1973). *The Men in Green: The Story of Irish Rugby*. London: Pelham.

Donnelly, P. (1993). 'Subcultures in Sport: Resilience and Transformation'. In A. Ingham & J. Loy (eds), *Sport in Social Development* (pp. 119–146). Champaign: Human Kinetics.

Duke, V. (1994). 'The Drive to Modernization and the Supermarket Imperative: Who Needs a New Football Stadium?' In R. Giulianotti & J. Williams (eds), *Game Without Frontiers* (pp. 129–149). Aldershot: Arena.

Dunn, R. (1986). 'Television, Consumption and the Commodity Form'. *Theory, Culture & Society*, 3, 49–64.

Dunning, E. & Rojek, C. (1992). 'Introduction: Sociological Approaches to the Study of Sport and Leisure'. In E. Dunning & C. Rojek (eds), *Sport and Leisure in the Civilizing Process* (pp. xi–xix). London: Macmillan.

Edgell, S. & Jary, D. (1973). 'Football: A Sociological Eulogy'. In M. Smith, S. Parker & C. Smith (eds), *Leisure and Society in Britain* (pp. 214–229). London: Allen Lane.

Eisenberg, D (2001). 'The NBA's Global Game Plan'. *Time*, 17 March.

Eisenstadt, S. N. (2001). 'The Civilizational Dimension of Modernity: Modernity as a Distinct Civilization'. *International Sociology*, 16(3), 320–340.

Elias, N. (1965). In Elias, N. & Scotson, J. L. (1965/1994). *The established and the outsiders: a sociological enquiry into community problems*. London: Frank Cass.

Elias, N. (1971). 'Sociology of Knowledge: New Perspectives'. *Sociology*, 5, 149–168.

Elias, N. (1974). 'The Sciences: Towards a Theory'. In R. Whitley (ed.), *Social Processes of Scientific Development* (pp. 21–42). London: Routledge & Kegan Paul.

Elias, N. (1978). *What is Sociology?* New York: Columbia University Press.

Elias, N. (1982). 'Scientific Establishments'. In N. Elias, R. Whitley & H. G. Martins, (eds), *Scientific Establishments and Hierarchies* (pp. 3–69). Dordrecht: Reidal.

Elias, N. (1987a). 'On Human Beings and their Emotions: A Process-Sociological Essay'. *Theory, Culture & Society*, 4, 339–361.

Elias, N. (1987b). *Involvement and Detachment*. Oxford: Basil Blackwell.

Elias, N. (1991). *The Society of Individuals*. Oxford: Basil Blackwell.

Elias, N. (1939/1994). *The Civilizing Process: The History of Manners and State Formation and Civilization*. Oxford: Blackwell.

Elias, N. (1995). 'Technization and Civilization'. *Theory, Culture & Society*, 3, 18–41.

Elias, N. (1996). *The Germans: Power Struggles and the Development of Habitus in the Nineteenth and Twentieth Centuries*. Cambridge: Polity.

Elias, N. & Dunning, E. (1986). *Quest for Excitement: Sport and Leisure in the Civilizing Process*. Oxford: Blackwell.

Elias, N. & Scotson, L. (1965/1994). *The Established and the Outsiders*. London: Frank Cass/Sage Publications.

Emerson, R. (1994). 'Globalball'. *The Bulletin*, 8 November, 77–82.

Ensor, R. C. K. (1936). *England 1870–1914. The Oxford History of England*. Oxford: Clarendon Press.

Everitt, R. (1991). 'Battle for the Valley'. *Greenwich Borough Planning Report: January 1990*. London: Voice of The Valley.

Falcous, M. (1998). 'TV made it all a New Game: Not again! A Case Study of the European Superleague'. *Occasional Papers in Football Studies*, 1(1), 4–22.

Falcous, M. & Maguire, J. (2005). 'Making it Local? NBA Expansion and the English Basketball Subculture'. In M. Silk, D. Andrews & C. Cole (eds), *Corporate Nationalisms: Sport, Cultural Identity and Transnational Marketing* (pp. 13–34). Oxford: Berg Publishers.

Fennell, D. (1989). *The Revision of Irish Nationalism*. Dublin: Open Air.

Fletcher, J. (1997). *Violence & Civilization: An Introduction to the Work of Norbert Elias*. Cambridge: Polity.

Frisby, D. (1992). *Simmel and Since: Essays on Georg Simmel's Social Theory*. London: Routledge.

Fukuyama, F. (1992). *The End of History and the Last Man*. New York: Free Press.

Galtung, J. (1991). 'The Sport System as a Metaphor for the World System'. In Landry, F., Landry, M. & Yerles, M. (eds), *Sport... the third millennium* (pp. 147–156). University of Laval Press: Quebec.

Galily, Y. & Sheard, K. (2002). 'Cultural Imperialism and Sport: the Americanization of Israeli Basketball'. *Culture, Sport, Society*, 5(2), 55–78.

Galtung, J. (1982). 'Sport as Carrier of Deep Culture and Structure'. *Current Research on Peace and Violence*, 5, 133–143.

Gellner, E. (1983). *Nations and Nationalism*. Oxford: Basil Blackwell.

Giddens, A. (1986). *The Constitution of Society*. Cambridge: Polity Press.

Giddens, A. (2000). *Runaway World*. London: Profile Books.

Gilroy, P. (2001). Preface. In B. Carrington & I. McDonald (eds), *'Race', Sport and British Society* (pp. xi–xvii). London: Routledge.

Giulianotti, R. (ed.) (2004). *Sport and Modern Social Theorists*. London: Palgrave Macmillan.

Golding, P. & Murdock, G. (1991). 'Culture, Communications and Political Economy'. In J. Curran & M. Gurevitch (eds), *Mass media and society* (pp. 15–32). London. Edward Arnold.

Goodwin, C. (1986). *West Indians at the Wicket*. London: Macmillan.

Gouldner, A. (1976). *The Dialectic of Ideology and Technology*. London: Macmillan.

Graham, C. (2001). *Deconstructing Ireland. Identity, Theory, Culture*. Edinburgh: Edinburgh University Press.

Greer, L. & Lawrence, G. (2001). Book Review [Review of the book *Global Sport*]. *International Review for the Sociology of Sport*, 36(1), 94–96.

Gruneau, R. (1989). 'Television, the Olympics and the Question of Ideology'. In R. Jackson & T. McPhail (eds), *The Olympic Movement and the Mass Media: Past, Present and Future Issues* (pp. 2.3–2.7). Calgary: Hurford Enterprises Ltd.

Gruneau, R. (1999). *Sport, Class and Social Development* (2nd edition). Champaign: Human Kinetics.

Gruneau, R. & Cantelon, H. (1988). 'Capitalism, Commercialism and the Olympics'. In J. Segrave & D. Chu (eds), *The Olympic Games In Transition* (pp. 345–364). Champaign: Human Kinetics.

Gruneau, R. & Whitson, D. (2001). 'Upmarket Continentalism: Major League Sport, Promotional Culture, and Corporate Integration'. In V. Mosco & D. Schiller (eds), *Continental Order? Integrating North America for Cybercapitalism* (pp. 235–264). New York: Rowman & Littlefield.

182   *References*

Guha, R. (2002). *A Corner of a Foreign Field: The Indian History of a British Sport*. London: Picador.

Guttmann, A. (1994). *Games and Empires: Modern Sports and Cultural Imperialism*. New York: Columbia University Press.

Habermas, J. (1972). *Knowledge and Human Interests*. London: Heineman.

Hall, A. (1996). *Feminism and Sporting Bodies: Essays on Theory and Practice*. Champaign: Human Kinetics.

Harding, H. (2001). 'Discussion of "International Political Economy from a Chinese Angle"'. *Journal of Contemporary China*, 10, 55–60.

Hardman, A. E. & Stensel, D. J. (2003). *Physical Activity and Health: The Evidence Explained*. London: Routledge.

Hargreaves, J. (2002). 'Globalisation Theory, Global Sport, and Nations and Nationalism'. In J. Sugden & A. Tomlinson (eds), *Power Games* (pp. 25–43). London: Routledge.

Hargreaves, J. & McDonald, I. (2000). 'Cultural Studies and the Sociology of Sport'. In J. Coakley & E. Dunning (eds), *Handbook of Sports Studies* (pp. 48–60). London: Sage.

Harvey, J., Law, A., & Cantelon, M. (2001). 'North American Professional Sport Team Franchises, Ownership Patterns and Global Entertainment Conglomerates'. *Sociology of Sport Journal*, 4, 435–457.

Hayter, R. (ed.) (1981). *The Best of the Cricketer 1921–1981*. London: Cassell.

Heinilä, K. (1984/1998). 'The Totalization Process in International Sport'. In K. Heinilä (ed.) *Sport in Social Context* (pp. 123–140). Jyväskylä: University of Jyväskylä Press.

Held, D. (2000). 'Regulating Globalization? The Reinvention of Politics'. *International Sociology*, 15(2), 394–408.

Held, D., & McGrew, A. G. (eds) (2000). *The Global Transformations Reader: An Introduction to the Globalisation Debate*. Cambridge: Polity Press.

Held, D., & McGrew, A. (2002). *Globalization/Anti-Globalization*. London: Polity.

Held, D., McGrew, A., Goldblatt, D. & Perraton, J. (1999). *Global Transformations: Politics, Economics and Culture*. Cambridge: Polity.

Henderson, R. (1995) 'Is it in the Blood?' *Wisden Cricket Monthly*, July, 9–10.

Hoberman, J. (1988). 'Sport and the technological View of Man.' In W. Morgan & K. Meier (eds), *Philosophic Inquiry in Sport* (pp. 319–327). Champaign: Human Kinetics.

Hoberman, J. (1992). *Mortal Engines. The Science of Performance and the Dehumanization of Sport*. New York: Free Press.

Hobsbawm, E. J., & Ranger, T. (eds) (1983). *The Invention of Tradition*. Cambridge: Cambridge University Press.

Holt, R. (1989). *Sport and the British: A Modern History*. Oxford: Clarendon Press.

Hoogvelt, A. (2001). *Globalisation and the Postcolonial World: The New Political Economy of Development* (2nd edition). Basingstoke: Palgrave.

Hopcraft, A. (1968/1971). *The Football Man*. Harmondsworth: Penguin.

Hornby, N. (1992). *Fever Pitch*. London: Victor Gollancz.

Horne, J. (1998). 'The Politics of Sport and Leisure in Japan'. *International Review for the Sociology of Sport*, 33(2), 171–182.

Hsu, C-Y. (2001). 'Chinese Encounters with other Civilisations'. *International Sociology*, 16(3), 438–454.

Huizinga, J. (1949/1970). *Homo Ludens: A Study of the Play Element in Culture*. London: Temple Smith.

Huntingdon, S. P. (1996). *The Clash of Civilizations and the Remaking of the World Order*. New York: Simon and Schuster.

ICSSPE (2003). *Science, Service, Advocacy*. Berlin: ICSSPE.

Ingham, A. (1997). 'Towards a Department of Physical Cultural Studies and an end to Tribal Warfare'. In J-M. Fernandez-Balboa (ed.), *Critical Postmodernism in Human Movement, Physical Education, and Sport* (pp. 157–180). New York: SUNY Press.

Ingham, A., & Lawson, H. (1999). 'Prolympism and Globalization: Knowledge for Whom, by Whom?' Paper presented at the *German Association of Sport Science* in Heidelberg, Germany, June.

Ingham, A., Chase, M. & Butt, J. (2002). 'From the Performance Principle to the Developmental Principle: Every Kid a Winner?' *Quest*, 54(4), 308–331.

Inglis, S. (1987). *The Football Grounds of Great Britain*. London: Collins Willow.

International Olympic Commitee (2005). 'Olympic Charter'. Retrieved 20 March 2005, from http://multimedia.olympic.org/pdf/en_report_122.pdf.

Jackson, S. & Andrews, D. (1996). 'Excavating the (Trans) National Basketball Association: Locating the Global/Local Nexus of America's World and the World's America'. *Australiasian Journal of American Studies*, 15, 57–64.

Jackson, S. & Andrews, D. (1999). 'Between and Beyond the Global and the Local'. *International Review for the Sociology of Sport*, 43(1), 31–42.

James. C. L. R. (1963). *Beyond a Boundary*. London: Stanley Paul.

Jarvie, G. & Maguire, J. (1994). *Sport and Leisure in Social Thought*. London: Routledge.

Jeanrenaud, C. & Kesenne, S. (eds) (1999) *Competition Policy on Professional Sports*. Antwerp: Standard.

Jhally, S. (1989). 'Cultural Studies and the Sports/Media Complex'. In L. Wenner (ed.), *Media, Sports and Society* (pp. 70–96). Newbury Park: Sage.

Kanazawa, M. & Fund, J. (2001). 'Racial Division in Professional Basketball: Evidence from Nielsen Ratings'. *Economic Enquiry*, 39, 599–608.

Kellner, D. (1996). 'Sports, Media Culture, and Race – Some Reflections on Michael Jordan'. *Sociology of Sport Journal*, 13, 458–467.

Kelner, S. (1996). *To Jerusalem and Back*. London. Macmillan.

Kemp. M. & Wallace, M. (2000). *Spectacular Bodies. The Art and Science of the Human Body from Leonardo to Now*. Berkeley: University of California Press.

Kervin, A. (1995). 'Slam-dunk drama proves sadly lacking in subtlety'. *The Times*, 23 October.

King, A. (1997). 'New directors, Customers, and Fans: the Transformation of English Football in the 1990s'. *Sociology of Sport Journal*. 14(3), 224–240.

King, A. (1998). *The End of the Terraces: The Transformation of English Football in the 1990s*. London: Leicester University Press.

Klein, N. (2000). *No Logo*. London: Harper Collins.

Korr, C. (1986). *West Ham United*. Urbana: University of Illinois Press.

Krüger, M. (ed.) (2003). *Menschenbilder im Sport*. Schorndorf: Hofmann.

Kudo, Y., Nogawa, H. & Kudo, Y. (2003). 'Migration of Japanese Top Athletes and the Emergence of Sport Tourism'. Paper presented at the 2nd World Congress for the Sociology of Sport in Koln, Germany, June.

Lanfranchi, P. & Taylor, M. (2001). *Moving with the Ball: The Migration of Professional Footballers*. Oxford: Berg.

Leiss, W., Kline, S. & Jhally, S. (1997). *Social Communication in Advertising. Persons, Products and Images of Well-Being*. London: Routledge.

Lemmon, D. (1987). *Cricket Mercenaries – Overseas Players in English Cricket*. London, Pavilion Books Ltd.

Lenskyl, H. (2000). *Inside the Olympic Industry*. New York: SUNY.

Linklater, A. (2004). 'Norbert Elias, the 'Civilising Process' and the Sociology of International Relations'. *International Politics*, 41, 3–35.

Li, Xing. (2000). 'The Conundrum of the Chinese–United States' Relationship'. *Journal of International Relations and Development*, 3, (4), 325–346.

Longmore, A. (1995). 'NBA orders limited retreat from decibel hell'. *The Times*, 19 October.

Luschen, G. (1967). 'The Interdependence of Sport and Culture'. *International Review of Sport Sociology*, 2, 127–139.

MacAloon, J. (1999). 'Anthropology at the Olympic games: an Overview'. In A. M. Klausen (ed.), *Olympic Games as Public Performance and Public Event: The Case of the XVII Winter Olympic Games in Norway* (pp. 9–26). New York: Berghahn.

McCrone, D. (1998). *The Sociology of Nationalism*. London: Routledge.

McGovern, P. (2000). 'The Irish Brawn Drain: English League Clubs and Irish Footballers, 1946–1995'. *British Journal of Sociology*, 51(3), 401–418.

McGovern, P. (2002). 'Globalisation or Internationalisation? Foreign Footballers in the English League, 1946–95'. *Sociology*, 36, 23–42.

McGrew, A. (2000). 'Power Shifts: From National Government to Global Governance'. In D. Held (ed.), *A Globalizing World? Culture, Economics, Politics* (pp. 127–168). London: Routledge.

McIntosh, P. C. (1968). *Physical Education in England Since 1800*. London: Bell.

McKay, J. (1991). *No Pain, No Gain? Sport and Australian Culture*. London: Prentice Hall.

McKay, J., Lawrence, J., Miller, T. & Rowe, D. (1993). 'Globalization and Australian Sport'. *Sport Science Review*, 2(1), 10–28.

McLellan, A. (1994). *The Enemy Within – The Impact of Overseas Players on English Cricket*. London, Blandford.

Magee, J. & Sugden, J. (2002). '"The World at Their Feet": Professional Football and International Labour Migration'. *Journal of Sport and Social Issues*, 26(4), 421–437.

Maguire, J. (1988). 'The Commercialization of English Elite Basketball 1972–1988: A Figurational Perspective'. *International Review for the Sociology of Sport*, 23(4), 305–322.

Maguire, J. (1990). 'More than a Sporting Touchdown: the Making of American Football in England 1982–1990. *Sociology of Sport Journal*, 7(3), 213–237.

Maguire, J. (1991a). 'Human Sciences, Sports Sciences and the Need to Study People "in the round"'. *Quest*, 2, 190–206.

Maguire, J. (1991b). 'The Media–Sport Production Complex: the Case of American Football in Western European Societies'. *European Journal of Communication*, 6(3), 315–335.

Maguire, J. (1992). 'Towards a Sociological Theory of Sport and the Emotions: a Process-sociological Perspective'. In E. Dunning & C. Rojek (eds), *Sport and Leisure in the Civilising Process: Critique and Counter-critique* (pp. 96–120). London: Macmillan.

Maguire, J. (1993a). 'Globalisation, Sport and National Identities: "The Empire Strikes Back"?', *Loisir et Société*, 16(2), 293–322.

Maguire, J. (1993b). 'American Football, British Society and Global Sport Development'. In E. Dunning, J. Maguire & R. Pearton (eds), *The Sports Process* (pp. 207–230). Champaign: Human Kinetics.

Maguire, J. (1994a). 'Sport, Identity Politics, and Globalization: Diminishing Contrasts and Increasing Varieties'. *Sociology of Sport Journal*, 11, 398–427.

Maguire, J. (1994b). 'Preliminary Observations of Globalisation and the Migration of Sports Labour'. *Sociological Review*, 42(3), 452–480.

Maguire, J. (1995). 'Sport, the Stadium and Metropolitan Life'. In J. Bale & O. Moen (eds), *The Stadium and the City* (pp. 45–57). Staffordshire: Keele University Press.

Maguire, J. (1996). Blade Runners: Canadian Migrants, Ice Hockey and the Global Sports Process'. *Journal of Sport and Social Issues*, 21(3), 335–360.

Maguire, J. (1998). 'Globalization and Sportization: a Figurational Process/sociological Perspective'. *Avante*, 4(1), 67–89.

Maguire, J. (1999). *Global Sport: Identities, Societies, Civilizations*. Cambridge: Polity Press.

Maguire, J. (2002). 'Civilisational Games and Cultural Struggles: US media representations of the Beijing bid for the 2008 Olympics'. Paper presented at the North American Society for the Sociology of Sport in Indianapolis, November.

Maguire, J. (2003). 'Modern Sport, Sport Science and Images of Humans: Habitus, Diversity, Sustainability'. In M. Krüger (ed.), *Menschenbilder im Sport* (pp. 117–131). Schorndorf: Hofmann.

Maguire, J. (2004). 'Body Cultures: Diversity, Sustainability, Globalisation'. In G. Pfister (ed.), *Games of the Past – Sports for the Future?: Globalisation, Diversification, Transformation* (pp. 22–27). Duderstadt: ISHPES.

Maguire, J. & Pearton, R. (2000a). 'Global Sport and the Migration Patterns of France 1998 World Cup Finals Players: some Preliminary Observations'. *Soccer and Society*, 1, 175–189 .

Maguire, J. & Pearton, R. (2000b). 'The Impact of Elite Labour Migration on the Identification, Selection and Development of European Soccer Players'. *Journal of Sports Sciences*, 18, 759–769.

Maguire, J. & Poulton, E. (1999). 'European Identity Politics in Euro 96: Invented Traditions, Imagined Communities and National Habitus Codes'. *International Review for the Sociology of Sport*, 34(1), 17–29.

Maguire, J. & Stead, D. (1996). 'Far pavilions?: Cricket Migrants, Foreign Sojourns and Contested Identities'. *International Review for the Sociology of Sport*, 31(1), 1–21.

Maguire, J. & Tuck, J. (1998). 'Global Sports and Patriot Games: Rugby Union and National Identity in a United Sporting Kingdom Since 1945'. *Immigrants and Minorities*, 17(1), 103–126.

Maguire J. & Tuck, J. (1999). 'Making Sense of Global Patriot Games: Rugby Players' Perceptions of National Identity Politics'. *Football Studies*, 2, 26–54.

Maguire, J. & Young, K. (2002). 'Back to the Future: Thinking Sociologically About Sport'. In J. Maguire & K. Young (eds), *Theory, Sport & Society* (pp. 1–22). Oxford: Elsevier Press.

Maguire, J. Poulton, E. & Possamai, K. (1999). 'Weltkrieg III? Media Coverage of England versus Germany in Euro 96'. *Journal of Sport & Social Issues*, 23(4), 439–454.

Maguire, J., Jarvie, G., Mansfield, L. & Bradley, J. (2002). *Sport Worlds: A Sociological Perspective*. Champaign: Human Kinetics.

Majors, R. (1986). 'Cool Pose: the Proud Signature of Black Survival'. *Changing Men: issues in Gender, Sex and Politics*, 17, 184–185.

Majors, R. (1990). 'Cool Pose: Black Masculinity and Sports'. In M. Messner & D. Sabo (eds), *Sport, Men and the Gender Order: Critical Feminist Perspectives* (pp. 109–114). Champaign: Human Kinetics.

Mangan, J. A. (1986). *The Games Ethic and Imperialism*. London: Viking Press.

Mangan, J. A. (ed.) (1988). *Pleasure, Profit and Proselytism: British Culture and Sport at Home and Abroad 1700–1914*. London: Frank Cass.

Mangan, J. & Hong, F. (2003). *Sport in Asian Society: Past and Present*. London: Cass.

Markovits, A. (1990). 'The Other "American Exceptionalism": Why is there no Soccer in the United States?' *International Journal of the History of Sport*, 7(2), 230–264.

Martinelli, A. (2003). 'Markets, Governments, Communities and Global Governance'. *International Sociology*, 18, 291–324.

Martin-Jenkins, C. (1984). *Twenty Years On – Cricket's Years of Change 1963–1983*. London: Willow Books.

Mazrui, A. (1987). 'Africa's Triple Heritage of Play: Reflections on the Gender Gap'. In W. Baker & J. A. Mangan (eds), *Sport in Africa: Essays in Social History* (pp. 217–228). New York: Africana.

Mennell, S. (1994). 'The Formation of We-Images: a Process Theory'. In C. Calhoun (ed.), *Social Theory and the Politics of Identity*. Oxford: Blackwell.

Midwinter, E. (1992). *The Illustrated History of County Cricket*. London: Kingswood Press.

Milleker, E. J. (ed.) (2000). *Year One Art of the Ancient World: East and West*. New York: Metropolitan Museum of Art.

Miller, T., Lawrence, G., McKay, J. & Rowe, D. (2001). *Globalisation and Sport*. London: Sage.

Miller, T., Rowe, D., McKay, J. & Lawrence, G. (2003). 'The Over-Production of US Sports and the New International Division of Cultural Labour'. *International Review for the Sociology of Sport*, 38(4), 427–440.

Moorhouse, H. F. (1996). 'One State, Several Countries: Soccer and Nationality in a "United" Kingdom'. In J. Mangan (ed.), *Tribal Identities: Nationalism, Europe, Sport* (pp. 55–74). London: Cass.

Murphy, P., Sheard, K. & Waddington, I. (2000). 'Figurational Sociology and its Application to Sport'. In J. Coakley & E. Dunning (eds), *Handbook of Sports Studies* (pp. 92–105). London: Sage.

Nairn, T. (1977). *The Break-Up of Britain: Crisis and Neo-Nationalism*. London: NLB.

O'Donnell, H. (1994). 'Mapping the Mythical: a Geopolitics of National Sporting Stereotypes'. *Discourse & Society*, 5(3), 345–380.

O'Mahony, P. & Delanty, G. (1998). *Rethinking Irish History*. London: Macmillan.

Page, S. & Dowling, R. (2002). *Ecotourism*. London: Prentice Hall.

Postman, N. & Weingartner, C. (1969). *Teaching as a Subversive Activity*. London. Penguin.

Puijk, R. (2000). 'A Global Media Event? Coverage of the 1994 Lillehammer Olympic Games'. *International Review for the Sociology of Sport*, 3, 309–330.

Pyykkönen, T. (2003). 'Elite Sport is a Lot, but not Everything'. *Motion – Sport in Finland*, 2, 22–23.

Rail, G. (ed.) (1998). *Sport and Postmodern Times*. Albany: SUNY Press.

Ram, U. (2004). 'Glocommodification: How the Global Consumes the Local – McDonald's in Israel'. *Current Sociology*, 52(1), 11–31.

Real, M. (1989). *Super media: a cultural studies approach*. Newbury Park: Sage.

Real, M. (1996). 'The Post-modern Olympics: Technology and the Commodification of the Olympic Movement'. *Quest*, 48, 9–24.

Relph, E. (1989). 'Responsive Methods, Geographical Imagination and the Study of Landscapes'. In A. Kobayashi & A. McKenzie (eds), *Remaking Human Geography* (pp. 149–163). London: Unwin Hyman.

Reng, R. (2003). *Keeper of Dreams: The Incredible Story of a Goalkeeper*. London: Yellow Jersey Press.

Richards, V. & Foot, D. (1979). *Viv Richards*. Surrey: The Windmill Press.

Robertson, R. (1990). 'Mapping the Global Condition: Globalization as the Central Concept'. *Theory, Culture & Society*, 7, 15–30.

Robins, K. (1997). What in the World is going on? In P. DuGay (ed.), *Production of Culture/Cultures of Production* (pp. 11–67). London: Sage.

Roche, M. (2000). *Mega-Events and Modernity: Olympics and Expos in the Growth of Global Culture*. New York: Routledge.

Rojek, C. (1992). 'The Field of Play in Sport and Leisure Studies'. In E. Dunning & C. Rojek (eds), *Sport and Leisure in the Civilising Process* (pp. 1–35). London: Macmillan.

Rowe, D. (1995). *Popular Cultures: Rock Music, Sport and the Politics of Pleasure*. London: Sage.

Rowe, D. (1999). *Sport, Culture and the Media*. Buckinghamshire: Open University Press.

Rowe, D. (2003). 'Sport and the Repudiation of the Global'. *International Review for the Sociology of Sport*, 38, 281–294.

Rowe, D. & Lawrence, G. (1996). 'Beyond National Sport: Sociology, History and Postmodernity'. *Journal of the Australian Society for Sports History*, 12(2), 3–16.

Sagan, C. (1997). *The Demon-Haunted World. Science as a Candle in the Dark*. London: Headline Press.

Sage, G. (1990). *Power and Ideology in American Sport*. Champaign: Human Kinetics.

Sage, G. (1993). 'The impact of European unification on American sports'. *Journal of Comparative Physical Education and Sport*, 15, 21–29.

Sage, G. (1999). 'Justice do it! The Nike Transnational Advocacy Network: Organization, Collective Actions, and Outcomes'. *Sociology of Sport Journal*, 16, 206–235.

Sanderson, S. K. (ed.) (1995). *Civilization and World Systems: Studying World-Historical Change*. London: AltaMira.

Sassen, S. (1996). *Losing Control? Sovereignty in an Age of Globalisation*. New York: Columbia University Press.

Schäfer, W. (2001). 'Global Civilization and Local Cultures: A Crude Look at the Whole'. *International Sociology*, 16(3), 301–319.

Schwarz, B. (1992). 'England in Europe: Reflections on National Identity and Cultural Theory'. *Cultural Studies*, 6, 198–206.

Scraton, S. & Flintoff, A. (eds) (2002). *Gender and Sport: A Reader*. London: Routledge.

Segrave, J. (2000). 'The (neo)Modern Olympics: the Revolution in Europe and the Resurgence of Universalism'. *International Review for the Sociology of Sport*, 3, 268–281.

Shank, M. D. (1999). *Sports Marketing: A Strategic Perspective*. New Jersey: Prentice Hall.

Silk, M. & Andrews, D. (2001). 'Beyond a Boundary: Sport, Transnational Advertising, and the Reimagining of National Culture'. *Journal of Sport and Social Issues*, 25(2), 180–202.

Sissons, R. (1988). *The Players – A Social History of the Professional Cricketer*. London: Kingswood Press.

Sklair, L. (1991). *Sociology of the Global System*. London: Harvester Wheatsheaf.

Slater, J. (1998). 'Changing Partners: The Relationship Between the Mass Media and the Olympic Games'. In R. Barney, K. Wamsley, S. Martyn & G. MacDonald (eds), *Fourth International Symposium for Olympic Research* (pp. 49–69). Ontario: University of Western Ontario.

Smith, A. D. (1991). *National Identity*. Harmondsworth: Penguin.

Smith, A. D. (1995). *Nations and Nationalism in a Global Era*. London: Polity Press.

Stalker, P. (2000). *Workers Without Frontiers: The Impact of Globalisation on International Migration*. Colorado: Lynne Rienner.

Starr, M. & Samuels, A. (2001). 'The NBA's No-Shows'. *Newsweek*, 19 February, pp. 42–53.

Stead, D. & Maguire, J. (1998a). 'The Northern Invaders: Nordic/Scandinavian involvement in English Elite Soccer'. In P. Murphy (ed.), *Review 1997–98 Association Football Season* (pp. 10–12). London: Singer & Friedlander.

Stead, D. & Maguire, J. (1998b). 'View from the North: the Experiences of Nordic/Scandinavian Players in English Soccer'. In P. Murphy (ed.), *Review 1997–98 Association Football Season* (pp. 34–36). London: Singer and Friedlander.

Stead, D. & Maguire, J. (2000a). 'No Boundaries to Ambition – Soccer Labour Migration and the Case of Nordic/Scandinavian Players in England'. In J. Bangsbo (ed.), *Soccer and Science in an Interdisciplinary Perspective* (pp. 35–55). Copenhagen: University of Copenhagen Press.

Stead, D. & Maguire, J. (2000b). 'Rite de Passage or Passage to Riches?: The Motivation and Objectives of Nordic/Scandinavian Players in English League Soccer'. *Journal of Sport and Social Issues*, 24, 36–60.

Stoddart, B. (1979). 'Cricket's Imperial Crisis: the 1932–33 MCC Tour of Australia'. In R. Cashman & M. McKernan (eds), *Sport in History* (pp. 124–147). St Lucia: University of Queensland Press.

Stoddart, B. (1988). 'Sport, Cultural Imperialism, and Colonial Response in the British Empire'. *Society for Comparative Study of Society and History*, 649–673.

Sugden, J. & Bairner, A. (1993). *Sport, Sectarianism and Society in a Divided Ireland*. Leicester: Leicester University Press.

Szymanski, S. (1999). 'The Market for Soccer Players in England after Bosman: Winners and Losers'. In C. Jeanrenaud & S. Kesenne (eds), *Competition Policy on Professional Sports: Europe after the Bosman Case* (pp. 133–160). Antwerp: Standard Publishers.

The Economist (2004). 'For a Wreath, a Flag – or Cash?' 14 August, p. 31.

Therborn, G. (2000). 'Globalisations: Dimensions, Historical Waves, Regional Effects, Normative Governance'. *International Sociology*, 15, 151–170.

Thomas, C. (1996). *The History of the British Lions*. Edinburgh: Mainstream Publishing.

Tiryakian, E. A. (2001). 'Introduction: The Civilization of Modernity and the Modernity of Civilizations'. *International Sociology*, 16(3), 277–292.

Tomlinson, J. (1996). 'Olympic Spectacle: Opening Ceremonies and Some Paradoxes of Globalization'. *Media, Culture & Society*, 18, 583–602.

Tomlinson, J. (1999). *Globalisation and Culture*. Cambridge: Polity.

Toohey, K. & Veal, A. J. (1999). *The Olympic Games: A Social Science Perspective*. New York: CAB.

Truss, L. (1997). 'Bulls hit town for lesson in jargon'. *The Times*, 20 October.

Tuan, Y. F. (1974). *Topophilia*. Englewood Cliffs: Prentice Hall.

Tuck, J.(2003). 'The Men in White: Reflections on Rugby Union, the Media and Englishness'. *International Review for the Sociology of Sport*, 38(2), 177–199.

Tuck, J. & Maguire, J. (1999). 'Making Sense of Global Patriot Games: Rugby Players' Perceptions of National Identity Politics'. *Football Studies*, 2(1), 26–54.

Tudor, A. (1992). 'Them and Us: Story and Stereotype in TV World Cup Coverage'. *European Journal of Communication*, 7, 391–413.

UK Sport (2001). Annual Report: *Golden Opportunities 2000/2001*. London: UK Sport.

UK Sport (2003). *Countdown To Athens*. London: UK Sport.

UNDP and Sport for Development and Peace (2003). *Towards Achieving the Millennium Development Goals*. Retrieved 1 March 2005, from www.undp.bg/user_files/en/documents/fast_facts/sports_peace.pdf.

UN Press Release (2001) SG/SM/7523. 31 August.

Van Bottenburg, M. (2001). *Global Games*. Chicago: University of Chicago Press.

Van Bottenburg, M. (2003). 'Thrown for a Loss? (American) Football and the European Sport Space'. *American Behavioural Scientist*, 46(11), 1550–1562.

Van Esbeck, E. (1974). *One Hundred Years of Irish Rugby: the Official History of the Irish RFU*. Dublin: Gill & Macmillan.

Van Esbeck, E. (1986). *The Story of Irish Rugby*. London: Stanley Paul.

Van Esbeck, E. (1999). *Irish Rugby 1874–1999: A History*. Dublin: Gill & Macmillan.

VanWynsberghe, R. & Ritchie, I. (1998). '(Ir)Relevant Rings: the Symbolic Consumption of the Olympic Logo in Postmodern Media Culture'. In G. Rail (ed.), *Sport and Postmodern Times* (pp. 367–384). New York: SUNY.

Voy, R. (1991). *Drugs, Sports, and Politics*. Champaign: Leisure Press.

Waddington, I. (2000). *Sport, Health and Drugs*. London: Spon.

Wamsley, K., & Heine, M. (1996). 'Tradition, Modernity, and the Construction of Civic Identity: the Calgary Olympics'. *Olympika*, 5, 81–91.

Wasserstrom, J. (2002). 'Using History to Think about the Beijing Olympics: the Use and Abuse of the Seoul 1988 Analogy'. *Harvard International Journal of Press/Politics* 7, (1) 126–129.

Waters, M. (1995). *Globalization*. London: Routledge.

Weber, M. (1949). *The Methodology of the Social Sciences*. New York: Free Press.

Wenner, L. (ed.) (1989). *Media, Sports and Society*. Newbury Park: Sage.

Wenner, L. (ed.) (1998). *MediaSport*. London: Routledge.

Westerbeek, H. & Smith, A. (2003). *Sport Business in the Global Marketplace*. London: Palgrave Macmillan.

Whannel, G. (1992). *Fields in Vision: Television Sport and Cultural Transformation*. London: Routledge.

Whitson, D. (1998). 'Circuits of Promotion: Media, Marketing and the Globalization of Sport'. In L. Wenner (ed.), *MediaSport* (pp. 57–72). London: Routledge.

Whitson, D. & Macintosh, D. (1990). 'The Scientization of Physical Education Discourses of Performance'. *Quest*, 42, 40–51.

Whyte, D. (1995). 'Houston in control of the mission'. *Independent on Sunday*, 22 October.

Wilcox, R. (1994). 'Imperialism or Globalism?: A Conceptual Framework for the Study of American Sport and Culture in Contemporary Europe'. *Journal of Comparative Physical Education and Sport*, 15(1), 30–40.

Williams, R. (1977). *Marxism and Literature*. Oxford: Oxford University Press.

Wilson, B. (1997). '"Good Blacks" and "Bad Blacks": Media Constructions of African-American Athletes in Canadian Basketball'. *International Review for the Sociology of Sport*, 32(2), 177–189.

Wilson, B. (1999). '"Cool Pose" Incorporated: the Marketing of Black Masculinity in Canadian NBA Coverage'. In P. White & K. Young. (eds), *Sport and Gender in Canada* (pp. 232–253). Oxford: Oxford University Press.

Wright-Mills, C. (1959). *The Power Elite*. Oxford: Penguin.

Wuolio, T. (2004). 'Elite Sport: On the Trail of Sustainable Development'. *Motion – Sport in Finland*. 1, 38–39

Yeung, H. (2000). 'Economic Globalization, Crisis and the Emergence of Chinese Business Communities in Southeast Asia'. *International Sociology*, 15(2), 266–287.

Young, M. F. D. (1971). *Knowledge and Control: New Directions for the Sociology of Education*. London: Collier-Macmillan.

Zimbalist, A. (2001). *Unpaid Professionals*. New Jersey: Princeton University Press.

Index